$55.00

Censorship in Canadian Literature

MARK COHEN

McGill-Queen's University Press
Montreal & Kingston · London · Ithaca

© McGill-Queen's University Press 2001
ISBN 0-7735-2214-X

Legal deposit fourth quarter 2001
Bibliothèque nationale du Québec

Printed in Canada on acid-free paper

This book has been published with the help of a grant
from the Humanities and Social Sciences Federation of
Canada, using funds provided by the Social Sciences
and Humanities Research Council of Canada.

McGill-Queen's University Press acknowledges the
financial support of the Government of Canada through
the Book Publishing Industry Development Program
(BPIDP) for its activities. It also acknowledges the
support of the Canada Council for the Arts for its
publishing program.

National Library of Canadian Cataloguing
in Publication Data

Cohen, Mark, 1966–
Censorship in Canadian literature
Includes bibliographical references and index.
ISBN 0-7735-2214-X
1. Censorship – Canada. 2. Censorship in literature.
3. Canadian fiction (English) – 20th century – History of
criticism. I. Title.
PN156.C64 2001   c813'.5409   C2001-900233-5

Typeset in Palatino 10/12
by Caractéra inc., Quebec City

Contents

Preface

There is a large body of academic work devoted to the subject of censorship, including many books on censorship as a philosophical or moral issue, numerous historical reviews, and several studies of the censorship of specific works of literature. The overwhelming majority of these inquiries focus on censorship in Europe or the United States. This makes sense when we consider that official censorship dates back to the advent of the printing press in Europe and that the First Amendment has been an overwhelmingly important provision in American law. It also makes sense since the most notorious literary censorship cases have involved works – either of international stature, such as *Lady Chatterley's Lover* and *Fleurs du Mal*, or of great popularity, such as *The Catcher in the Rye* – that are European or American. Understandably, then, thinking about censorship has come late to the Canadian academy. Canada has neither a history of official censorship nor an American-style preoccupation with free speech (the less glorified Canadian version of the First Amendment was ensconced in the Charter of Rights and Freedoms only in 1982). Furthermore, while Canadian schools and libraries have frequently participated in the banning of those foreign texts traditionally subject to censorship, there has been little to analyse from a uniquely Canadian perspective in these incidents. As a result, writing about censorship of literature in Canada has been limited,[1] consisting mostly of formal listings of texts that have come under fire in the classroom and the public library.[2]

There are several possible explanations for the dearth of detailed study of censorship involving English Canadian literature. First, literary critics may have been reticent about undertaking a study that draws extensively on disciplines outside of literature, such as philosophy, law, and sociology (all of which I utilize in this book). With the emergence of interdisciplinary studies in recent years, however, this kind of analysis seems less unusual. Second, the relatively unified voice with which Canadian authors have condemned censorship attacks may have given critics the impression that the issues involved are clear, the conclusions foregone, and that these controversies therefore require little study. I will show that this impression is far from the reality. The third and most compelling reason, though, is simply that until comparatively recently Canadian literature had neither the status nor the reputation of foreign literature and was therefore not widely consumed in this country. Limited in its distribution, its chances of being subjected to censorship were limited as well.

Over the course of the last thirty years, however, there has been a dramatic change in the fate of literary writing in Canada. With the ascendancy of Canadian literature in quality and quantity since the 1960s – what Linda Hutcheon terms the "flowering of Canadian fiction" (1) – censorship has become an issue in Canadian writing for two reasons. First, more Canadian literature is stocked by libraries and more of it is taught in schools. An increase in the sheer volume of Canadian books used in these institutions has led in turn to more controversies in which Canadian literary works are the objects of censorship attacks. With these attacks happening in their own backyards, Canadian writers have taken notice and responded to the censorship attacks *of* their writing *in* their writing. Second, a rise in standing of Canadian literature internationally has given writers a sense of confidence in commenting on censorship issues more broadly, a feeling that writing about the Rushdie affair or pornography or changes to Canada's obscenity laws would wield some power in national and international arenas. Canadian writers, therefore, have recently had occasion to think deeply and write extensively about censorship. To put it briefly, censorship has become an issue within the Canadian literary establishment, if not yet among critics of Canadian literature.

It is this relationship between the growing stature of Canadian literature and the corresponding increase in the prominence of the issue of censorship among its writers that has led me to the three principal figures of my analysis: Timothy Findley, Margaret Atwood, and Margaret Laurence. Arguably among the five most prominent authors of English Canadian literature, these three writers, partly because of their stature, have all experienced attempts to censor their work, and all three have responded to these attacks on their work in writing. Furthermore, all three have gone beyond defences of their own work to write about censorship in other contexts and in more general or philosophical terms. They have chosen to do this most directly through non-fiction (articles, memoirs, etc.), and one of the purposes of this book is to enumerate their explicit arguments, both to establish the writers' positions on censorship and to shed light on the role of censorship as it appears in their fiction. My close reading of their fictional works – *The Wars* and *Headhunter* by Findley; *Bodily Harm* and *The Handmaid's Tale* by Atwood; and a draft of an unfinished novel by Laurence – aims to uncover the positions on censorship implicit within these works.

Both explicitly in their non-fiction and implicitly through their fiction, these well-known authors invoke many of the most fundamental arguments regarding censorship. It is for these reasons that I have also chosen to examine the work of Beatrice Culleton and Marlene Nourbese Philip, who, though not yet considered to be "major" Canadian authors, have both experienced censorship of their writing, have commented explicitly on censorship, and, most importantly, have conveyed their ideas on the subject through their fiction (and in the case of Philip, through her poetry). The ideas on censorship of all these writers are key to the development of my position on the issue: by engaging the arguments that they raise, exposing weaknesses and underlining strengths, I present a new picture of censorship that aims to ease the acrimonious nature of many censorship disputes and offer suggestions for resolving some of the most troublesome controversies.

Acknowledgments

I wish to acknowledge first the Estate of Margaret Laurence, for granting me permission to quote from Laurence's private papers. Timothy Findley also graciously allowed me to quote from his private papers. The staff at the William Ready Archives at McMaster University in Hamilton, at the York University Archives in Toronto, and at the National Archives in Ottawa aided me in my work with this archival material. I am grateful to the *Journal of Canadian Studies* for allowing me to reprint an article that appeared in its Winter 1998–99 issue (vol. 33, no. 4), entitled "'Singing Our Way Out of Darkness': Findley's Anti-Censorship Argument in *Headhunter*," and to Kerry Cannon, Charmaine Eddy, and Michael Peterman, who edited the article. I also thank the *Zeitschrift fur Kanada-Studien (ZKS)* for permission to reprint "A Dystopia of Silence: Atwood's Anti-Censorship Arguments in *The Handmaid's Tale*" (20. Jahrgang, Nr. 1, Band 37 [2000]).

I wish to thank Aurèle Parisien and Joan McGilvray at McGill-Queen's University Press for their sure-handed editorial guidance, and Susan Kent Davidson for her formidable copy-editing skill.

Though I cannot acknowledge everyone who was generous enough to converse with me about censorship, I would like to thank David Ainsworth, Lisa Ariemma, Martin Behr, Anne Blott, Genevieve Cimon, Tracie Gemmel, Karin Flemig, Paul Hedlin, Sabine Sautter-Léger, Esme Terry, Kendal Young, and Grant Zubis for listening to my ramblings and providing me with insights that profoundly shaped my thoughts. For reading the manuscript at its various stages and providing me with crucial critical feedback I am obliged to Charles Blattberg, Maeve Haldane, Mary Ellen Macdonald, Marianne Stenbaek, and Brian Trehearne.

I owe a deep debt of gratitude to Susan Dalton, who challenged me, comforted me, and just plain made a pleasure of the years during which this work evolved.

And in conveying my thanks to Nathalie Cooke, words such as admiration, respect, and affection only serve to confirm Offred's observation that "It's impossible to say a thing exactly the way it was, because what you say can never be exact, you always have to leave something out." Professor Cooke consistently balanced rigorous criticism with warm encouragement, and I will never be able adequately to thank her for her commitment to the success of this project.

Finally, I wish to thank my family, without whose support this work would have been impossible.

Censorship in Canadian Literature

1 Introduction: Justifying Just Judgment

The main goal of this book is to explicate and comment on the views – both explicit and implicit – of some of our most prominent Canadian writers on censorship, but before I can begin this work I must clarify what I mean by that term. The *Oxford English Dictionary* defines a censor (the noun) in four ways. The first refers to the original use of the term to refer to the Roman magistrates who took the census of the citizens. The last is used in psychology to describe the mental faculty that represses certain elements of the unconscious. My definition, which does not deal particularly with classical history or Freudian psychology, derives primarily from the other two meanings. A censor, according to the first of these, is "one who exercises official or officious supervision over morals and conduct," and this includes "an official in some countries whose duty it is to inspect all books, journals, dramatic pieces, etc., before publication, to secure that they shall contain nothing immoral, heretical, or offensive to the government" (1029). The OED's other definition of a censor is "one who judges or criticizes," especially "one who censures or blames" (1029). This definition, according to the dictionary, has become obsolete: before the twelfth century, "censurer" and "censor" had the same meaning, which included the non-pejorative sense of one who judges or evaluates; as this definition fell out of use, "censor" came to mean an official who suppresses, while "censurer" became one who finds fault, blames, or condemns (OED, 1029). I believe that the loss of this early meaning of "censor" has deprived the word of its most salient characteristic, namely the quality of judgment – the word comes, after all, from the Latin *censere*, meaning to assess, estimate, judge – which in turn has led to confusion regarding what practices are and are not covered by the word.

Before I attempt to justify my belief that the element of judgment should be returned to the definition of censorship, I want to situate the two pertinent OED definitions in the context of intellectual history, a context that will provide a theoretical frame for my own definition. The first definition, that censorship is government suppression, is a product of the Enlightenment. For Enlightenment thinkers – from Bacon and Locke through Voltaire and Diderot to Franklin and Jefferson – society's crucial problems could be solved and reliable norms established through the use of reason. Of course reason could only be freely exercised when people were liberated from the tyranny of authoritarian institutions such as the Church and the state, and this included being free of their agents of censorship, who regulated the expression of reason. John Milton's *Areopagitica* is directed at the English Parliament, as is J.S. Mill's treatise "On the Liberty of Thought and Discussion," which is aimed at the "legislature or [its] executive" (78). The American First Amendment stipulates that "*Congress* shall make no law abridging the freedom of speech, or of the press." Because the Enlightenment project was so concerned with the emancipation of reason through the liberation of the rights of the individual, the Enlightenment model of censorship came to be the institutional – primarily governmental – control of expression.

We are still living with the Enlightenment conception of censorship, and there are still those in the West who explicitly adhere to a definition of censorship as government suppression. John Leo, writing from a particularly conservative perspective, is one such adherent: "In normal English," he argues, "'censorship' means control of utterance by government." He dismisses the claims of censorship made by artists who are denied grants, and by those squeezed out of the marketplace by corporate interests, as "word games ... [that] are generating suspect statistics and polluting public discussion" (31). Explicit positions such as Leo's are rare.[1] More commonly the Enlightenment definition is simply assumed: it has become a traditional way of thinking about censorship and constitutes the semantic background out of which censorship debates emerge. It is the assumption, for example, behind the liberal assertion, formulated by Oliver Wendell Holmes (inspired by Mill and echoed by Ronald Dworkin), that "the best test of truth is the power of the thought to get itself accepted in the competition of the market" (Abrams v. United States, 616). This argument, a central one in free-speech debates, holds that, as long as government suppression is absent from society, members of the society will be able to express and exchange ideas freely. It maintains that there is no censorship inherent in a marketplace of ideas.

There are a couple of problems with the Enlightenment definition of censorship and the arguments that proceed from it. First, this definition simply fails to describe accurately the relationship between power and the control of discourse in our society. In his influential book *Questions of Censorship* David Tribe challenges this definition of censorship as government suppression: "In this narrow sense, which some pedants, I believe wrongly, regard as its true meaning, censorship of printed material disappeared in Britain in 1695, and of plays in 1968. Only in totalitarian lands of the Right or the Left does it, by and large, remain in this form. Yet it would seem perverse to say there is no censorship in the liberal democracies" (17). As Tribe points out, the definition of censorship as suppression by government has led to the (mistaken) belief that, as the Enlightenment project was gradually realized in the West in the decline of the power of the Church and the replacement of authoritarian rulers with democratic practices, censorship has been eradicated. Censorship has not been eliminated in liberal democracies. The marketplace of ideas, left to function on its own without government censorship, has not resulted in the open and free expression of ideas among people. I will demonstrate in this book that there exist, in our society, a whole range of censors – from government to agents in the private sector to the writers themselves.

Another problem with the Enlightenment definition is the demonization of censorship. As a tool of government control of its citizens, censorship came to be known as the enemy of reason and therefore an enemy of freedom and democracy. As Sue Curry Jansen points out, in Enlightenment discourse "censorship is a devil term. It refers 'back to' a Dark Age in Western history. It refers 'down to' reactionary elements: un-Enlightened or foreign elements which threaten to reverse the tide of progress in Liberal societies" (4). As a result, censorship has come to acquire, in liberal democracies, especially in the United States, a reputation of being a practice that is *always* wrong. A related problem is the rhetorical effect this demonization of censorship has had on discussion of the issue. Whenever a proposal surfaces for the control of some discourse – be it pornography, hate literature, or offensive art – those making the proposal are labelled censors. This portrayal is not inaccurate, but the effect of calling individuals censors is immediately to cast them as anti-democratic, intolerant, and immoral, even before any of their arguments or the discourse in question is examined. It is very difficult for would-be censors to have their reasons for advocating censorship heeded when they have already been written off for that advocacy in the first place. Deprived of moral efficacy, arguments for the control of particular discourses must give way to anti-censorship feeling that, having hardened into an absolute principle on the moral high ground, is applied procedurally, without care for context, with significant deleterious results.[2]

If the Enlightenment position is one camp on the conceptual field defining censorship, then the other is what I wish to call the constructivist position. The constructivist position defines censorship as a process embedded in the forces that shape society. It derives from the ideas of thinkers such as Michel Foucault, who challenge the Enlightenment notion that truth can be arrived at or that knowledge can be produced by an autonomous individual using "objective" reasoning. For these thinkers, knowledge is at least partially a product of forces outside the individual. For Foucault, those forces are ones of power: "We should admit rather that power produces knowledge (and not simply by encouraging it because it serves power or by applying it because it is useful); that power and knowledge imply one another; that there is no power relation without the correlative constitution of a field of knowledge, nor any knowledge that does not presuppose and constitute at the same time power relations" (*Discipline and Punish*, 29).[3] It is a logical step from the idea that all knowledge proceeds from the interaction of social forces to the related idea that the absence or exclusion of any knowledge is the result of the interplay of social forces as well. In this view government, which suppresses the free expression of reason, is not the only censor in society: any time a social force causes expression to be excluded, or "disempowers" expression, censorship is taking place.

This is the broader view held by critics such as Richard Burt, who revises the Enlightenment definition of censorship and dispenses with the public/private divide that sees censorship as something performed only by governments: "I will contend that censorship operates not only in repressive terms (as in the confiscation and destruction of art, say), but also as a complex network of productive discursive practices that legitimate and delegitimate the production and reception of the aesthetic in general and of the avant garde in particular" ("Degenerate 'Art,'" 220). Burt relies on the constructivist idea that the existence (and therefore exclusion) of any discourse depends not on the intentions of any particular agent but on social forces that shape the context of that discourse. Sue Curry Jansen relies on this kind of thinking as well in her reformulation of censorship, which is similar to Burt's: "My definition of the term encompasses all socially structured proscriptions or prescriptions which inhibit or prohibit dissemination of ideas, information, images, and other messages through a society's channels of communication whether these obstructions are secured by political, economic, religious, or other systems of authority. It includes both overt and covert proscriptions and prescriptions" (221n1). In constructing these broader definitions, both Burt and Jansen come to reject the view of censorship as a strictly repressive, negative, demonic process that must be eliminated; instead, they take the view that censorship occurs wherever social forces contend, making it "an enduring feature of all human communities" (Jansen, 4). While both critics' intellectual projects echo my own in attempting to rehabilitate the concept of censorship by extending the traditional Enlightenment definition in several ways, their books limit the application of a revised definition: for Burt to the realm of aesthetics and for Jansen to the realm of economics (what she calls "material or market censorship" [222n1]).[4]

While my redefinition of censorship will be applicable beyond the realms of aesthetics and economics, I believe there is a danger in taking this constructivist approach too far. Michael Holquist, building on the same constructivist terrain as Burt and Jansen, does not observe their limits but ends up with a redefinition of censorship that has little use. His approach is tied closely to the structuralist view of language, in which signs gain their identity only through relational contrast with other signs. Echoing Ferdinand de Saussure's idea of linguistic difference, he writes: "Censorship is a necessary moment in all perception (to see a tree, I must cut out of my purview the rest of the forest). And it is an ineluctable feature of the grammatical aspect of language (to say "cat" in the noun slot of an English sentence is to exclude "dog," "zebra," "heffalump," etc.). In some measure, then, all texts are censored. Imposed censorship occupies a small segment in the arc of prohibition ... At this overabstracted level, the concept begins to lose its usefulness but not, perhaps, before demonstrating that all experience is a reading between the lines" (23n2). As Holquist himself recognizes, this definition is overly broad, to the extent that it becomes synonymous with the generic capacity to distinguish one thing from among others (whether it be a tree in a forest, a word in a sentence, or one book from others). This definition provides no answers to questions regarding the parameters of censorship – whether it is public or private, intentional or unintentional, whether it occurs before or after publication, and for what reasons – because it observes no such boundaries. Ultimately, under this definition, because everything is censorship, nothing is.

Holquist's definition of censorship is interesting, however, because it comes so close to duplicating the definition of the word "judgment," which is "the mental ability to perceive and distinguish relationships; discernment" (*Nelson Canadian Dictionary*, 735). What am I doing when I see Holquist's tree if not perceiving and distinguishing the relationship between that individual tree and those that make up the surrounding forest, or, in other words, using my faculty of judgment to pick out and comprehend that individual tree? This brings me back to the point of departure of my discussion of definitions, which was the historical connotations of the word "censor" and, by extension, "censorship." Quite some time ago, according to the OED definitions outlined above, censorship was simply the act of judging or criticizing. During the Enlightenment the word came to mean the governmental suppression of discourse. But this later meaning is in fact a much more specific version, a subset of the earlier one, for the government censorship of some work is a *negative* judgment of the work, backed up by the power to enforce that judgment. In recent times, however, it has become evident that governments are not the only authorities that exercise the judgment of censorship: Jansen argues that the economic market does so; Holquist that we *all* do. My point here is that, again, any discussion of censorship must acknowledge that judgment is at the base of this activity. Anti-censorship forces are loath to admit this because judgment is not a pejorative term; the words they *do* focus on, "suppression" and "control," when placed beside "government" are much more effective in achieving the demonizing effect they are after.

It is appropriate, therefore, to see all definitions of censorship on a spectrum of judgment, with the very narrow Enlightenment definition (Leo's, for example) at one end and a very diffuse constructivist one (Holquist's, for example, which comprises the judgment of anything by anyone) at the other. Most other definitions of censorship will generally fall somewhere between these poles.[5] The definition I use in this book does so as well. I would define censorship as the exclusion of some discourse as the result of a judgment by an authoritative agent based on some ideological predisposition.[6] The definition borrows from but is certainly broader than the Enlightenment definition: the idea that censorship is practised by someone in power is maintained, for example, but the government official is changed to any authoritative agent. It is naturally narrower than the all-encompassing constructivist definition contemplated by Holquist: judgment is the prime activity of the censor; it is not just any judgment, however, but judgment based on some ideological ground (so Holquist's physiological example would not qualify).

Let me expand on some of the characteristics of this definition. First, who can be a censor? Is censorship a practice solely within the purview of the government (that which is public) or can it be a private practice as well? If censorship can be private as well as public, then another question arises: can a person censor him/herself? That is, is censorship performed only by a third party, or can it also take the form of self-suppression? As is evident from the definitions of censorship I have highlighted so far, constructivist definitions diverge from the traditional Enlightenment one mainly in asserting that governments are not the only censors in society. Gara LaMarche argues that "censorship functions at three levels: governmental, through legislatures and school boards and arts councils; nongovernmental, through decisions by editors and producers, publishers and studios, booksellers and theaters; and the personal" (58). Like Lamarche, I will contend that private censorship and self-censorship are not different in kind from governmental censorship and that all three are covered by my definition.

What is the difference between government and private censorship? Let us take an example to consider the justification of such a distinction. It is 1947 in Moscow. I write a letter to the editor spelling out the evils of Communism and hope to have it published in the newspaper. Under the regime of the day all letters appearing in the Communist Party newspaper (the only newspaper permitted) must be screened by government officials before being authorized for publication. My work is duly examined, fails the test, and is refused publication. I am sent a terse note directing me to stop writing capitalist propaganda, and my friends tell me I am lucky to be alive. Clearly this is censorship (it epitomizes the traditional Enlightenment definition). Now let us imagine that at the same time I have a cousin who lives in the United States and holds views on political economy diametrically opposed to mine. My cousin writes a letter on the benefits of Communism, and while the Soviet government is considering my letter, he sends his to an American newspaper editor who, after considering the content of his polemic, not surprisingly turns him down. How are these two scenarios different?

Noted First Amendment scholar Frederick Schauer takes up the issue of public versus private censorship and gives two main reasons for viewing them as different. One difference he identifies is that suppression of speech in the private realm "is almost always trivial. Speakers and listeners can move to different locations" (125). Schauer's point is that private suppression is usually local, while public suppression extends systematically throughout the domain of the government. Applied to my example, this argument would hold that, while government rejection of my letter barred it from every newspaper in the land, my cousin could turn to other newspaper publishers. But given the Cold War hysteria in the United States at the time of our example, is it not conceivable that my cousin would send his letter to newspaper after newspaper with no success at publication? Would an industry ban be any different from a government one? For South African novelist and social commentator J.M. Coetzee, writing in 1996, this is the answer to Schauer's argument: "When censure is not only expressed but acted upon by bodies that hold an effective monopoly on particular media of expression (via, for instance, distribution or retail networks), freedom of expression may be stifled as effectively as under outright legal ban. This is a significant problem for anyone who tries to distinguish sharply between censorship and censure, or what Frederick Schauer calls public and private censorship" (235). Furthermore, while private suppression can be *as* effective as a public ban, sometimes it can be *more* effective. If the Soviet government for some reason decided my letter would be barred only from newspapers distributed in Moscow, and my cousin was refused by every newspaper in New York State, it could be argued that the private suppression was more robust than the public. Finally, just as the subject of private suppression can move to another location to speak his piece (or in my cousin's case to another newspaper if he can find one), there is nothing inherently immobilizing in censorship wielded by government. It is true that the Soviet authorities would not have let me pass into West Germany to publish my letter, but that is not because they practised censorship but because they believed in restricting the movement of their citizens. Other countries that censor (like Canada, which has hate laws) are not concerned with such restriction of movement. So it is not necessarily true that private censorship is trivial or local compared to public censorship, and to distinguish between them based on this view would be a mistake.

The other distinction Schauer makes between public and private suppression of discourse is that private suppression may be an act of expression. The *New York Times* may decide to suppress my cousin's letter, but if the state tells the newspaper it must be more tolerant and publish his letter, the *Times* is being censored. Forcing the newspaper to include something it would prefer not to include interferes with *its* freedom of expression. Schauer concludes that "the act of censoring by a private agent can in many instances be an act of speech by that agent, and … remedying this act of censorship by a private agent can be a governmental restriction on that act of speech ... This additional dimension of private suppression as an act of speech, or at least a corollary to it, distinguishes private from government censorship, and makes the notion of private censorship almost self-contradictory" (122–3). Schauer's argument is faulty, however, because it does not consider that government suppression can be an act of expression as well. The City of New York could decide to ban any newspapers containing pro-Communist sentiment from its streets, but if the federal government tells the city it must be more tolerant and allow these newspapers, the city is being censored. It wishes to express its anti-Communist feeling, but its freedom to do so is being curtailed in a way similar to the curtailment of the *Times* by the government.[7] Thus suppression can be an act of speech not only for private agents but for public ones as well. Schauer's second distinction is no more justified than his first, and I would contend there is no good reason to observe a difference in kind between public and private censorship.

The continuity between public and private censorship lends support to my definition, in which censorship can be performed by *any* authoritative agent. But does this formulation include self-censorship? Can an artist (who has, after all, a certain authority over his or her own work) who ends up excluding his or her own discourse be considered to be a censor? Before I can answer this question I need to consider some of the characteristics of censorship that are implied by my definition. These include the question of when censorship can occur, whether it is intentional or unintentional, and the reasons for its occurrence.

When can censorship occur? The traditional definition holds that censorship is "prior restraint," which consists either of a licensing system in which a work must be submitted to a government agent for inspection before publication or of a court injunction prohibiting the dissemination of some information. Within Western democracies the former kind of prior restraint has, for the most part, been done away with for written material like books, and is found only in pockets of other forms of cultural production (films, for example, are still reviewed before release in some Canadian provinces). The latter kind, court injunction, is used sparingly (sometimes judges impose a publication ban on the proceedings of a trial to ensure the accused gets a fair hearing). Though incidences of prior restraint are now rare, there is a constant stream of disputes, both inside and outside the courtroom, in which censorship is considered to be the issue of contention. This fact suggests that censorship does not consist only of occurrences of prior restraint. As Cass R. Sunstein points out, "There is a major obstacle to free speech if someone who utters a criticism of the President is subject to a sentence of life imprisonment; but there is no prior restraint. Most censorship occurs through subsequent punishment" (xiii). Perhaps, however, we are using the wrong word when we call these cases censorship. These instances of post-publication suppression, as Sunstein says, consist of punishment. Prior restraint, by contrast, aims to prevent certain material from being published. If censorship is exclusion or suppression, then isn't prevention a much more comprehensive mode of exclusion than punishment?

The answer is no, for two reasons. First, punishment *is* prevention. The infliction of some penalty in retribution for someone's act is usually only one goal of punishment; the other is to prevent that person from committing the act again and to send a warning to others who would commit such an act. Deterrence makes post-publication suppression as effective a form of censorship as prior restraint. In fact, it may be more rigorous. For in a state that punishes after publication, to reduce their risk authors will tend not to produce material they fear will come close to what is considered punishable by the authorities (this is an example of self-censorship). In a system of prior restraint authors will feel more at ease producing this marginal material since the only risk they incur is having their work rejected. We see the deterrent capacity of post-publication suppression in the effect of libel law known as "libel chill," whereby authors fearing retribution refrain from making claims that, though perhaps controversial, would not be actionable under the law. Second, one may argue that post-publication suppression is not "true" censorship because individuals under this system have an autonomy unlike those subject to prior restraint. At least they are free to publish their work: if it is suppressed afterward, that is another matter. But this is only to say that these individuals are free to break the law. The same can be said of authors in a system of prior restraint, for they too are free to break the law by flouting government inspectors and publishing, while facing the consequences afterward.

Not only do I believe that censorship can occur both before and after a work's publication; I would go further to argue that censorship can occur even before the work is written. With this claim I am concerned not so much with the timing of the suppression but with its nature: is censorship always direct, overt, and intended? The traditional Enlightenment definition of censorship would answer this question in the affirmative: faced with an offensive work, the government intervenes without an intermediary, openly carrying out its purpose, which is to suppress the work. Some of the constructivist definitions I have discussed, however, present censorship as a more subtle, systemic discursive process that shapes the very boundaries of what can be said. Richard Burt calls this "structural censorship": "Censorship may be seen, then, not only in terms of repressed and free discourses but also in terms of the receivable and the unreceivable – what cannot be heard or spoken without risk of being delegitimated as beyond the pale of discourse" ("Introduction," xvii). Judith Butler refers to a similar phenomenon when she writes of "implicit censorship" (she also calls it "foreclosure") that "operate[s] on a level prior to speech, namely, as the constituting norm by which the speakable is differentiated from the unspeakable" (137–8). The "unreceivable," the "unspeakable," are not lacunae in discourse that are produced by the direct and overt intervention of an intentional agent. At the level of language, if I cannot express some idea because the requisite words do not exist in my lexicon, I am being constrained indirectly and covertly by the social forces (not an intentional agent) that have constructed my vocabulary. At the level of speech act, if I refrain from interrupting a play to roundly curse the actors for their bad performance, it is not because of any government prohibition but because of social mores that deem it unacceptable. In both examples I can break free of the restraints only by a radical act of social transgression (in the first case by creating the words I need and having them understood by others, in the second by defying social convention).

One might argue, however, that these are not cases of censorship precisely because they are not direct and overt, and no intentional agent is present. But surely these attributes are not required in all incidents in which we would consider censorship to be a factor. If a government decides to give grants only to artists who sing the praises of that government, it is not censoring directly and overtly: it is not openly preventing its critics from voicing their views through prior restraint or punishment. Yet while the awarding of a government grant is a reward, the withholding of it is a punishment, and again, to punish for the expression of some idea is often as effective as to prevent it. In this way the outcome of the government's action will be to inhibit speech. This *is* censorship, albeit of an indirect and covert nature.[8] Nor does censorship need to be intentional. During an election campaign the media may agree to disseminate candidates' views only if the candidates can afford to purchase expensive ads. The media's intent, no doubt, is merely to make money, not to suppress particular political views. The effect, however, is to censor those who are financially disadvantaged. In Canada the government recognizes this threat of inadvertent censorship and counters it by obliging the public broadcaster to air political ads free of charge.

Taken together, the arguments I have been making about censorship lay the foundations for my claim that self-censorship is a form of censorship not unlike the others I have been discussing. Some of the examples I have used – when I refrain from saying something about someone because I am afraid of being sued for libel; when I suppress my urge to interrupt a play; or when I refrain from criticizing the government to win a grant – show self-censorship in action even as they illustrate these arguments. Self-censorship often occurs before a discourse is even articulated. It is often indirect: I may decide not to say something, but it may be because a third party has put pressure on me to keep silent. That third party may be the government, but it may also be a private interest. Self-censorship can be intentional (I may choose to keep my criticism of the government to myself because I know it is the only way of obtaining a grant), but it may also be unintentional: I may have so completely assimilated the values of society that my suppression of my opinion may be unthinking and automatic (in which case it becomes difficult to identify). Since, as we have seen, censorship can be private; since it can occur before a discourse is even articulated; and since it need not be direct, overt, or intentional, we can conclude that self-censorship is not different in kind from other forms of censorship.[9]

One problematic issue that arises when we consider self-censorship is its relation to artistic revision. What is the difference between self-censorship and editing? When a novelist reluctantly bows to pressure from a publisher to remove a scene that the publisher feels will be controversial, the novelist is clearly performing an act of self-censorship. When the novelist agrees to make certain stylistic changes demanded by the publisher, such as modification of grammar or punctuation, we call it editing. What determines the difference between these activities, and where is the line drawn between them? At first glance it would appear that the answer depends on the nature of the motivation of the revision. The motivation in the first case is political or ideological (I prefer the latter word as per my definition of censorship), while in the second it is aesthetic. But poststructuralist critics have suggested that there is no pure, objective, aesthetic realm, that aesthetic judgments do not exist independent of the ideological forces (economic, social, historical, etc.) that shape them. Ideological foundations can affect judgments of style no less than they do other kinds of aesthetic judgments (such as "quality"). Consider the Black Canadian writer who is told that her novel, written in Nation Language (a Black English dialect) will only be published if she "cleans up" the grammar to comply with standard English. The publisher's demand is ideological, and should the writer comply, she will be censoring herself. Clearly the difference between self-censorship and editing is not the latter's aesthetic motivation. Perhaps the difference relies on there being a disagreement between writer and publisher: when the writer endorses the changes it is editing; when she makes them against her wishes, when she bows to outside pressure, it is self-censorship. But if a writer goes along with changes merely because she has assimilated the ideological values that inform them, she is participating in the "implicit censorship" to which Butler refers. In this way, making "grammatical" corrections to get published is like keeping silent during an awful play to avoid incurring public displeasure.

While I think it is very difficult to formulate a difference between editing and self-censorship when artistic revision is instigated by a third party (including when a writer, of her own accord, makes changes to her work to align it with some externally set standard), I am reluctant to class editing choices made solely by the author for "personal" (non-ideological) reasons as self-censorship. This feeling rests on the assumption that individuals have a certain authoritative autonomy, that they can make some choices, including some aesthetic ones, independently of the social forces at work in the background. Determining the validity of the extreme constructivist position that proffers these social forces as fundamental to human endeavour, that decentres the subject and questions the subject's authority, even posits the death of the author,[10] is beyond my purview here. Thus, in trying to determine whether an author is performing self-censorship by altering a text based on what appear to be autonomous, personal reasons – as I do with Findley in chapter 2 – I rely on a case-by-case approach that takes in the context of the act (the nature of the changes, the author's stated intent, etc.).

All the characteristics of censorship I have been discussing are implicit in my definition, in which censorship is the exclusion of some discourse as the result of a judgment made by an authoritative agent based on some ideological predisposition. By an authoritative agent I mean someone with the power to enforce the judgment, whether it be a public agent, a private agent, or the producer of the discourse herself. Rather than attach a clear subject to the act of exclusion I use the rather passive "as a result of" to allow for censorship that is indirect and covert and may not always be intentional. The definition also stipulates that there must be a certain driving factor behind the suppression for it to be censorship (even if it is indirect), namely a judgment driven by ideology. This rules out arbitrary and physiological acts of differentiation or selection. The most important word in the definition, however, is judgment. Censorship is the result of a mental activity in which the censor perceives and distinguishes relationships or alternatives with respect to the discourse being judged. This judgment can be better – it can be more "just" – when it manages to take in much of the context surrounding the discourse (whether the discourse is art, whether it is intended to be ironic, the identity of its target audience, etc.), or worse, when it fails to do so, but it will never be perfect (the entire context can never be known), and it is not always pernicious. We can no more rid ourselves of censorship than we can of our capacity and proclivity to judge; all we can do is try to bring about the conditions that make these judgments more appropriate and constructive. Censorship is just (merely) judgment, so what we need to focus on is making just (fair) judgments.[11]

CENSORSHIP AND CANADIAN WRITING

The definition of censorship I have been discussing informs the following chapters of this book. I use it both to identify the arguments about censorship that these Canadian writers make (either explicitly or implicitly) and to expose some of the contradictions in these arguments. In chapter 2, I show that Timothy Findley has taken up the traditional position, which sees censorship as a sinister force in society. He takes this position in part in response to a number of controversies involving the exclusion or alteration of his own writing, including the rejection of one of his novels by publishers and the decision not to publish another because of the threat of a libel suit. *The Wars* in particular shows signs of censorship (either attempted or accomplished) by Findley's editors, the creators of the film version of the novel, and Findley himself. Much of the source material in this section of chapter 2 comes from unpublished writings by Findley, making this the first critical study to compare early versions of *The Wars* with the final, published one. My goal in examining these incidents of exclusion and alteration of Findley's work is to show that they are examples of censorship and, as such, illustrate the point that censorship can take forms other than government suppression of expression. In fact these censoring activities – such as selection by publishers, for example – are widespread and inevitable in our society, so when we argue about censorship it is not the practice itself we should be evaluating but the reasons behind this practice. In this section I also explore some of Findley's more wide-ranging philosophical attacks against censorship. He condemns the practice explicitly in some of his non-fiction work, where he advances several different anti-censorship arguments. I demonstrate that his arguments are undermined by discrepancies within this non-fiction writing as well as by contradictory evidence provided by a thematic reading of *The Wars*.

The second half of the chapter on Findley is devoted to a close reading of *Headhunter* that emphasizes the novel's implicit anti-censorship position. The novel makes more sense, for example, when we see that the birds – supposed to carry disease – represent books and the D-squads represent censors, and that Findley based his malevolent artist, Julian Slade, on the real-life painter Attila Richard Lukacs. Observations of this sort, taken together, reveal that in *Headhunter* Findley proffers a traditional neutralist liberal attack characterized by two arguments, the non-consequentialist and consequentialist claims for free speech, aimed at discrediting censorship. I counter the first, non-consequentialist claim by asserting that it does not really exist, that in fact it is always a species of the second, consequentialist approach. The consequentialist position in turn relies on the "slippery-slope" argument, which rejects the possibility of drawing a line between acceptable and unacceptable speech. I challenge this argument by invoking my definition of censorship and maintaining that all exercises of judgment involve the drawing of lines, and that the judgment or censorship of discourse should not be, cannot be, any exception.

The second writer that I study, Margaret Atwood, also puts forward the slippery-slope argument in her fiction, but in the context of the pornography debate. Chapter 3 traces the development of Atwood's attitudes towards the censorship of pornography. It begins with an analysis of *Bodily Harm*, the novel in which Atwood is interested in the relationships between censorship, pornography, and violence. This analysis reads the novel against three other texts that deal with pornography: *I Never Promised You a Rose Garden*, *Autobiography of a Schizophrenic Girl*, and *Story of O*. Although they may seem unlikely books to compare with Atwood's, the striking resemblances between these works and *Bodily Harm* provide a new explanation of the character Rennie's attitude towards her own body and of the importance of hands in the novel. Certain elements of my definition of censorship come into play in this analysis as I show that one of the major obstacles to the growth of the protagonist is marketplace censorship, the suppression of certain kinds of discourse through economic pressure. This kind of censorship often transforms into self-censorship, as economic values are internalized by individuals, and this is what happens to Rennie. Another kind of censorship afflicting Rennie, remarkably, is pornography. The equation between censorship and pornography is Atwood's, but it meshes with my definition of censorship as the exclusion of some discourse as a result of ideological judgment (with pornography it is the exclusion of certain depictions of sexuality as a result of patriarchal judgments). Reflecting anti-pornography feminist theory of the time, *Bodily Harm* puts forward several arguments linking pornography with male violence, ultimately making the case for the censorship of pornography. It may sound contradictory to discuss the censorship of pornography when pornography is equated with censorship, but this equation fits with the controlling idea of the novel: *Bodily Harm* calls for the exclusion of an exclusionary practice.

Atwood's change in thinking on the censorship of pornography is signalled by an article she wrote for *Chatelaine* magazine in which she attacks pornography, but which ends by sounding a note of warning about the oppressive potential of censorship. The article was published two years after *Bodily Harm* and two years before *The Handmaid's Tale*; in the latter novel Atwood picks up that note of warning to structure a full-blown dystopia. The second half of my chapter on Atwood is a close reading of *The Handmaid's Tale*. I argue, for example, contrary to most critics, who believe that the character Serena Joy (Commander Fred's wife) is based on conservative Republican Phyllis Schlafly, that in fact she is modelled on television evangelist Tammy Faye Bakker. I also add fresh evidence to the established view that Gilead bears many similarities to Nazi Germany and, more importantly, explain why Atwood relies on this comparison. In addition, in my discussion of taboo, I show that the restrictions attached to sex in the novel have clear analogues in the suppression of discourse, or in censorship. More important than the novelty of these observations is their role as elements in an overall interpretation that sees Atwood making four (albeit implicit) arguments against censorship: first, that truth and meaning are subjective – what is profane and should be censored for one person is sacred for another; second, that censorship will result in a slippery slope that eventually engulfs "inoffensive" works; third, that pornography is harmless; and fourth, that suppressing some discourse only makes that discourse more attractive (I call this the "compression-explosion" model of censorship). I believe that the presence of these ideas in the novel suggests that, by the time she wrote *The Handmaid's Tale*, Atwood had come to question the view that pornography is more dangerous than censorship. At the same time I maintain that objections to her four arguments are contained within the novel itself, challenging this anti-censorship position.

Chapter 4 also deals with the censorship of pornography, but my study of Margaret Laurence's work shows that, though writing at approximately the same time as Atwood, Laurence arrived at very different conclusions regarding the benefits of eliminating pornography. In this chapter I am less interested in implicit arguments about censorship to be found *in* Laurence's fiction (a large part of my work with the other writers) than in an aspect of her explicit commentary on the subject that has remained, so far, unknown to her readers. The most important unpublished piece of writing by Laurence involving censorship is a draft manuscript of a novel now held at the William Ready Archives at McMaster University. Laurence began work on this draft shortly after an attack on her work *The Diviners* was mounted in 1976 in her own town of Lakefield, Ontario. Censorship is a more personal issue for Laurence than it is for the other writers I study because of this event (and a similar attack that took place in 1985), so any understanding of Laurence's position on censorship must take into account the consequences of these biographical episodes. I begin my study by looking at the effects on the writer of the first attack, tracing the evolution of her response from the germination of the idea to write a novel about the attack, to her struggle to create characters with whom she could not sympathize, to her final abandonment of the project. I examine the draft material for this project that Laurence left behind, showing how it reflects the 1976 attack – in its characters, the attackers' motivations, the material in question, and the protagonist's reaction – and is a response to it.

Though this response remained incomplete and unpublished, Laurence did find other written forms through which to channel her feelings about censorship: her children's book *The Christmas Birthday Story,* and her article "The Greater Evil," which appeared in *Toronto Life* in 1984. The second half of my chapter on Laurence is a re-reading of this article – in which Laurence weighs the relative dangers of pornography and of censorship – in the light of its more lengthy and complex unpublished precursor, a speech Laurence gave to Ontario judges in 1983. In this light the powerful arguments she makes for banning pornography show up much more clearly, and as a result Laurence's position on censorship is revealed to be much closer to the one that derives from my definition of censorship as judgment than to the liberal anti-censorship position that might otherwise be ascribed to her based on a reading of the article alone.

Of all the chapters in this book, chapter 5 illustrates most clearly the definition I have constructed of censorship. In it I look at types of censorship that occur as a result of the competition of social groups in the cultural sphere. "Socio-cultural censorship," as I call it, is practised by four different groups of agents: educators, who censor through the exclusion of certain languages and histories from the classroom; "cultural gatekeepers," such as publishers, critics, anthologists, and the distributors of awards, who mediate between cultural producers and the public, deciding what material will be disseminated; some cultural producers who appropriate the voice or subject of a social group that is not their own, thereby excluding members of that group from the cultural arena; and some cultural producers themselves who practice self-censorship.

This socio-cultural censorship derives from competition among social groups in society, so it is typically most often perpetrated by members of a dominant group over members of a disadvantaged one. In chapter 5 I look at the socio-cultural censorship of two marginalized groups in Canada: Native and Black writers. To illustrate the way this kind of censorship affects Native Canadian writers I focus on Beatrice Culleton, a Métis writer whose autobiographical novel, *In Search of April Raintree*, was either the subject of or implicitly portrays socio-cultural censorship at the hands of all four kinds of agents I mentioned above. In the second half of the chapter I turn to the Black Canadian writer Marlene Nourbese Philip, who writes about the censorship of Black language and the appropriation of Black culture in her book of poetry *She Tries Her Tongue, Her Silence Softly Breaks*; she discusses the agents I describe as cultural gatekeepers in non-fiction essays and letters; and she shows how self-censorship works within the Black community in her novel for young adults, *Harriet's Daughter*. My goal in accumulating evidence that these two writers implicitly and, along with many scholars who write on marginalized cultures, explicitly view these exclusionary activities as censorship is to lend support to my definition of the term as a practice based on judgment. While I decry the racist ideology behind much of the socio-cultural censorship illustrated in this chapter, I maintain that, were racism to disappear, censorship would remain, for socio-cultural judgments by their very nature are based on ideological predispositions. This inevitability suggests that we should be looking at ways to make socio-cultural censorship more just rather than trying to rid our society of it along with other forms of censorship.

While there has been much written on censorship, from John Milton to Stanley Fish, almost none of it has focused on Canadian literature. I hope that, by exploring issues of censorship in English Canadian literature specifically, this study will shed new light on Canadian literary practice and, at the same time, will sharpen our ideas about how censorship works, its inevitability and value, and the importance that context plays in making judgments in all censorship disputes.

2 The Case against Censorship: Timothy Findley

> They haven't understood. That person who wants that book
> removed for that reason, I would say, is a rapist of a kind,
> a cultural rapist, because he's taken an event and hasn't seen
> through what the artist has done with it and has intended by it.
>
> Timothy Findley

Although the metaphor of censorship as rape is a common one
among writers – we will see it subtly surfacing in the writing of
Margaret Atwood and Beatrice Culleton and more overtly in the
work of Marlene Nourbese Philip – it nevertheless points to the
power of the issue of censorship to provoke strong, visceral
responses. Findley's use of the metaphor above comes in an interview with Johan Aitken in which he criticizes those who attempted
to have *The Wars* banned because of its homosexual rape scene. Judging by his responses to episodes of censorship such as this one and
the position he takes on censorship in general, it seems Findley sees
few grounds on which censorship could be justified.

Each of the controversies he faced provoked Findley to defend
himself and his work, and rebuttals to his attackers figure prominently in his discussions of the novels in interviews, opinion pieces,
and his memoir. Findley has not, however, limited his reactions
against censorship to defences of his own work; he has also defended
other writers. He has a great affinity for Salman Rushdie and Arthur
Miller, of whom he writes: "Both have been vilified. Both have survived the vilification. Both – in the course of that survival – have
continued to give voice to all the voices in them, as writers, that
speak without compromise" (*Inside Memory*, 189). He has even
expressed support for such surprising subjects of censorship as Beatrix
Potter, as when he read *The Tale of Peter Rabbit* at a public forum in
aid of PEN International in 1987 – the children's book had recently
come under fire from the London Council on Education in England

(*Inside Memory*, 163–5). And, of course, he has come to the aid of his closest writer friends, as evidenced by his impassioned vindication of Margaret Laurence's *The Diviners* in "Better Dead than Read? An Opposing View." There he argues that censorship stems "from a truly evil manipulation of people's genuine fear and uncertainty about the world we live in" (4), illustrating the rhetoric of demonization so often underwriting discussions of censorship.[1]

What emerges is a picture of an author for whom censorship is a major concern. Censorship has touched him personally, and he has felt constrained to answer his opponents and the opponents of other authors he admires. I suggest that these experiences have caused Findley to think about the issue extensively and to take an active stand on the subject generally.[2] His work as chairman of the Writers' Union of Canada, a prominent anti-censorship organization, his numerous non-fiction pieces on the subject, and his outspoken comments in interviews all point to a position on censorship that has been developed over many years and is held with the firmest of convictions. Put briefly, the position Findley takes is one of opposition to *all* censorship. As Diana Brydon states, "Findley believes that literature should never be censored because its value lies in testing limits and putting the assumptions of civilisation itself on trial" (*Writing on Trial*, 13). His position is similar to the Enlightenment view that censorship is an evil that should be eliminated in society. The fervent passage at the end of his memoir concisely sums up his view: "In recent times, the subject of banning books and censorship has been the cause of grave and increasing concern. The gulf between those who favour and those who oppose these things is growing wider and deeper. For myself, I am on the side of opposition. Nothing can make me believe another human being should have the power to prevent me from reading what I want or what I need to read" (*Inside Memory*, 315).

In this chapter I will examine issues of censorship involving Findley's work first by looking at several incidents of exclusion or alteration that have befallen his writing, from rejection by publishers to the threat of a libel suit to removal of his books from schools. My analysis of *The Wars* suggests that censorship was attempted or accomplished by Findley's editors, the makers of the film version of the novel, and Findley himself. My purpose is to show that censorship is not just an exclusionary procedure practised by governments (the traditional view) but includes activities many of us engage in that we would not want to outlaw. I argue, therefore, that it is not, as Findley maintains, censorship that is the problem in our society but rather, as the example of censorship of Findley's work shows, the errors of judgment in given cases of censorship. I then explore some of Findley's more specific critiques of censorship explicitly articulated in his non-fiction writing, in particular his essay "Censorship by Every Other Name." Findley makes several different arguments here against censorship, but I show that these arguments are undermined by the exceptions they allow and by contradictory evidence provided by a thematic reading of *The Wars*. Finally, I highlight the implicit anti-censorship position Findley puts forward in *Headhunter*, which rests on two main arguments – the non-consequentialist and consequentialist approaches to freedom of speech – both of which are central to the neutralist liberal polemic against censorship (see, for example, Ronald Dworkin). My critiques of both these arguments lend support to this study's goal of rehabilitating the concept of censorship and revealing it as an activity that we must practise not less frequently but more carefully.

CENSORING TIMOTHY FINDLEY

Findley's work has been at the centre of censorship controversies that are surprisingly numerous and diverse in kind. Sometimes these attacks succeeded; sometimes they were resisted or defeated. His first novel, *The Last of the Crazy People*, was published in the United States in 1967 but rejected by Canadian publishers (it was distributed in Canada at the time by General Publishing; its first Canadian publisher was Macmillan in 1977). Findley recalls that the novel, which tells the story of an eleven-year-old boy who kills his family, was rebuffed by Canadian publishing houses because they contended "that children don't do that kind of thing in Canada" (quoted in Benson, 109). This rejection constitutes censorship according to the definition I adopted in my Introduction: Findley's work was excluded for a time from the cultural arena because of the judgment of an authoritative agent (the publisher) based on an ideological predisposition. The nature of the ideological predisposition is not clear: is the publisher's justification – that a story like Findley's would not happen in Canada – an economic one (Canadians, not being able to identify with the story, would not buy the book) or an aesthetic one (the book fails because it is not realistic)? Regardless of its nature, ideological bias is evident in the rejection of the book based on its content.

This incident is not the only example of censorship of Findley's work. The stage adaptation of *Not Wanted on the Voyage*, an irreverent retelling of the Bible story of the great flood, which includes a cross-dressing archangel Lucifer, sparked an outcry when it was put on in Winnipeg in 1992. Manitoba vice officers investigated the performance for obscenity, their interest aroused specifically by a scene in which a young woman is violated by a unicorn's horn (262–5 in the novel). In the end the police decided against laying charges (Wagner, J1).

In addition to third-party interference, Findley has also suppressed his own work. He decided to delay the publication of *Famous Last Words* in Britain and France after being "strongly advised" (*Inside Memory*, 204) that he could be sued for libel by the Duchess of Windsor. The book portrays the Duke and Duchess of Windsor as Nazi collaborators during the Second World War. It was finally published in Britain in 1987, after the Duchess's death (to critical condemnation and a place on the bestseller lists); but, as Findley observes, for six years "it was completely denied two of its major European markets" (*Inside Memory*, 205). This decision to refrain from publishing out of fear of a libel suit is a typical example of "libel chill." As Frederick Schauer points out, faced with the risk of defamatory liability, a publisher or writer may "refrain from publishing owing to a desire to avoid that risk. To the extent that [that] course of action is chosen, some degree of *self-censorship* exists" (170). Self-censorship on Findley's part for a time kept *Famous Last Words* from wider distribution.

While censorship of the works I have mentioned so far was relatively isolated and temporary, censorship of Findley's Governor-General's Award–winning novel *The Wars* has been more widespread, sustained, and complex. Censorship of *The Wars* can be divided into two categories: pre-publication and post-publication. Findley resisted one attempt at pre-publication censorship that involved a scene in the novel in which the hero, Robert Ross, is raped by fellow soldiers (165–9). Ironically, one person who pressured Findley to remove the scene was fellow free-speech advocate Margaret Laurence. Findley reports the following exchange:

It would be tragic if something went wrong because you're being pig-headed … Tell me why it has to be there," she said.

"It has to be there because it is my belief that Robert Ross and his generation of young men were raped, in effect, by the people who made that war. Basically, their fathers did it to them."

Margaret said: "Yes, I agree with you. But surely that's implicit in the book already. You don't have to *say* so."   (*Inside Memory*, 151)

More serious objections to the scene came from Findley's editor, John Pearce, and his typist, Ellen Powers, who, writes Findley, were "concerned … because they think it will get the book in trouble … Ellen said the scene *had rung a warning bell* – and Pearce has attempted a diplomatic, roundabout route, whereby I will come to the decision to cut the scene myself" (*Inside Memory*, 150). Notice that Findley's description of his editor's approach clearly captures the covert, indirect nature that, I argue, often characterizes incidents of self-censorship. Often the pressure of an outside force will be insidious, making it appear to others and to the cultural producer himself that what is at work in the excision of some text is the cultural producer's choice and not self-censorship.

I believe this dynamic, where a writer is convinced he is making a free aesthetic choice but is actually censoring himself, may have been at work in the production of *The Wars* even before it was submitted for publication. There are a number of scenes in the novel that, in early drafts, contain more explicit or profane language than appears in the published version. This is evident in revisions with respect to the word "fuck" (a word that has been the bane of many a liberal-minded author, from Daniel Keyes to J.D. Salinger). In the crater scene Robert saves his men from poison gas by having them breathe through pieces of urine-soaked cloth. At first Robert orders the men to get out their handkerchiefs, and when his second-in-command Corporal Bates responds that they have no handkerchiefs, Robert explodes. In the draft manuscript this explosion appears as, "THEN TEAR THE FUCKING TAILS OFF YOUR FUCKING SHIRTS" (Ms/ TsN, file 17-4:149).[3] In the published version Robert's response is more polite: "THEN TEAR THE TAILS OFF YOUR GOD DAMNED SHIRTS!" (124).

Is this self-censorship on Findley's part? It certainly seems that the author's original and lasting impulse was to use the more explicit language, for the more profane passage occurs at least four times in three separate draft manuscripts before being revised in the published version.[4] But Findley maintains his revision decision was not self-censorship. In a letter responding to my queries on the removal of certain material from the novel, he explains his decision: "Yes, in earlier drafts, I tried to have Robert Ross use the kind of language I assumed was common amongst young Canadians fighting in World War I. However, as I went along with the writing, I discovered something both interesting and immutable about Robert Ross. He simply wouldn't say 'fuck.' Or 'shit.' It wasn't a question of self-censorship, but of being obedient to the integrity of a character." So, according to Findley, he removed the profane language neither because he was worried about offending his publishers or readers nor because he was concerned about an explicit version of the book selling poorly (common reasons for self-censorship) but rather because it did not match Robert's character. This is an aesthetic decision and, though in the Introduction I argued that some aesthetic judgments can rely on ideological predispositions, I cannot see an ideological force or a set of beliefs at work in this one (I think the argument that Findley is applying an assimilated penchant for realism is a weak one).

Yet Findley's explanation seems less convincing when we consider that other speakers in the novel have their language sanitized as well. Soon after Robert arrives in France for the first time, he finds himself trapped and slowly sinking into a poisonous sea of mud. In a draft manuscript of this scene the narrator provides this description of his struggle: "He began to push again and to lift – thrusting his pelvis upward harder and harder – faster and faster against the mud. He was fucking the mud. It made him laugh. His hat fell off. The wind and the fog were dabbling in his hair" (TsO, file 17-9:115).[5] This passage is part of a much longer paragraph that is almost identical with the one appearing in the published novel. There is, however, one notable difference in the two versions. In the novel the narrator says: "He began to push again and to lift – thrusting his pelvis upward harder and harder – faster and faster against the mud. His hat fell off. The wind and the fog were dabbling in his hair" (80). Is it likely that Findley revised his copy, specifically to avoid using the offensive four-letter word, because he came to realize it would be out of character for his narrator to swear? There is little evidence in the novel that refinement and sensitivity are as integral to the narrator's character as they are to Robert's. Yet it could be argued that the scene in the mud is being described from Robert's point of view (through the narrator) and should therefore reflect the words Robert might use.

The same argument, that a kind of third-person limited narration necessitated the expurgation of the diction, cannot, however, explain the alteration of the language of Corporal Bates. When Robert and his men first set out for the crater to instal their guns, Corporal Bates warns the troops not to waver. In a draft manuscript he cries: "Jesus – don't you fuckers stop for nothin' or I'll shoot youse myself!" (TsC, file 17-7:141).[6] In the novel he yells: "Don't you stop for nothin' or I'll shoot youse myself!" (117). Of course we could consider an explanation analogous to Findley's original claim for Robert, that Bates's language is changed to fit more naturally to his character. But Bates is nothing like Robert. He does not have Robert's education or breeding (Robert would never say "youse"; Bates also uses the slang negative "ain't" [117, 123] and refers to the "cyclone of 19-0-12" [117]); nor does he manifest Robert's sensitivity (Bates's reaction when two men are killed by exploding shells is the imperative quoted above that produces fear in Robert's heart). It is perfectly imaginable that Bates would say "fuck."

In short, while the defence of faithfulness to character may justify the bowdlerization of Robert's lexicon, it is less compelling when applied to the alteration of other speakers' remarks. As Findley says in his letter, he changed Robert's speech *from* the kind of language he assumed was common amongst young Canadians fighting in the First World War. Yet that common language does not appear in the novel, for there is not a single occurrence of the word "fuck" in the published version.[7] Unless it is a coincidence that all the novel's characters happen to have unusual personality types, like Robert, that cause them to refrain from language that would otherwise be common among them, some other factor seems to be at work. I suggest that this factor was Findley's concern for the propriety of his readers (either his publisher or his public) and that, as propriety derives from the ideological mores of society, this concern resulted in self-censorship.

This claim is strengthened by the fact that, in the 1982 film version of *The Wars*, for which Findley wrote the screenplay, swearing is reintroduced into the speech of some of the characters. On board ship for England, Robert shows his two cabin-mates his gun, observing that it can fire seven rounds rather than the standard six. The seventh is for the soldier to shoot himself, remarks one of his comrades, to which the other responds, "Bullshit." In the crater scene in the film the word "fuck," excised from the scene in the novel, is spoken by one of Robert's men in response to Robert's directive that each man tear off a strip of cloth and urinate on it: "Why the fuck are we doin' this?" demands the soldier. Finally, near the end of the story, in freeing the horses from a compound under heavy bombardment, Robert disobeys his commanding officer, Captain Leather. In the film Leather runs after Robert waving his gun and screaming: "Come back here Ross. Ross. Ross, you fucking toad, I'll have you court-martialled"; this profanity does not appear in the novel. The explanation for this divergence most likely lies in the difference in genre of the two works. The novel has become an exemplum of good literature in Canada, and if Findley was aiming to write a "literary" work – that is, a work of high art – he may have decided to remove profanity, which is more common in popular fiction.[8] The motion picture, by contrast, as the twentieth century's most "realistic" medium, frequently features profanity. Also, there may have been a sense that the novel, which resides on one's bookshelf and can be consulted again and again, is a more permanent and accessible record than a film. Profanity in a novel is there forever; profanity in a film flits across the mind of the viewer and is quickly supplanted by the next scene. Whatever the reason, the presence of profanity in the film makes its absence in the novel conspicuous, suggesting self-censorship was at work in creation of the latter.

In addition to suggesting self-censorship in the novel, the film version of *The Wars* itself displays several striking examples of Findley's self-censorship. As is bound to happen with any literary work made into a motion picture, a number of scenes in the novel do not appear in the film version. What is striking, however, is that all traces of violent sexuality or homosexuality – elements that are key in the novel – are completely eliminated in the film. The only pictured sex in the film is the scene in which the young Juliet d'Orsey stumbles upon Robert and her sister in bed. In the novel Juliet's description is of "Two people *hurting* one another ... and the violence. Barbara was lying on the bed, so her head hung down and I thought that Robert must be trying to kill her ... Robert's neck was full of blood and his veins stood out. He hated her" (156). In the film Robert and Barbara appear to be "making love." There is no violence, no blood-filled veins, and certainly no hate. Evidently, Findley's original intention was not to soften the scene. In his first draft for the filmscript the violence is present: "Robert is lying on top of Barbara apparently strangling her ... Robert appears to be 'angry' – almost in a fit of fury" (Fts1, file 18-6:216). But while love scenes are fairly common in motion pictures, violent sex takes a director on to thin ice and has been grounds for banning films in certain provinces in Canada.

Add homosexuality to violent sex scenes, and you have a film ripe for controversy. The closest the film version of *The Wars* comes, however, to depicting homosexuality is a scene in which Robert, soon after joining the army, is shown showering with his fellow soldiers. But there is no sex; there are no stolen glances, and to read homosexuality into the scene would be an interpretive blunder. The absence of homosexuality in the film is curious, given that one of the most important scenes in the novel, one that is formative of Robert's character, involves two men engaging in violent sex. The passage in the whorehouse in which Ella forces Robert to watch Taffler being "ridden" (44–5) by the Swede does not appear in the film. Once again, Findley originally included the scene in his draft: "The giant blond bouncer who carried Clifford away – sits on Taffler in such a way as to suggest sodomy" (Fts1, file 18-4:77). For the second draft he made the scene less explicit, more suggestive: "They [Robert and Ella] both look through the hole at someone making slapping and thumping noises, but we are not shown what they see" (AM, 61). In the final version the voyeurism is cut altogether, and with it, the potentially controversial homosexuality.

Even more important to Robert's development and the theme of the barbarity of war in the novel is the scene in which Robert is raped by fellow soldiers. This is the passage that his editors and even Margaret Laurence urged him to remove from the book. It is present in a very early filmscript outline of 1979, but the rape scene is gone by the first draft and in all subsequent drafts of the filmscript. Its absence is remarkable given how passionately Findley says he fought for it to appear in the novel. In his memoir, after he records his tussle with Laurence over the controversial passage, he writes:

But I cannot remove it. As a scene, it is intrinsic – deeply meshed in the fabric of the book as I first conceived it. I cannot cut away its arms and legs – no matter how convinced other people are that the book will stand and function without them ...

It *was* rape.

The scene stays.   (*Inside Memory*, 151)

That this scene was removed from the film clearly indicates a difference in opinion between Findley and those employing him to write the filmscript which resulted in Findley censoring his copy.

There does, in fact, seem to have been some tension between Findley's vision for the film and that of director Robin Phillips. In a note to Phillips dated January 1981, between his second and third drafts of the filmscript, Findley writes:

We need an example of Robert's fury: something of the repressed rage that he can never get out as words. In the book, the examples range from breaking the mirror and water jug at the whorehouse – through his shooting at the tree (witnessed by Juliet) to his destruction of the room at Bailleul after he's been raped. We see it in action when he attacks Teddy Budge: when he is fucking Barbara and when he shoots Captain Leather ... To me, these gestures of rage are vital to Robert's character.   (FtsN, file 19-5)

This note suggests that Findley did in fact want included Robert and Barbara's violent love-making, the whorehouse scene involving Taffler and the Swede, and the rape of Robert. In the end, however, Phillips' decision to cut the scenes to "tone down" the violence and rage held sway.

Findley has been questioned about omissions in the film. In an interview in 1986 Eugene Benson asked him, "You wrote the script for the film of your novel *The Wars*. Did you have to omit any portions of the book? Did the director or producer overrule you in any sense?" (111). In response Findley makes no mention of censorship, and his denial of the "aesthetic" motivations behind the excisions seems to be an attempt to deflect any accusations that the makers of the film suppressed scenes for ideological or political reasons: "The producer overruled not from an aesthetic point of view but from a practical point of view. There were some things that he said there simply wasn't money for … And the war sequences were very costly. Therefore, what is not in that film is not there for two reasons – time, money" (111–12). This "practicality" explanation may account for the absence of scenes of mass destruction, like the explosive air raid on the road near St Eloi (173–4), or the depiction of German soldiers using flame-throwers to lay waste to the French countryside (132), for these would be costly to produce on film. But cost cannot have been much of a factor in the decisions to cut or alter any of the three scenes I have been discussing. Surely the lengthy crater scene that occurs in the film would have cost much more than either the scene with Taffler and the Swede or the one in which Robert is raped. The latter two scenes would have been relatively short, and required nothing more than a couple of extra actors and a room (the rape scene even occurs in the dark). It appears that, in the interview, Findley was covering for the director and producer of the film. He voiced no objections to the absent scenes upon the film's release and, in an interchange with the director, called the film "a great, great gift" (quoted in Jay Scott, E5).

Findley gives the real reason for the excision of the rape scene in the recent letter in which he addresses questions about self-censorship. After reiterating the importance of the scene, he writes, "Well, not only was the scene absolutely banned from the script by the Producers (Nielsen-Ferns) – when one of the major investors (The National Film Board of Canada) sent its representatives to a screening of the rough-cut, their *second* comment was 'What is this? A fag film?'" The homophobic slur is not made about the rape scene, which had long since been removed, but it nevertheless shows the ideological predisposition behind the producers' judgment that caused Findley to remove the rape scene. Furthermore, it explains why all traces of homosexuality are excised from the film and confirms that Findley was constrained to censor his work on the screenplay.

In addition to pre-publication censorship – that is, exclusion of material from the novel and film before they reached the public – the novel was the subject of post-publication attacks as well. Most of these attacks resulted, not surprisingly, from reactions to the controversial rape scene in the novel.[9] In 1991 a student at a high school in Sarnia, Ontario, asked that the book be removed from the school curriculum. According to the *Globe and Mail*, the student said she "finds the depiction of the rape offensive and that studying the book pressures students to accept homosexuality" ("Student," C5). The high school's English department defended the book, as did the school board, and the student transferred to a class in which the novel was not being taught. A similar incident occurred as recently as 1994 at a Catholic high school in Calgary. There Cyril Doll, a grade 12 student, objected to the sexual content of the novel, arguing that "it was pornography, and that my parents sent me to a Catholic school so I wouldn't be exposed to that sort of smut." He was initially assigned a different novel to read, but his father (a teacher at another school) maintained that "the issue is a homosexual book in a Catholic school" ("Steamy," 27) and tried to have *The Wars* banned from the institution. When the school board administration refused his request, he pulled Cyril out of the school to finish his final months of study at home.

My goal in highlighting these different incidents is, at one level, to show that they are all examples of censorship (either attempted or accomplished). All involve the exclusion of some aspect of Findley's work as the result of a judgment made by an authoritative agent for ideological reasons. But my goal is also to demonstrate that, once we acknowledge that these types of activities are censorship, it becomes much easier to see that the problem is not with censorship itself but rather with some of the motivating ideologies behind it. Libel law, for example, is a means of censorship, but few would call for the abolition of such legislation.[10] Rather we demand that libel laws distinguish between speech that harms a person's reputation and speech that does not; we expect interpreters of this law to use judgment, taking into account the context of each case. The same can be said for publishers who reject or alter a writer's work. While we may decry a publisher who attempts to censor homosexual material in a novel, we would be more willing to accept a publisher's censorship of blatantly racist or otherwise hateful material. The fault lies with the producers of the film version of *The Wars* not because they excluded certain portions of the novel – for they couldn't include everything – but because their censorship was based on homophobia. Censorship is merely judgment, and we cannot fault people for undertaking that process. We can, however, fault them when we perceive their judgments to be unjust. I acknowledge that concepts of justice change over time and vary among different communities, but I believe it would be more fruitful to struggle over conflicting concepts of justice than over the benefits or harms of the "principle" of censorship.

Findley has shown some reticence in accepting as censorship some of the events I have described: he rejected my suggestion that his expurgation of the profanity in *The Wars* was self-censorship and did not at first appear to see that censorship was a factor in the alteration of the film (though in his letter to me he acknowledges it). This reaction is not surprising for two reasons. First, the term "censorship" has become demonized, so it is natural that an author would not want to apply it to himself or to people he feels beholden to, such as the director and producers of his film shortly after its release. Second, once we accept that censorship includes things like libel laws, publishers' selections, and film producers' dictums, it becomes much harder to hurl the word "censor" as an epithet, to condemn other would-be banners – whether they are government or religious conservatives – even before hearing their reasons. I am not defending any of the agents who have tried to censor Findley's work. I am merely arguing that what they are doing is not different in kind, only in degree, from what we all do all the time in excluding discourse based on our judgments, and that they should have as much opportunity to justify their views as we would expect would be given to us.

"CENSORSHIP BY EVERY OTHER NAME"

While Findley's stance against censorship is problematized by my expansion of the Enlightenment definition of the term, some of the more specific arguments the author makes against censorship need to be addressed as well. These arguments appear in the published text of a speech he gave in 1983 called "Censorship by Every Other Name." In this article Findley attacks censorship from several different angles, but he begins the piece in a rather curious way:

Let me begin with an example of self-censorship:
   "Gosh, I hope I don't say anything that's going to offend anyone here tonight. I hope I don't say anything wrong ... "   (14)

It may sound as if Findley is invoking a definition of self-censorship very similar to mine, which I use to discredit the principled stand against censorship, Findley's own position. This impression is furthered by what follows:

Censorship by Every Other Name. And, in this case, the name can be anything from "fear-ship" to "self-esteem-ship"; from "Obsequiousness-ship" to "shyness-ship" to "lack-of-integrity-ship" and "Isn't-he-thoughtful-he-doesn't-want-to-offend-us-*ship*"!
   ...
   Censorship now goes under so many names: "concern" – "anti-pornography" ... "official secrets" ... "native interests" ... "rhetoric," etc.   (14)

In other words, many activities we generally call by other names constitute censorship. People who are silent out of fear ("fear-ship") are censoring themselves. A government agency that denies a grant

to a White writer in order to promote "Native interests" is also censoring. Findley probably presents this broad definition as a "hook"
to interest the reader in his article (or the listener in his speech): it is
radically different from what people think of as the "traditional"
definition of censorship. This broader definition also allows him to
target several different forms of censorship rather than just the
narrow government sort (which is hardly a subject of contention):
later in the article he attacks censorship in the form of rhetoric and
anti-pornography advocacy.

Yet Findley's opening is curious because it would seem to under-
mine the purpose of his article, which is to show that censorship is
wrong. For while, in his example of self-censorship, he is condemning a person who refrains from speaking a truth because she is afraid
of offending someone, I suspect he would not condemn someone
who, out of fear, censors herself from making racist or sexist remarks.
He condemns as censorship the government that keeps "official
secrets" from the public, but I contend that the government that
withholds from the public personal information it has on file about
him is censoring as well, though I am sure he would not object to it.
Once again, the argument with which he begins his article does not
show that censorship is wrong (in fact it shows that censorship is
inevitable) but that sometimes the driving forces, the ideological
motivations behind censorship can be wrong. I agree.

Nevertheless, Findley continues with his goal of showing "the
problems of book banning and censorship" (15). As examples of
"those who want to censor the news, fig-leaf the statues, and ban
books [in order] to wipe out a large part of reality" he first cites
"Hitler's censorship of the fact that Jews are human beings – making
way for the news ... that the Jews, not being human, could be done
away with," and then points to the Alberta school teacher James
Keegstra, "who succeeded in censoring the news that Hitler's final
solution had ever taken place" (15). Findley's argument here seems
to be that censorship is bad because it can be used by despots (Hitler
in Germany, Keegstra in the classroom) who suppress truth in order
to spread lies for evil ends. I find the choice of examples to support
this argument against censorship strange, since Hitler and Keegstra
are usually named as subjects of whom censorship would be particularly appropriate. The real issue regarding Hitler was not that he
censored the view that Jews were human beings but that he was
allowed to spout his hate propaganda freely enough that people were
swayed by him. If Germany at the time had had censorious hate laws
such as Canada has now, perhaps Hitler's evil program would have
been less destructive than it was. As for Keegstra, the Supreme Court

ruled, by way of a conviction under these hate laws, that censorship was an appropriate response to his anti-Semitic polemics in the classroom. These cases are much more compelling as instances where censorship has (or would have) gone right than where it has gone wrong. I do not disagree with Findley that the exclusion of truth in favour of lies by Hitler and Keegstra is censorship and that it is unjust censorship. I am arguing that we cannot rid ourselves of censorship (if we allow these men to speak, they censor; if we disallow them to speak, we censor them). The best we can do is work for the most just censorship possible (which in these specific cases I believe to be the censorship of Hitler and Keegstra).

Findley proceeds to admit, in the article, that not all censorship is motivated by the evil intentions of a Hitler or a Keegstra: "I do not believe for one moment that everyone who proposes censorship and the banning of books is motivated by a desire to suppress the past or to do harm to the future" (17). He points to the "sincerity of the convictions" held by some parents who take up the fight to ban certain books in schools. Good intentions, however, for Findley, are not sufficient reason to justify censorship: "It is one thing to speak out against material (this is everyone's right) but it is quite another thing to remove, or to attempt to remove material from the public domain" (17). Yet Findley would allow parents to censor material to which *their* children have access: "The problem here is not in what they desire for their own children, but in their belief that they have the right to censor material for others ... The only place parents or guardians have the right to ban books or concepts is in the home" (17).

Is there not a contradiction, a double standard in this remark? When we censor material for our children, are we not censoring others? It is clear to me that parents should indeed have the power to control what their children watch or read, but I do not observe definitive lines between one's responsibility to one's own children, to others' children, and to other adults in society.[11] Certainly there are no such obvious lines in the realm of action. If I see my neighbour viciously beating his six-year-old, I feel justified in intervening either personally or via the police. (Some members of society, such as educators, are legally obliged to do so.) We frequently control the behaviour of other adults when we elect governments that pass laws to restrict behaviour. Furthermore, we *do* control what the children of other parents read in school by voting for school boards that set curriculum standards. When we tell the children of religious parents that they cannot get a public education based solely on a Bible-centred curriculum, we are censoring them. I happen to agree with this censorship (I value a liberal approach to education and feel it is justified by the availability of sectarian teaching in private, denominational schools). The point is that once we start making these exceptions – it's acceptable to censor our children; it's acceptable to censor religious children – it becomes very difficult to maintain the position that we are against *all* censorship.

One last form of censorship that Findley condemns is rhetoric: "It seems to me, the first victim of rhetoric is language. Therefore, rhetoric, in itself, is a form of censorship ... Rhetoric – like censorship itself – is a tool of repression. And it is wielded with a will – and for a purpose. Its purpose is to silence opposition to its aims" (19). Now Findley is talking about the evils of political rhetoric, the rhetoric of corrupt governments defending their policies, but I would submit that all speech designed to convince or move a listener (or reader) uses rhetorical devices. Findley's article, for example, is replete with rhetoric, as demonstrated by his suggestion that censors have motives ulterior to aesthetic concerns. He writes:

What is *really* being suppressed?
　Ask it.
　Ask it.   (17)

The rhetorical question and repeated imperative are basic tools of the propaganda speech-maker, but Findley does not seem aware of the irony of their use in a piece that condemns rhetoric. This contradiction is part of a larger irony that sees Findley implying that rhetoric (the "tool of repression") should be quelled because it is a form of censorship, which, in this article, he says he opposes. More importantly, his argument reminds us that, since we all use rhetoric regularly in expressing ourselves, we cannot genuinely say we are against all censorship.

That rhetoric, and therefore censorship, is present whenever a view is expressed on a subject is admirably illustrated by one of the general themes in *The Wars*. M.L. McKenzie has shown that the novel is situated in a vein of war writing that replaces traditional depictions of the glory of war with a portrayal of "war as a dehumanising purveyor of destruction" (396). *The Wars* is very much about how the received official stories of war are rhetorically sanitized, censored versions of the truth. The novel's narrator gives the following ironic description of how wartime deaths are typically depicted: "Someone will hold my hand and I won't really suffer pain because I've suffered that already and survived. In paintings – and in photographs – there's never any blood. At most, the hero sighs his way to death while linen handkerchiefs are held against his wounds. His wounds are poems. *I'll faint away in glory hearing music and my name*" (49). This account – written in roughly metrical phrases (in an early draft made explicit by caesurae) to enhance the effect (a rhetorical one on Findley's part) – reminds us that romantic, poetic war stories are rhetorical. These rhetorical narratives privilege certain versions of the truth for ideological reasons (to arouse patriotism, for example), thereby censoring other versions.

But we must ask what censorship *The Wars*, as a rhetorical text, itself exerts on our view of war. If Findley is trying to replace traditional historical accounts with the kind of tale that Peter Klovan says is of "mythological proportions" (58), then is this new myth not also privileging a particular view and, in effect, censoring the one it is designed to replace? Coral Ann Howells argues that, in *The Wars*, Findley turns history into myth, and she asserts that "myths *un-write* traditional meanings and *re-write* new meanings into the language of historical fact" ("'Tis Sixty Years Since," 131). As Diana Brydon points out, "Any telling silences alternative versions" ("It could not be told," 69). My point is that, as Findley says, rhetoric is a kind of censorship, and when we acknowledge that a rhetorical text such as *The Wars* performs this kind of censorship by rewriting the First World War (even if it is a rewriting we think is more accurate), we must conclude that there are times when censorship is admissible, even commendable (I believe, or "judge," that Findley's censoring version of war is much more credible, or "just," than those glorifying war).

FINDLEY AS LIBERAL

In part, then, on the basis of the arguments I have highlighted (and criticized), Findley takes a rigid stand against censorship. His is a neutralist liberal attitude,[12] of the variety propounded by Milton and Mill, that all speech must be allowed in an open marketplace of ideas where received views may gain the authority of truth only through vigorous contestation by ideas that might be considered offensive. As Mill writes, "it is only by the collision of adverse opinions that the ... truth has any chance of being supplied" (111). Another related liberal tenet that Findley echoes is the view that moral truth is contingent and fallible, and that, therefore, "we can never be sure that the opinion we are endeavouring to stifle is a false opinion" (Mill, 79). Findley, like Mill, believes that a certain piece of writing, though the whole world find it offensive, may come eventually to be regarded as truth, and that therefore no offensive writing should be disallowed. Earlier in his memoir he approvingly cites Rushdie's idea that "a book is a version of the world," and adds, "it couldn't matter less, in the long run, if the version being depicted is scandalous or laudatory, nihilistic or celebratory" (188). He drives the point home by quoting Rushdie directly: "What is freedom of expression? Without the freedom to offend, it ceases to exist" (187).

These arguments for unrestricted freedom of speech are neither self-evident nor supported by historical experience. There is no natural law that says that, when confronted with both truth and falsehood, humans consistently recognize and adopt the former. As Schauer points out, "History provides too many examples of falsity triumphant over truth to justify the assertion that truth will inevitably prevail" (26–7). Slavery and genocide are only two painfully obvious examples of instances in which truth, lacking any intrinsic persuasiveness, has been trounced by lies on the battlefield of ideas. One might counter, as Mill does (82), that, though mistakes may occur in the short term, in the long run the truth does emerge: slavery was a mistake, but with time, the truth about the evils of slavery has prevailed. But is there any compelling reason to believe that we will never again take up the practice of slavery? Surely, given the bloodiness of the twentieth century, we are not beyond believing and acting on lies that are presented as truths. The only way the "long run" argument works is if the period designated the "long run" has no end. But as Schauer observes, "If there is no limit to its duration, the assertion that knowledge advances in the long run is both irrefutable and meaningless" (27).

As we have seen, there are contradictions and exceptions that render Findley's anti-censorship view problematic. In his insightful book *There's No Such Thing as Free Speech, and It's a Good Thing, Too*, Stanley Fish points out that contradictions of this sort are common within the neutralist liberal position in general. He observes that Milton, for example, urges the merits of unrestricted publication, but stipulates that speech by Catholics "itself should be extirpate" (103). Liberals like Ronald Dworkin call for unlimited free speech, but not for the young and the "incompetent" (Dworkin, 57). Despite what advocates of free speech say, Fish argues, free speech is never an absolute principle but rather one that will be trumped by any other principle that the advocate values more highly: "Speech, in short, is never a value in and of itself but is always produced within the precincts of some assumed conception of the good to which it must yield in the event of conflict" (104–5). Why do these liberals not admit that free speech is a principle in competition with other principles and not the transcendent axiom they idealistically espouse? As I have argued in my Introduction, claiming that you are in favour of unrestricted free speech is a way of gaining the moral high ground in any argument about censorship. What reasonable person, contends this liberal thought, could be against free speech, a concept that treats all expression in a "neutral," "objective" way? But because speech is always in the service of some higher good, free speech can never be a neutral principle. As Fish says, free speech always means "free speech so long as it furthers rather than subverts our core values" (14). In other words, liberals who say they oppose censorship on principle, in reality oppose censorship of works that they value.

"Once and for all, let it be said," declares Findley to his censorious opponents, "that the only kind of 'free love' advocated by Margaret Laurence is compassion. And that is not an opinion. That is a fact" ("Better Dead," 4). Of course it *is* an opinion, but Findley calls it a fact in order to claim, before his opponents do, the ground of "neutrality" and "objectivity." Facts are neutral, or so this brand of liberal argument goes, and if I invoke facts, you cannot accuse me of being biased, and you cannot hope to win the argument by bringing forward interested arguments of your own. This is the same kind of rhetoric of neutrality that Findley uses when arguing about censorship. He defends his work and the work of others on the grounds that free speech is a neutral, objective good. This leads him to contradict himself, however, when he finds some speech that is not valuable. A more fruitful approach would be to defend the works he values (this is the ultimate aim of his censorship argument anyway) on an individual basis, showing why the work in question deserves to be disseminated. Just as *The Wars* shows us there was no monolithic First World War, the conclusions we draw from a study of the novel's relationship to the issue of censorship show us that there is not one war against censorship but rather many battles, each involving a different controversial work and each requiring the application of judgment.

I want to turn now from Findley's explicit remarks against censorship in his non-fiction to the implicit argument he makes against censorship in his novel *Headhunter*. There Findley mounts a two-pronged attack on censorship, an attack that, like the position he sets out in his non-fiction, has its roots in a reductive liberal ideology. The novel promotes both the non-consequentialist and consequentialist defences of freedom of speech. The non-consequentialist argument, according to Ronald Dworkin, asserts that free speech is an end in itself, that "freedom of speech is valuable, not just in virtue of the consequences it has, but because it is an essential and 'constitutive' feature of a just political society" (56). The consequentialist or instrumentalist argument, by contrast, maintains that free speech is important as a means, that, as Dworkin writes, free speech is good "not because people have any intrinsic moral right to say what they wish, but because allowing them to do so will produce good effects for the rest of us" (56). Dworkin points out that most strong anti-censorship positions make use of both arguments (57); that *Headhunter* does so situates Findley's futuristic novel solidly in this tradition of liberal thought.

While the novel represents these free-speech arguments, it also contains the flaws inherent in them. First, the distinction between the two arguments becomes questionable when we realize that speech is never treated as valuable in itself but is always valued according to how it is used or what it can do. As Fish writes, "The trouble ... with a nonconsequentialist position is that no one can maintain it because it is always sliding over into consequentialism" (14). This becomes evident when we examine Dworkin's self-contradictory definition of the non-consequentialist justification. While it purports to argue that the principle of free speech is inherently valuable ("not just in virtue of its consequences"), the definition's last phrase ("it is an essential and 'constitutive' feature") postulates a just political society as the end to which free speech is one of the key means ("constitutive" connotes a thing that makes something else what it is). Dworkin's admission that the non-consequentialist argument is not absolute and that there may be certain necessary curtailments of free speech (censorship of military information is the example he gives [57]) further illustrates that the value of free speech is not inherent but is contingent on what kind of information is used for what purposes. This collapse of the non-consequentialist argument into the consequentialist is apparent in *Headhunter*.

Secondly, the consequentialist approach, while presented in the novel, is also undermined by the work itself. This argument promotes the protection of all manner of discourse on the presumption that "the truth ... is more likely to emerge if no idea is excluded from the discussion" (Ronald Dworkin, 58). It reasons that this process is jeopardized by any censorship since no dependable line can be drawn between unacceptable and acceptable discourse. The error in this argument is its failure to recognize that there are criteria available (and in current use) for judging different kinds of discourse. It is possible to bar harmful speech without jeopardizing all speech.

In *Headhunter* the principle of free speech is represented by books, while censorship is represented by their destruction. The most blatant example of the destruction of books in the novel, the burning down of the Rosedale library, is not an accident but is purposefully perpetrated by Otto, "the student whom Doctor Goebbels had chosen to ignite the pile of books when burning them had been the first Nazi gesture of contempt for German culture" (60–1). That Lilah Kemp conjures Otto not from some Second World War history text but from Ray Bradbury's *Fahrenheit 451* (a classic anti-censorship text that I discuss below) underscores the notion that books are to be seen as the embodiment of free speech.

THE NON-CONSEQUENTIALIST APPROACH

Findley's novel puts forth the non-consequentialist argument – that books (and, therefore, free speech) are inherently valuable – by linking books with nature, which the author appears to value for its inherent worth rather than its instrumental potential. As M.L. McKenzie points out, for example, in *The Wars* Findley explores the "philosophical opposition between the transcendent and the pragmatic" approaches to nature, ultimately rejecting the latter (409). The transcendent quality of the value of nature is echoed in Findley's pantheistic musings: "If God is really everywhere ... then why not pray to God through rivers, trees and animals? God isn't somewhere out of sight. At least not my god ... That god exists in everything that breathes" (quoted in Twigg, 89). God is generally considered an end, not a means, so Findley's placement of the deity in nature suggests a non-consequential valuation of nature.

In *Headhunter* books are linked to nature primarily through living things. A principal conflation is of books and human beings, and it is Lilah, a character who serves in the novel as one of the reader's main touchstones, who constantly invokes this conflation: "*Oh, world without books – what would you be*? Lilah did not dare to think. Her world would have no population at all, if someone had not put it there with pens" (314). Lilah not only conflates books and people; she also conflates the content of those books, their ideas, with human beings. Lilah's friends and family are fictional characters (therefore ideas contained in books): "Books were her centre, and from them she drew the majority of her companions. Neither had the distant past been greatly populated. [She was shy] of strangers, whose lives had not been delineated on the page" (31). An interesting example of her linkage of books and people is the result of a mysterious tryst with Heathcliff, from *Wuthering Heights*, which leads to the birth of her baby boy, Linton, physically embodied by Bronte's novel. In the following passage an idea – the fictional character, Linton – is represented by a book that is treated as if it were a real person:

She turned then towards the baby carriage.
   "You," she said, "must be tired unto death."

There was no reply.

Lilah bent down and pushed her canvas bags of books aside and reached in under the blankets.

There it was – safe and sound and warm in spite of its ride through the storm. *Wuthering Heights* – in blue.

She kissed it and held it up to her cheek.   (14)

Through Lilah, a character with whom we are clearly meant to sympathize, Findley compares books and the ideas they contain to human beings, suggesting that we should valorize the former to the degree to which we do the latter. This non-consequentialist argument for free speech proposes that if people are inherently valuable, and books and ideas are as valuable as people (and they are to Lilah), then books and ideas are inherently valuable as well.

Books, and therefore free speech, are not only linked to humans in the novel; they are linked to other living beings as well. Findley equates books with animals, primarily birds, through the novel's subplot involving the battle against "sturnusemia," a plague thought to be spread by birds. This subplot directly parallels the main plot of *Fahrenheit 451* and invites us to see the destruction of the birds as a metaphor for the destruction of books, or for censorship. I have already mentioned Findley's explicit reference to the novel, in which, he reminds his reader, "Ray Bradbury ... had wanted to address the question of censorship in the time of McCarthy ... [and] chose the theme of book-burning as a way of showing a world without words and a world without imagination" (*Headhunter*, 60). Findley echoes the bird-book metaphor that is prominent in *Fahrenheit 451* from the first page, where books, set on fire, are described by Bradbury's narrator as "flapping, pigeon-winged" (3).[13] Like Bradbury, Findley chooses fire as the means by which the object of his fictional society's phobia will be destroyed. His D-Squads obviously echo Bradbury's storm-troopers in their inversion of the fireman's role. These firemen set rather than quell fires. They respond to tips from the public, arrive quickly in their fire trucks, and "within an hour or two of their arrival, the fires would be lit and the birds would be ash" (*Headhunter*, 8).

Aside from clear parallels with Bradbury's novel, there are other ways in which Findley suggests that the D-Squads represent censors and birds represent books. During the winter, when there are fewer birds to exterminate, the firemen go "from school to school, informing teachers and students of the dangers inherent in flocking birds" (8). Given Findley's personal experience with censorship, this would appear to be a thinly veiled reference to the censorship of books in the classroom. Then there is Marlow, for whom the birds are the embodiment of art (see his tribute to their singing [519]), and who views the D-Squads with trepidation. He asks, "*Why are all bright creatures doomed?*" and answers his own question: "Plumage. Song. Intolerance" (433). "Intolerance," of course, is the key word in many anti-censorship arguments, and it prompts us to take plumage to stand for art and song to stand for speech, emphasizing the link between birds and artistic or literary publications. Finally, the narrator of the novel tells us that opponents of the D-Squads are arrested for posting bills, "an act which was forbidden" (491), hence explicitly linking the D-Squads with censorship.

The character in the novel who, more than any other, takes the side of the birds (and other animals) and tries to save them is Amy Wylie. As Rosemary Sullivan has observed, Findley makes it clear that he modelled this character on the poet Gwendolyn MacEwen, who, at one point in her life, waged a campaign to save Toronto's stray cats: "Timothy Findley was one of the people deeply moved by Gwen's campaign to save the cats. The image of Gwen feeding the cats in the back alleys of the Annex in a winter blizzard became the inspiration for his character Amy Wylie, in *Headhunter*, who fights against the extermination of birds in a plague-ridden city. For Findley, Wylie is the 'embodiment of the truly civilized' in his novel" (*Shadow Maker*, 432n11). It is significant that Findley makes Amy Wylie a poet – what other profession has such a stake in the fight against censorship? – and models her on MacEwen. Some of these dangers of being a poet are captured in MacEwen's poem "Icarus," in which the title character is a poet who views his feathers as "a quill to write / poetry across the sky" (11). He flies too high, of course, and the burning sun sees

> the lean poem's flesh
> tattered and torn
> by a hook
> of vengeful fire
> Combustion of brief feathers.   (13)

MacEwen's poem offers themes and images I have been tracing as central to *Headhunter*. Both Icarus and Amy see things that others cannot (Amy sees birds and their value where no one else does); both articulate a vision that defies convention. In both works there is the metaphor of discourse as feathered messenger and its ultimate destruction by fire. That Findley intends his reader to make these connections is confirmed by the fact that the one poem by Amy Wylie that appears in the novel is entitled "Icarus" (476).

As with Lilah, we are meant to sympathize with Amy (the birds, after all, turn out to be scapegoats in the fight against sturnusemia [585]) and to admire the lengths to which people go to support her cause. When Amy is in the mental hospital, her sister Peggy secretly goes to her house to feed Amy's birds: "in ever-widening circles, she spread the rest of the corn and the peanuts and all the bread. If anyone had seen her, they would have assumed that Peggy Webster was a dancer. But she was simply imagining freedom – for her sister, Amy, and for herself – a thought that had never occurred to her. To be free, after all, one must break the law" (531). In this passage art (dancing) and freedom can be had only by saving the birds, even if it means doing so illegally. Earlier in the novel we are told that Amy, in her early twenties, had staged "a hunger strike for endangered species – setting up a tent in the wolf compound of the Metro Zoo, where fellow students kept her alive with orange juice and tea during a three-week siege" (320). If animals, particularly birds, represent books in this novel, Findley's ultimate message is that we should be willing to break the law, even lay down our lives, to protect free speech.

I have been contending that, in *Headhunter*, Findley chooses his metaphors for books and ideas carefully in order to promote a non-consequentialist argument against censorship. He compares the vehicles of free speech with human beings and animals: as Lilah's mentor, Nicholas Fagan, says, *"These characters drawn on the page by the makers of literature ... are distillations of our thwarted selves"* (138). The comparison suggests that we should value the former principle in the same way that we value living beings: that is, for their inherent qualities, and not for instrumental purposes. This non-consequentialist argument fails, however, for the same reason that Dworkin's non-consequentialist argument against censorship fails: both inevitably end up as consequentialist polemics. In *Headhunter* it becomes clear that humans and animals are valued not as ends in themselves but as instruments. Kurtz manifests his evil motives by using his patients to satisfy his own monetary and career ambitions, while the photographer John Dai Bowen exploits children for his own sexual and perverted artistic gratification.

Instrumental motives can also be ascribed to characters we are meant to admire, not condemn. Amy values animals because they give her a sense of purpose, assuaging the most perilous symptoms of her madness and allowing her to continue to write poetry. Marlow concludes that her return from incarceration to caring for her birds "would give Amy back the only life in which she can function – in which she is happy" (572). The birds perform a similar functional role for Amy's sister Peggy, granting her a sense of freedom (531).

Marlow acknowledges his own complicity in a world that treats people like Emma Berry and birds as instruments: *"Show me your feathers. Let me hear you sing. I will use you, then I will destroy you. Yes? I will wear you. Yes? I will dine on your flesh. Yes? ... Everyone had used her, just as he had used the bird to lift his spirits"* (433). Even Lilah, who makes the most explicit link between people and books, values her "good companions waiting to be introduced" (364) for what they provide for her: friendship and a sense of family and belonging. There are no characters in *Headhunter* who can be said to value living things for solely unselfish, therefore non-consequential reasons. If living things are a metaphor for free speech but are valued only as instruments (even of positive effects), then it becomes clear that there can be no non-consequentialist claim for free speech.

THE CONSEQUENTIALIST APPROACH

Findley does not, however, base his argument against censorship solely on the non-consequentialist approach. He also posits the consequentialist or instrumentalist notion, which claims that free speech is valuable because it is capable of producing good effects in society. In a section on book-banning near the end of *Inside Memory* Findley calls the censorship of literature a war against the imagination and stresses the importance of imaginative expression:

I know that human imagination can save us; save the human race and save all the rest of what is alive and save this place – the earth – that is itself alive.
  Imagination is our greatest gift.   (314)

That books can be seen to be tools of human salvation is echoed in *Headhunter* by Fagan, a spokesperson for the power of words: *"A book is a way of singing ... our way out of darkness"* (138). Indeed, it is the written word and pictures contained in the files of the sexually abused children that help Marlow and Lilah to discover the secret at the heart of the darkness that is the world run by Kurtz (482–4).

One of the ways the written word can lead the world out of darkness is through its power to make us "pay attention." This phrase is a leitmotiv in Findley's thinking. As he says, "The words 'pay attention' echoed through my life, and I must have heard it from a lot of people, it keeps coming out – 'pay attention! pay attention!'" (Aitken, 82). He talks about paying attention in *Inside Memory* (31) and on numerous other occasions in interviews (Benson, 111, 115; Mellor, 98; Summers, 107, 110). In one interview, when asked what we can do to save our society, Findley replies: "Pay attention. Pay attention to real reality ... But art is also reality. The mind is reality. The imagination is reality" (Meyer, 11). In *Headhunter* this paying attention is the effect that the mad poet Amy Wylie has on her mother: "I have to pay attention" (23), says Eloise Wylie, referring to her daughter's behaviour. It is the goal of Amy's cousin, who, like the poet figure in the poem "Icarus," dives to his death: "He would have called that *paying attention*. At last" (474). It is the moral of Fagan's story about the murder of Jean-Paul Sartre and Simone de Beauvoir, which he summarizes as "the dangerous consequence of failing to pay attention" and which Marlow links to the bleak scene outside his window caused by the D-Squads (387), agents who represent censors. All these examples involve poets or philosophers who urge that attention be paid to their words.

If words are the key to making people pay attention, it is partly because of their power to menace. Interestingly, Findley casts the menacing artist in a positive, socially useful light. In a 1992 *Toronto Star* interview he remarks: "Arthur Miller once said this wonderful thing: that the job of art is to menace. Wow!" (quoted in Wagner, J1). Explaining his admiration, Findley adds, "There's a lot out there that needs to be menaced because we've got to stop it." The *Star* reporter goes on to explain that "'It' refers to Findley's abiding fear that corporate North America is itself conspiring to create a society of bland, unquestioning consumers" (Wagner, J1). This is a standard argument made by those who oppose censorship because, they say, it restricts the ability of artists to challenge a complacent, conservative, and sometimes unjust society. In so far as artists menace by promoting reasonably progressive, constructive ideas, the argument has merit. But what kind of ideas do certain of the menacing artists in *Headhunter* endorse within the perimeter of the view that any kind of art is acceptable? One of the foremost artistic menacers in *Headhunter* is the painter Julian Slade, who, like the writers Salman Rushdie and Arthur Miller (so admired by Findley), is a rebellious artist intent on challenging the limits of convention. However, the extremes to which he goes to fulfil this role seriously compromise his claim to free expression.

Julian Slade is described as a painter who, through his work, "never failed to challenge his audience ... And there was always an overpowering sense of menace staring down from a Slade canvas" (91). Indeed, Findley models Slade on the iconoclastic Canadian artist Attila Richard Lukacs. The resemblance between the fictional and the real artists' work is clear. Both produce pieces on a huge scale: two of Slade's paintings are "sixteen feet in length and ten feet high – one of them larger still" (96); Lukacs's are equally large, the centrepiece of a 1989 exhibit attaining nine feet by twenty-two feet (Ken Johnson, 204). Both use a technique involving the layering of gold leaf (*Headhunter*, 97; Smolik, 145). The resemblance is furthered by the content of Slade's *The Collection of Golden Chambers*, which Findley describes at some length: "a panoply of naked men in thrall of other naked men, males in thrall of being male, boys and youths in thrall of masculine strength – and strength itself in thrall of force … Every hair and every nuance of veined muscle, every toe and finger, every penis and nipple, every folded, curving buttock was exposed as if prepared for manipulation or consumption" (98). This could easily be a description of a number of Lukacs's paintings, including *The Young Spartans Challenge the Boys To Fight*, in which "five naked life-size youths" confront "six beetle-browed hunks, in typical skinhead regalia" (Ken Johnson, 204). Findley's familiarity with Lukacs's work is confirmed by the use of the artist's 1987 painting *Where the Finest Young Men* as the cover illustration for the French translation of *Headhunter*. It is clear that Findley has chosen Lukacs as a model because of the artist's capacity to shock, to menace. Lukacs's work has been described as depicting "rituals of pain, violence, and eroticism [that] lie outside the moral categories of good and evil" (Smolik, 145). This is precisely the nature of the work of Slade, who is described by one character, albeit the fascistic Griffin Price, as "the Mengele of art" (86).

It might seem, from the novel's depiction of this artist, that Slade is in a category apart from other, more conventional artists. Findley's consequentialist opposition to censorship rests, however, on the premise that the menacing artist is precisely the role that freedom of expression is designed to protect and that Slade is like other artists in his adoption of this role. In a scene at Robert Ireland's house Kurtz admires one of Slade's paintings, which is mounted among the works of other famous artists: Francis Bacon, Thomas Eakins, Alex Colville. The gallery owner, Fabiana Holbach, stands beside Kurtz looking at the Colville and muses: "That's the other thing about a lot of Colville's paintings – they're unnaturally quiet. The word *menace* seems appropriate" (262). Clearly, by having Ireland hang Slade's painting with the work of other recognized artists, and by stressing that both Slade and Colville produce menacing work, Findley means us to view Slade as fulfilling his role as artist and as one who is therefore entitled to protection from censorship.[14]

In *Headhunter*, therefore, Findley is positing a spectrum of menace along which all works of art lie. He places Slade's work at the extremely menacing end but connects it to Colville's (among others), which is somewhere on the spectrum as well. By presenting this spectrum he seems to be asking: If you start banning works like those of Slade, where will it end? What will prevent Lukacs from being banned, or even Colville? What will prevent a book like *Famous Last Words*, which threatens accepted versions of history, from being banned? This is the liberal argument known as the "slippery-slope" argument, which holds that once you begin to regulate, there is no natural place to stop, and what begins as a minor restriction may in time blossom into full-fledged tyranny. With no natural place to stop, neutralist liberals feel compelled to do away with the judging of art altogether and any censorship that might arise from such judgment. This is, of course, a consequential argument, in that it warns that the application of censorship anywhere on the spectrum of menace could lead to the loss of the positive effects of free speech in society.

Once again I find it necessary to disagree with the anti-censorship argument being made here. There are ways to make distinctions among works on the spectrum of art. As Fish notes, "Slippery slope trajectories are inevitable only in the head, where you can slide from A to B to Z with nothing to retard the acceleration of the logic" (130).[15] In the real world there are tests that we apply to determine the acceptability of forms of expression. One such test involves the degree of harm risked by allowing some utterance. We do not allow someone to cry "Fire" in a crowded theatre because that utterance, in those circumstances, can cause great harm. Findley appears to recognize this idea on some level, for he chooses to preface one of his chapters in *Headhunter* with an epigraph from Conrad that reflects it: *"There is a weird power in a spoken word ... And a word carries far – very far – deals destruction through time as the bullets go flying through space"* (389). But can we say that Slade's work actually causes harm, and if so, is it of a kind grave enough to warrant censorship?

There are suggestions in *Headhunter* that Slade's art is linked to and, in fact, inspires the activities of the Club of Men, a circle of influential masked males who meet to watch and eventually participate in sexual acts involving children.[16] First, Slade describes his *Golden Chambers* paintings, which depict the violent eroticization of boys, as the portrayal of *"savage acts which have been done too long in darkness. It is my belief they should be done in the light. And to that end – these paintings"* (95–6). His end is realized in the practices of the Club of Men, even to the extent of their use of common techniques. In the *Shreds* series Slade slashes his canvases with what he calls a flaying knife. Upon examining one of these paintings, Kurtz notes the similarity of the technique to that used by Robert Ireland, a member of the Club of Men: "The shredding had been accomplished in much the same manner as Robert must have shaved away the pubic hair from a boy he had talked about once – with lingering, sensuous strokes – each stroke a considered work of art … Kurtz, in his mind, could hear the slow, hoarse voice of the knife as it broke through the canvas skin – not unlike the voice of Robert's silver razor" (261). When we realize that in the sexual violation and ultimate murder of the boy George Shapiro, "Apparently, a razor had been used" (406), Slade's choice of tool (and name for that tool – to flay means to strip the skin off) implies that the Club of Men takes its cue, in part, from Slade's work.

Furthermore, as Marlow discovers near the end of the book, it is Kurtz who is ultimately responsible for the actions of the Club of Men: through his role as therapist to many of its members he not only absolves them of guilt for their perversions but actually provides them with the drug Obedion, which they use to induce the children to perform sex with each other and with the club's members. And it is Kurtz who is in thrall to Slade's work. On his deathbed Kurtz tells Marlow of his involvement in the unsavoury series of events, and Marlow realizes that "All along, it now seemed, Kurtz had been standing in front of his beloved triptych, watching Slade's horror unfold in perfect order" (616). While some menacing art can be desirable for its capacity to challenge outdated modes of thought, some art (some would prefer the word "pornography") can do harm to society. Slade's work, given his intention and capacity to produce harm, not good, appears to be in the latter category.

As with Findley's non-consequentialist reasoning, then, the fictional construction in *Headhunter* that represents the consequentialist argument against censorship serves to contradict that argument. Findley is right in making the consequentialist claim that art must be protected because it is an important vehicle with which to challenge conventional thinking. But if we accept that there are books and ideas that can do good work and should be protected, we must also recognize that there are those that can do bad work. To protect the former does not mean we must take an inflexible stand against censorship and, in so doing, indiscriminately allow the latter. An overly rigid adherence to an absolute anti-censorship position is what causes neutralist liberals, often to their own consternation and clearly to the detriment of their societies, to support the right to free expression of the most heinous of hate-mongers and pornographers. As with most difficult moral issues in our society, the blind application of principle should give way to judgment. Judgment based on tests, such as the one measuring the risk of harm, should be exercised in order to draw lines in a wise manner across the spectrum of menace. Only then can we be confident of "singing our way out of darkness."

3 The Ambivalent Artist: Margaret Atwood

> The attempt to censor is the attempt to establish a Utopia, and people do need a vision of Utopia. You can't give up the vision of the perfect society. If you apply standards, you regulate it, though. It's one of the paradoxes of *the human condition*.
>
> Margaret Atwood

> INTERVIEWER: So would you say that you are against censorship?
> ATWOOD: This is another knotty problem. Censorship, yes. What censorship is, is the cutting off of a thing before it has been made public and I am against that with very, very few exceptions.

While Findley's position on censorship has remained relatively stable throughout his career, Margaret Atwood's seems to have altered somewhat during the time she was most concered with the issue, as illustrated by her two quite different comments above. In the first, made in an interview in 1979 (with Val Casselton), Atwood offers something of an apology for censorship by explaining it as the expression of the desire to bring into existence an ideal world by shutting out values contrary to that ideal. Quite a different sentiment is expressed in the second comment (quoted in Leckie, 187), made five years later, in which her stance against censorship has hardened into a more neutralist principle against the practice. What the two statements share is a built-in ambiguity or self-contradiction: in the first case, the acknowledgment that "if you apply standards, you regulate it," that striving for a utopia paradoxically involves limiting its citizens (through censorship); in the second case the qualification of Atwood's outright rejection of censorship by her admission of exceptions. In their changing attitudes and internal inconsistencies, these two comments provide a useful miniature of the position Atwood implicitly sets out in her fictional work most concerned with censorship, which is the study of this chapter.

Although censorship plays as important a role *in* Margaret Atwood's work as it does in the work of the other writers I study in this book, censorship *of* her writing appears to have been less common and consequential. Judith McCombs observes that many "overt, actively female-empowered" poems were removed from *The*

Circle Game at the insistence of Atwood's publisher, due, according to McCombs, to his "uneasiness with Atwood's content" (62). A teacher in Alabama lost her job after teaching the poem "A Women's Issue" (from *True Stories*) to her grade nine class because, according to the school board, it contained sexually explicit language (Jacobsen, 1). Asked about reaction to *The Handmaid's Tale* in the United States, Atwood says, "Oh, banned in high schools, death threats at the time of the movie" (Speech). And in an interview in the *Vancouver Courier* Atwood reports that "*Surfacing* was banned in Prince George, for instance – it had the word S-E-X in it" (quoted in Casselton, 16). That Atwood "spells [S-E-X] out wryly," according to the *Courier* interviewer, and that her admission of death threats in the above quotation is exceedingly blasé suggest that she did not take these attacks as personally as other writers, particularly Laurence, have done, and was able to make light of them (her tone almost suggests a kind of pride in these incidents, as if being censored is a mark of recognition of her accomplishment as a writer).[1] Despite the relatively (at least according to Atwood) minor incidents of censorship of her work, Atwood has been a vocal opponent of the censorship of others. In the course of the 1980s, the period during which her fiction was particularly concerned with issues related to censorship, she was president of both the Writer's Union of Canada (1982) and PEN International (1984), two organizations committed to eradicating censorship. Like Findley she made speeches and wrote articles in 1988 against Bill C-54 (see "And They Said"), the government's proposal for new laws on obscenity, which died on the order paper. Also like Findley, Atwood has publicly supported Salman Rushdie in his struggle in what she calls "the wars of the Imagination" (Fraser, C1).

The two works of fiction by Atwood that are markedly concerned with issues of censorship are *Bodily Harm* and *The Handmaid's Tale*. Close analysis of these books reveals that Atwood is against censorship, but this stand is rather more complex than simple opposition to banning any representation. In the former novel Atwood offers a critique of "marketplace censorship," the suppression of certain kinds of writing (often political) through economic pressure applied to the writer. In the protagonist, Rennie Wilford, she shows that this outside pressure can be assimilated by the writer to become self-censorship. This kind of censorship, the book implies, can lead to political violence.

The other form of censorship Atwood opposes is pornography. Atwood makes this striking equation herself, but in doing so she is voicing the opinion of other anti-pornography activists that, as Owen Fiss writes, pornography "induces fear in women and inculcates in them the habit of silence" (85). As with Findley's argument about rhetoric being censorship, pornography may be cast as a kind of censorship because it results in the exclusion of certain depictions (consensual, egalitarian, loving sex) for ideological (patriarchal) reasons. In *Bodily Harm* pornography is shown to be the source of considerable damage to society (and to women in particular). First the novel shows that pornography is responsible for the alienation women feel from their own bodies and their resulting dehumanization. Second, it illustrates how pornographic images are translated into real violence. In demonstrating the harm resulting from pornography, Atwood presents a prime argument used by feminists calling for the censorship of pornography at the time of *Bodily Harm*'s publication. That she can implicitly argue for the censorship of a kind of censorship (pornography) illustrates my point that any dispute that is ostensibly over censorship is really a debate about which party will have its views disseminated to the exclusion of others. In the pornography debate it is not really "censors" pitted against "pornographers"; rather it is one group of censors (feminists or the religious right) working against another group of censors (supporters of the patriarchy or libertarians) to convey their views.

Implicit in my discussion of pornography, then, are two interlocking definitions of the term, both of which Atwood uses herself. The first definition is that pornography, like censorship, is the exclusion and suppression of certain (non-patriarchal) depictions of sexuality. This definition supports the argument that the pornography debate is not about the censorship of pornographers as much as it is about which side will be able to censor the other. The second definition, a subset of the first one, is that pornography depicts sexual acts typically characterized by violence against and degradation of women (or children). It is this notion of pornography that lies behind legal formulations of the term such as that used in Section 138 of the Canadian Criminal Code and in the Model Ordinance put forward by Andrea Dworkin and Catharine MacKinnon to make pornography a civil rights violation in Minnesota (MacKinnon, 121–2n32). Margaret Laurence provides a definition that captures the way I use the term, in this sense: "Pornography ... is the portrayal of coercion and violence, usually with sexual connotations, and like rape in real life, it has less to do with sex than with subjugation and cruelty ... It is a repudiation of any feelings of love and tenderness and mutual passion. It is about hurting people, mainly women, and having that brutality seen as socially acceptable, even desirable" ("The Greater Evil," 268). It is this conception of pornography that is most commonly invoked by those advocating the censorship of pornography, and it is against this kind of pornography that Atwood sided with the pro-censorship feminists in her 1981 novel.

While in *Bodily Harm* Atwood sided with the advocates of censorship of pornography, her views on the matter seem to have changed as the 1980s wore on. The change is hinted at in a *Chatelaine* magazine article published in 1983, but it is with the publication of *The Handmaid's Tale* in 1985 that the full extent of her altered view becomes apparent. In that novel Atwood presents four arguments against censorship: (1) that truth and meaning are subjective; (2) that banning "offensive" discourse will lead to a "slippery slope" of censorship; (3) that pornography is harmless; and (4) that making some discourse taboo will only make it more desirable. The manifestation of these arguments in the novel suggests a changed position for Atwood in which she has come to see censorship as more detrimental than the expression of harmful ideas, including pornography. Each of these arguments against censorship, however, is flawed, and I contend that their counter-arguments are consistently depicted in the novel itself.

BODILY HARM: MARKETPLACE CENSORSHIP

One significant aspect of censorship that Atwood explores in *Bodily Harm* is the institutionalized, market-driven censorship practised by publishers and editors (either purposely or inadvertently) to sell their products. As William Gass has recently pointed out, "The chief mode of censorship in a commercial society is, naturally enough, the marketplace. What will the bookstore stock, the library lend, the papers report, the publishers publish? Chain stores are now reading manuscripts in order to advise publishers what books they might like to see on their shelves" (63). Atwood, too, recognizes this form of censorship. In an address delivered at a world meeting of Amnesty International the same year that saw the publication of *Bodily Harm*, she spoke out against the persecution of writers in non-democratic countries: "In some countries, an author is censored not only for what he says but for how he says it." Then she turns to Canada: "Our methods of controlling artists are not violent, but they do exist. We control through the marketplace and through critical opinion. We are also controlled by the economics of culture, which in Canada still happen to be those of a colonial branch-plant" ("Amnesty International," 395).[2]

In *Bodily Harm* marketplace censorship plays an important role in shaping Rennie, the principal character. The narrator tells us that Rennie began her work in journalism at college as an idealistic young writer who "believed there was a real story, not several and not almost real" (64). At the time (1970) her social conscience led her to write about callous city developers and the lack of day-care. In fact, she "decided to specialize in abuses: honesty would be her policy" (64). Soon, however, Rennie finds that her honesty conflicts with her ability to make money from her writing: "Several editors pointed out to her that she could write what she liked, there was no law against it, but no one was under any obligation to pay her for doing it, either" (64). The editors' claim that Rennie is free to write what she likes is clearly a naïve defence against any accusation of censorship, meant by Atwood to be read ironically. It would be censorship if there *were* a law against Rennie's preferred writing topics, and the grammatical construction of the phrase that follows ("but no one ... either") implies that financial control is comparable to legal censorship.

Diana Brydon confirms this interpretation – that market forces act as tools of censorship – when she notes that one of the things *Bodily Harm* explores is the suppression of discourse "as it occurs ... in Canada (through market and social pressures on Rennie) ... For Atwood ... the language of contemporary pop culture poses the greatest threat to Canadian writing" ("Caribbean Revolution," 182). She concludes her essay by stating that what the novel shows is "how opposition may be censored before it has ever surfaced: in the writer's selection of literary form and language" (185). With this last comment Brydon astutely underlines the shift from censorship institutionalized in the publishing and newspaper industries to the individual writer's self-censorship described in Atwood's novel. For after her earnest attempts at documenting social ills are rebuffed by editors, Rennie begins to censor the social commentary from her articles in favour of the fashion writing that her editors prefer. Atwood humourously shows how Rennie begins by compromising: she would write about "the *in* wardrobe for the picket line ... what the feminists eat for breakfast" (64). Then, in need of money she "did a quick piece on the return of hats with veils. It wasn't even radical, it was only chic, and she tried not to feel too guilty about it." Nearer to the narrative present or just before she goes on her trip we are told that "Now ... she no longer suffers from illusions," that she views honesty, as well as a social conscience, as "a professional liability" (64). Atwood's depiction of her character's conversion to self-censorship is complete, except for the occasional twinge of scruples on Rennie's part (64).

Through Rennie, Atwood shows both the cause and effect of self-censorship. As Gass puts it, "The self censors itself because it does not want to receive or inflict pain. The truth, of course, is a casualty" (59). But Atwood is not content, in the novel, to explain how the truth about housing or day-care problems in Canada becomes marginalized through self-censorship. Her intent in having Rennie visit the Caribbean islands of St Antoine and St Agathe is to show that this kind of censorship is a contributing factor to the kind of social unrest that leads to revolution, torture, and murder: to bodily harm. Self-censorship has been so ingrained in Rennie that she cannot even recognize the brutal political regime on St Antoine that is fomenting a dangerous political crisis. Like too many Canadians, Rennie goes along with a situation without speaking up. Dr Minnow, the one morally sensitive character who tries to enlist Rennie's journalistic aid, slyly jokes about this sheeplike mentality: "'I trained in Ontario, my friend,' he says. 'I was once a veterinarian. My specialty was the diseases of sheep. So I am familiar with the sweet Canadians'" (29). But Rennie resists Minnow's plea that she write about the political situation: "'It's not my thing,' she says. 'I just don't do that kind of thing. I do lifestyles'" (136).

A striking example of Rennie's self-imposed blindness occurs when Minnow takes her to visit "Fort Industry," which has been turned into St Antoine's prison. Tents pitched in the field outside its walls house women and children whose homes have been destroyed by a hurricane, those whom the government has refused to help. Among them Rennie comes across a "young girl" on a mattress nursing a baby. "'That's a beautiful baby,' Rennie says. In fact it isn't, it's pleated, shriveled, like a hand too long in water" (125).[3] Rennie ignores the malnourishment and poverty of these people, their socio-political situation (their lifestyle), focusing instead, in a manner typical of her moral detachment, on the aesthetic (their *style* of life). Not surprisingly, her observation ("That's a beautiful baby") is a lie.

Rennie has a similar attitude towards Lora Lucas, a fellow Canadian living in St Antoine. Lora tells Rennie the story of her life, a compelling description of poverty and brutality that Atwood, by including it in her text (110–15, 168–72), proves is worth being told. But Rennie tunes out soon after Lora begins telling it: "Rennie switches off the sound and concentrates only on the picture. Lora could definitely be improved … Rennie arranges her into a Makeover piece" (89). Once again, Rennie censors any information of a problematic social or political nature in favour of the purely aesthetic.

But it is with Lora that Rennie actually ends up a prisoner in Fort Industry towards the end of the novel, and after witnessing the brutality of the government towards its political opponents (including Dr Minnow and Lora) and suffering incarceration herself, Rennie's attitude begins to change. Towards the end of the novel, Lora, like Dr Minnow, implores Rennie to "Tell someone I'm here … Tell someone what happened" (282). Only when she witnesses Lora being savagely beaten does Rennie switch from detached self-censorship to fearful engagement: "She doesn't want to see, she has to see, why isn't someone covering her eyes?" (293). The answer is that it was *she* who was covering her eyes and can no longer tolerate such self-delusion.

Rennie imagines her future release from the jail cell, which she envisages the Canadian government's representative making conditional on her agreement not to report what she has witnessed: "I suppose you're telling me not to write about what happened to me, she says. Requesting, he says. Of course we believe in freedom of the press." The official goes on to make an unconvincing explanation of why Rennie should keep silent, to which she accedes: "I guess you're right, says Rennie. She wants her passport back, she wants to get out. Anyway it's not my thing, she says. It's not the sort of piece I usually do. I usually just do travel and fashion. Lifestyles" (295). This is precisely what she had said to Dr Minnow when he implored her not to keep silent. To the politically compromised Canadian official, however, her acquiescence is, as Roberta Rubenstein remarks, "one final – but this time, chosen – act of capitulation made in the name of her newly-won inner freedom and knowledge. Yet, in agreeing to such censorship, she sees for the first time the terrible consequences of neutrality or objectivity practised on a national scale" ("Pandora's Box," 273).

Rennie continues to imagine what her thoughts and actions will be after she leaves the islands, and foresees herself breaking her promise to the official, her self-imposed censorship. In the course of the story Rennie's attitude towards truth-telling has undergone significant change. As a young reporter she tries, perhaps naïvely, to tell people directly the social and political truths she sees around her. Met with their resistance, she abandons these truths for the safer but ultimately false reality of fashion. Finally, she comes to acknowledge that sometimes it is necessary to tell a lie in order for a greater truth to emerge. This is what she does when she agrees not to write about her experiences. For her agreement is a lie. "In any case she is a subversive. She was not one once but now she is. A reporter. She will pick her time; then she will report. For the first time in her life, she can't think of a title" (301). She can't think of a title because the title is the unessential, decorative part of the story. She has come to realize that it is the content, not the aesthetic packaging, that is important.

Thus, Rennie's journey from surfaces to depths,[4] from the purely aesthetic to the intensely political, dramatizes Atwood's view of the dangers of suppression. "The aim of all such suppression," writes Atwood, "is to silence the voice, abolish the word, so that the only voices and words left are those of the ones in power" ("An End to

Audience?" 350). This is precisely what happens on St Antoine and St Agathe as the corrupt ruler, Ellis, silences any opposition by killing his rivals, Prince, Marsdon, and Dr Minnow. Rennie comes to recognize her own culpability in this violence in picking up and delivering the gun for Lora and, more importantly, in keeping silent after internalizing the forces of censorship institutionalized in the Canadian capitalist society.

PORNOGRAPHY IS CENSORSHIP

Censorship is not the only practice that leads to violence in *Bodily Harm*. Pornography does as well. I have traced the causal chain that leads from censorship to violence, and will shortly trace a similar chain between pornography and violence, but I want to emphasize that it is not a coincidence that violence is the common outcome of both practices. For Atwood, and for other feminists writing at the end of the 1970s, pornography and censorship are similar activities. This view appears in "An End to Audience?" where Atwood criticizes the "stance" that some books in schools and libraries should be censored[5] due to their sexual content: "I happen to find this stance pornographic, for the following reason. Pornography is a presentation of sex in isolation from the matrix which surrounds it in real life; it is therefore exaggerated, distorted and untrue. To select the sexual bits from a novel like *The Diviners* and to discard the rest is simply to duplicate what pornographers themselves are doing" (353). According to Atwood's definition, then, Rennie is a pornographer when, in setting out to tell the truth about the world through her writing, she is forced, and later unknowingly agrees, to select certain bits of life and discard the rest. The view that Rennie, a prime censor in the novel, is implicated in this role is supported by the fact that the article she is writing at the time her cancer is discovered is about jewellery made from chains: "wear them on any part of your anatomy: wrists, neck, waist, even ankles, if you wanted the slave-girl effect" (23–4). Chains and slave-girls feature prominently in the favourite fantasy scenarios of pornographers; as Gloria Steinem reminds us, "'Pornography' begins with a root 'porno,' [connoting] … 'female captives'" (37). Rennie herself senses her implication in pornography as she compares the indigents stranded outside Fort Industry with wealthy European tourists: "That's what she herself must look like: a tourist. A spectator, a voyeur" (125). It is the last epithet that links Rennie's detached, apolitical behaviour to that of pornographers. Again, Steinem: pornography "ends with a root 'graphos,' meaning 'writing about' or 'description of,'" which implies "objectification and voyeurism" (37).

If *Bodily Harm* implies that the censor is a pornographer, then it suggests the inverse of this formula as well: that, as Susan Griffin writes, "the pornographer is a censor" (88). Griffin's book *Pornography and Silence* is one of the feminist anti-pornography pieces that, along with Andrea Dworkin's *Pornography* and the collection of essays *Take Back the Night*, edited by Laura Lederer, influenced Atwood's shaping of her characters' attitudes towards pornography (Howells, *Margaret Atwood*, 121). Like Atwood, Griffin means by this equation that the pornographer focuses on certain aspects of sexuality while obscuring or censoring others: "the pornographer, who says he would bring sexuality into consciousness, and who says that he desires the freedom to speak of sexuality, in fact wishes to suppress and silence sexual knowledge" (88). The intent behind this censoring is, according to Griffin, "to sever the connection between mind and body" (88).

The corollary and symbol of Rennie's lack of professional involvement with important political issues is her lack of personal involvement with her own body (both withdrawals are captured by her comment, "Massive involvement … It's never been my thing" [34]). After her operation for breast cancer, Rennie's doctor, Daniel, feels he must tell her that "The mind isn't separate from the body." This admonition is in response to her habit of seeing her body as other: "The body, sinister twin, taking its revenge for whatever crimes the mind was supposed to have committed on it" (82). Sonia Mycak notes that, after learning she has cancer, Rennie's "corporeal experience is one of fragmentation and dissolution" (158), while Howells observes, "In the first shock at the news Rennie's concept of her body changes, for she no longer sees it as a unified whole" (*Margaret Atwood*, 113). In addition to being a metaphor for the broader external political immorality in the novel, Rennie's breast cancer, in causing her mind/body split, represents pornography's corrupting influence in society. As J. Brooks Bouson observes, "Deliberately the text associates Rennie's breast surgery, which is described as a phallic-sadistic act that causes a severe narcissistic wound, with the violent attacks enacted on the female body – in particular on eroticized body parts like the female breast – in sadomasochistic pornography" (118).

In fact, this mind/body split links *Bodily Harm* with three other texts that, according to Griffin, portray the effects of pornography: *I Never Promised You a Rose Garden*, *Autobiography of a Schizophrenic Girl*, and *Story of O*. None of these three texts has been associated by critics with Atwood's novel, but there is ample reason to do so, for like Rennie in *Bodily Harm*, "In all three narratives, the heroines become alienated from their bodies, lose dignity, a sense of self, and a desire for freedom, and experience greater and greater degrees of 'unreality'"

(Griffin, 229). As in *Bodily Harm*, the heroine's alienation from her body in Hanna Green's *I Never Promised You a Rose Garden* is represented by the invasion of that body by a cancer. It is significant that in both cases the cancer attacks a sexual organ (Rennie's breast, Deborah's "feminine, secret part" [49]). For in a society profoundly influenced by pornography, the female sexual organs act as a nexus of sex and death. In *I Never Promised You a Rose Garden* Jacob, Deborah's father, causes his daughter to believe that "her shame-parts … had been diseased" (129) as a punishment for her sexual desires. In reality his explanation of her affliction is Jacob's way of denying his own sexual desire for his daughter. Griffin argues that fear of one's own sexual desire is, in one shaped by pornography such as Deborah's father, really a fear of death: "eros, nature, and woman, in the synapses of this mind, bring death into the world, and desire, this mind imagines, leads one to die" (13). The same fear grips Jake in *Bodily Harm*, when presented with the literal coalescence of sex and death after Rennie has had her breast operation: "He was afraid of her, she had the kiss of death on her, you could see the marks. Mortality infested her" (201). As we will see, Jake, like his namesake in Green's novel, is the product of a society in which pornography has far-reaching repercussions.

Like *I Never Promised You a Rose Garden*, the other two texts Griffin discusses are linked to Atwood's novel through the names of their characters and, more importantly, the nature of these characters' alienation from their bodies. Ildiko de Papp Carrington has pointed out how both "Renata" ("born again") and "Wilford" ("will cross over") suggest the ultimate success of the heroine's inner journey (49). But "Rennie," as she is called in the novel, also reminds us of Renee, the troubled girl of *Autobiography of a Schizophrenic Girl*, who, like Rennie, "referred to her body as to an object independent of, though linked to, her" (Sechehaye, 136). Renee's pathology can be traced to a childhood in which "her mother had refused to nourish, hence love, her" (Sechehaye, 118). In *Bodily Harm* Rennie comes to be dissociated from her own body through a lack of emotional nourishment by her grandmother, who punished her granddaughter by locking her in the cellar. The reason for this punishment is not given, but it seems instrumental in Rennie's dreamed adoption of her grandmother's senility-induced search for her own hands: "It's her hands [Rennie's] looking for, she knows she left them here somewhere, folded neatly in a drawer, like gloves" (116).

That Rennie is separated from her body specifically through alienation from her hands also links *Bodily Harm* to *Story of O* by Pauline Réage. In the latter text O, the principal female character, prostrates herself before every sadistic whim of her lover and tormentor, René (note again the coincidental names, in this case an alignment that suggests Rennie has internalized the pornographic side of patriarchy). As part of the abject surrender of her body, O is told, "Your hands are not your own" (15), and later she realizes that, "one of the things that most distressed her was the fact that she had been deprived of the use of her hands … O's hands had been taken away from her; her body beneath the fur was inaccessible to her. How strange it was not to be able to touch one's own knees, or the hollow of one's own belly. The lips between her legs, her burning lips were forbidden to her" (23). As Griffin remarks, in this passage "the idea that one can give oneself pleasure, which is the infant's first power over herself, is eradicated" (219).

Applied to Rennie, Griffin's interpretation helps to explain why she dreams she has lost her hands and why she is locked in the cellar by her grandmother (two points so far unexplained by critics). Although Rennie's sin is never explicitly identified, there is some evidence to suggest that her grandmother caught her sexually touching herself. First, as Bouson says, "the grandmother acts as a guardian of Griswold's repressive social code, a system of censorship and social conditioning that teaches the developing girl to maintain, at all costs, restraint and control" (121). This social code focuses largely on not touching things (*Bodily Harm*, 54) and sexual conservatism: "the standard aimed at was not beauty but decency" (54). Taken together, these prohibitions make masturbation a taboo. But the most suggestive indication comes in the last flashback involving the grandmother. The old woman approaches Rennie, holding out her arms and saying she cannot find her hands: "Rennie cannot bear to be touched by those groping hands, which seem to her like the hands of a blind person, a half-wit, a leper" (297). We have seen that Rennie identifies with her grandmother, particularly when it comes to her hands, so it is logical that this scene represents Rennie's fear and guilt at the groping (a sexually suggestive word) of her own hands. Finally, if, as is likely in a place like Griswold, Rennie was warned that masturbation would lead to blindness, insanity, or her hands falling off[6] (three common threats), then her identification of her grandmother (herself) with "a blind person, a half-wit, a leper" makes sense. The denial of Rennie's autoerotic pleasure is an example of a culture that disallows women to be sexual subjects, reserving them for the role of sexual objects for men. As Griffin points out, this triumph of "culture" over "nature" is pornography, "an expression not of human erotic feeling and desire, and not of a love of the life of the body, but of a fear of bodily knowledge, and a desire to silence eros" (1).

Another example of a product of the society influenced by pornography that Atwood's novel shares with *Story of O* is the professional
activity of their main female characters. O is a fashion photographer:
"Behind the camera, she is the aggressor, the one who captures, the
one who turns the real into the image and replaces nature with culture ... As the fashion photographer, she takes the same sexual attitude toward women, and in particular the women who fall under
the lens of her camera, that men have taken toward her" (Griffin,
221). Rennie is primarily a "lifestyles" writer, but photography is an
important aspect of her work, and, as Sharon Wilson documents in
depth, the camera serves her both as shield and weapon: "Operating
simultaneously as an unseeing or mirror eye and a pseudo-self, the
camera-narrator of *Bodily Harm* (Rennie's past self) is packager/pho-
tographer/victimizer as well as photo/product/victim" ("Turning
Life," 137). More importantly, Rennie's ambivalent role in this
dynamic of visual victimization is highlighted by her comments on
fashion photography: "she'd noted, many times, the typical pose of
performers, celebrities, in magazine shots and publicity stills and
especially on stage. Teeth bared in an ingratiating smile, arms flung
wide to the sides, hands open to show that there were no concealed
weapons, head thrown back, throat bared to the knife; an offering,
an exposure" (26). Rennie finds these displays (reminiscent in fact of
some of the tableaux presented in *Story of O*) "embarrassing" and is
glad she is not a performer of this sort, but feels no compunction (at
this stage in her development) about capturing them in print: "She
would much rather be the one who wrote things about people like
this than be the one they got written about" (26). Rennie, then, senses
the dehumanizing effects of pornography but, until the end of the
novel, is herself enmeshed in its value system.

PORNOGRAPHY IS HARMFUL

How does a woman like Rennie come to lose touch with her body,
to have her sexuality denied and objectified, and, in turn, to objectify
others through her writing and photography? In *Bodily Harm*
Atwood suggests that Rennie's co-option as an accomplice to the
propagators of pornography is one link in the causal chain that leads
from pornography to violence. As she does with marketplace censorship, Atwood uses literary techniques – repeated words and recur-
ring imagery – to show that pornography has significant harmful
effects on society. The argument based on harm against pornography
was a prime weapon in the feminist arsenal when Atwood was writing her novel. At that time women were "beginning to connect the

consumption of pornography with committing rape and other acts of sexual violence against women" (Longino, 47).

When we look in this novel for the basis of the argument that pornography leads to violence, we are inevitably drawn to Rennie's research visit to Project P at the police station. Howells' assessment of this passage is accurate: "I would suggest that the crisis point for Rennie is the article she is asked to write on pornography for the men's magazine *Visor*, which she researches but then refuses to write. Embedded in the text in Section 5, this episode provides an interesting crux for a woman's novel of the early 1980s written in the wake of vigorous American feminist anti-pornography campaigns which began in the late 1970s" (*Margaret Atwood*, 118). In this scene Atwood represents many of the different types of pornography studied by these feminists. Rennie views visual material featuring bestiality (see Griffin, 24–6); the sadism of Nazis (see Andrea Dworkin, 142–7, and Griffin, 156–99); and possibly snuff films (see LaBelle).

As with her reaction to political perversions, Rennie is able to maintain an emotional distance with respect to these film clips: these "Rennie watched with detachment" (210). But when she views a picture of a Black woman's pelvis with a rat "poking out from between the legs," her reaction is severe: "Rennie felt that a large gap had appeared in what she'd been used to thinking of as reality" (210).[7] The experience of "greater and greater degrees of 'unreality'" is the hallmark of the divided personality in some women whose malady has its roots in pornography (Griffin, 229). While Rennie does not share the pathology of her counterpart in *Autobiography of a Schizophrenic Girl*, she does question her perception of reality: "What if this is normal, she thought, and we just haven't been told yet?" (210).

While pornography is the social disease that causes Rennie to feel abnormal, cancer, her personal ailment, does so as well. After she discovers her breast cancer, she continually questions the normality of her life: "We'll get back to normal, she told herself, though she could not remember any longer what *normal* had been like" (35; see also 59, 84, and 163). That pornography and cancer both shake Rennie's sense of what is normal links them – as does the fact that Rennie witnesses the pornography a month before her operation (207) – as forces that alienate women from their bodies, depriving them of an important part of reality. In doing so they harm women (in both the body politic and the body), reinforcing the argument about the harmfulness of pornography that pro-censorship feminists make and confirming Rubenstein's comment that "the section describing Rennie's research is itself Atwood's own extremely powerful condemnation of pornography" ("Pandora's Box," 267).

It is not only by internalizing the values of pornography, however, that women are harmed in this novel. They are harmed by men as well. Atwood suggests a causal series that begins with confiscated pornography in the police station and extends through pornographic "art," mainstream art, and male fantasy, ending in the real enactment of pornographic images by real men. The first step in this progression is the link that the novel forges between pornography and what Rennie's editor calls "pornography as an art form" (207). Before she visits the police station Rennie is sent by her editor to do a story about the work of Frank, a Toronto artist who literally objectifies women by presenting nude mannequins moulded into household objects ("set on their hands and knees for the tables, locked into a sitting position for the chairs" [208]). In response to Rennie's negative reaction to his work, Frank comments that art merely mirrors reality: "Art is for contemplation. What art does is, it takes what society deals out and makes it visible, right?" (208). That art reflects, rather than shapes, societal values is a common argument among defenders of pornography who maintain its harmlessness (see, for example, Diamond, 47). Shortly thereafter, however, Frank suggests that Rennie should inspect his "raw material," which turns out to be not real people in society but rather other, more hard-core pornography: to be, in fact, as the novel implies (209), the very pornographic images Rennie encounters at the police station. The implication is that these images *influence* rather than just *reflect* people's attitudes towards women.

If Atwood establishes a relationship of influence between hard-core pornography and crank artists like Frank (there is an Atwoodian air of irony in Frank's query: "what's the difference between me and Salvador Dali, when you come right down to it" [208]), she establishes a similar relationship between pornographic art and more mainstream art: the kind of art that finds its way on to the apartment walls of people like Jake. In the living-room he hangs blown-up photographs of "three Mexican prostitutes looking out of wooden cubicles" (105). Clearly we are meant to think of pornography's original definition as "descriptions of the lives, manners, etc., of prostitutes and their patrons" (Copp, 17). A poster of a bound "brown-skinned woman … with thighs and buttocks exposed" (*Bodily Harm*, 105) reminds us of the racial film clip that so disturbed Rennie at the police station, while another features "a woman lying on a 1940s puffy sofa, like the one in their own living room. She was feet-first, and her head, up at the other end of the sofa, was tiny, featureless, and rounded like a doorknob" (105–6). Like the mannequins in Frank's work, the woman in the picture is primarily a body, her head, the site of a person's personality, reduced to a household object (a doorknob).

The fact that the sofa in this last picture is similar to the one owned by Jake and Rennie is a clue that these pictures are connected to their relationship. "These pictures ma[k]e Rennie slightly nervous" (106) because they not only reflect but in fact shape her problematic sexual relationship with Jake. Rubenstein points out that after her operation, Rennie finds herself positioned "in unconscious imitation of the poster above them on the wall" ("Pandora's Box," 262). When they try to make love, like the woman on the sofa in the picture, Rennie is "watching him from her head, which was up there on the pillow at the other end of her body" (199). An interchange with Jake makes the link between pornography and their relationship explicit:

Lately [says Rennie] I feel I'm being used; though not by you exactly.
  Used for what? said Jake.
  Rennie thought about it. Raw material, she said.   (212)

Rennie is beginning to identify with the women in the pornographic images at Project P, to become aware of her own objectification at the hands (and I use the phrase purposely) of people like Jake.

It is clear that Jake takes his values from and models his fantasies on the kind of art that is inspired by hard-core pornography. It is no coincidence that, while section 5's first five pages present the work of Frank and the pornography of Project P, its first paragraph describes Jake's preferred sexual games: "Jake liked to pin her hands down, he liked to hold her so she couldn't move. He liked that, he liked thinking of sex as something he could win at. Sometimes he really hurt her, once he put his arm across her throat and she really did stop breathing. Danger turns you on, he said. Admit it. It was a game, they both knew that ... So she didn't have to be afraid of him" (207). Sex for Jake enacts a rape fantasy, a contest for power ("something he could win at"). But it is important for Jake that Rennie should want to be overpowered. As Griffin points out, "when he is raping a woman [the] pornographic hero tells his victim, 'You really wanted this, didn't you?' thus implying to her that she is ... a whore" (23). After her operation Jake tries to enact this fantasy again: "He raised her arms, holding her wrists above her head. Fight me for it, he said. Tell me you want it. This was his ritual, one of them, it had once been hers too and now she could no longer perform it" (201). She can no longer perform this role because her cancer and her contact with Project P have begun to make her aware that the adherents of pornography and, by extension, Jake himself are using her as "raw material."

One of the ways Atwood consistently undercuts any notion that Jake's attitudes and fantasies are harmless is by use of a one-line ironic statement that usually follows a description of his views. "What is a woman, Jake said once. A head with a cunt attached or a cunt with a head attached? Depends which end you start at. It was understood between them that this was a joke" (235). There is frequently an ambivalence in these "punchlines" (in this quotation provided by the phrase "it was understood") that suggests an ironic reading of the line. In the description of Rennie's feelings towards Jake's posters it is the word "probably": "These pictures made Rennie slightly nervous, especially when she was lying on their bed with no clothes on. But that was probably her background" (106). When, after viewing Project P, Rennie asks Jake if he would be turned on by a rat in her vagina, Jake tries to distance himself from pornographers: "Come on, don't confuse me with that sick stuff. You think I'm some kind of a pervert? You think most men are like that?" The punchline, set apart for dramatic effect, is "Rennie said no" (212). While she *says* "no," the ironic implication is that she *thinks* "yes." So does the reader.

In fact, Atwood provides links between Jake and "real" perverts in the novel. This link represents the step in the anti-pornography argument that claims that fantasies inspired by pornography do not *remain* fantasies but are translated into reality in the form of harm to women. We have already seen that sometimes Jake really hurts Rennie as part of the exercise of his sexualized power (207). But Atwood also clearly identifies him with a source of real threat, of potential real violence: the intruder who breaks into Rennie's apartment and leaves a rope on her bed. Like this intruder, who "jimmied open [her] kitchen window" (13), sometimes Jake "would climb up the fire escape and in through the window" to surprise her (27). Through this identification Atwood questions the difference between the rapist who transgresses society's moral code and men like Jake, who bring violence into their relationships with women:

Pretend I just came through the window. Pretend you're being raped.
   What's pretend about it? said Rennie. Stop pinching.   (117)

Atwood implies, furthermore, that it is foolish to believe that men's violent, pornography-inspired fantasies will remain fantasies without eventually bleeding into their behaviour. When she considers telling Jake about the man with the rope, Rennie thinks: "What would Jake make of it, the sight of one of his playful fantasies walking around out there, growling and on all fours? He knew the difference between a game and the real thing, he said; a desire and a need. She was the confused one" (236). Again this final line has an air of irony about it, suggesting that men who adopt a pornographic view of women for their fantasies will be hard pressed not to bring this attitude to bear on the real women in their lives.

Finally, in a last link in the causal chain between pornography and violence, Atwood generalizes the connection between the consumption of pornography and real violence from the personal to its political and social manifestations. There may be many resemblances between Jake and the intruder with the rope, but it is only upon witnessing the extreme political violence from her jail cell on St Antoine that Rennie realizes, "She's seen the man with the rope, now she knows what he looks like" (290). In this scene, in which political prisoners are tortured in the courtyard of the jail, Rennie is reminded of the pornographic images she witnessed at the police station. Looking into the courtyard, she thinks, "It's indecent, it's not done with ketchup, nothing is inconceivable here, no rats in the vagina but only because they haven't thought of it yet, they're still amateurs" (290). Political violence, this passage implies, shares many of the assumptions of pornography. In fact, there is a sense, in the notion that there are pornographic horrors that the agents of violence on St Antoine "haven't thought of ... yet" (290), that this violence is performed in imitation of the acts depicted in pornography. We have already seen that the pornography of Project P causes Rennie to question her perception of reality, of what is normal. Jake is an accomplice to this disorientation; as Rubenstein points out, "Jake's very insistence upon the normalcy of his perverted view of Rennie and of women reinforces Atwood's point" ("Pandora's Box," 268]. That Rennie ironically sums up her ordeal on St Antoine as a "situation [that] is normalizing, all over the place, it's getting more and more normal all the time" (296), confirms this novel's assertion of the pornographic roots of political violence.

I have been arguing that *Bodily Harm* illustrates in detail the stance put forward by anti-pornography feminists in the late 1970s and early 1980s, whose principal argument is that pornography causes harm in society (an argument that Copp and Wendell call the "most central" to the pornography debate [12]). In addition to the alienation pornography causes women to feel from themselves, *Bodily Harm* traces the chain of influence that begins with hard-core pornography and leads to pornographic art, male fantasy, male behaviour within relationships, violence against women, and finally to violence in general. Based on this argument are many of the essays in the anti-pornography collection *Take Back the Night* that argue in favour of banning pornography. Susan Brownmiller calls for "restrictions on the public display of pornography" (255), and Helen Longino argues that "the prohibition of such [pornographic] speech is justified by the need for protection from … injury" (53). A year after the publication of this collection and during the same year that *Bodily Harm* was published, Atwood granted an interview to Tom Harpur in which she echoes these sentiments: "Those people [conservative religious groups] don't really impress me unless they are willing to go after the big fish. If they are going after Margaret Laurence, small potatoes; it's too easy, no forces on her side. It's easy to say, 'Let's stamp out Stone Angel.' If they said, 'Let's stamp out violent pornography, let's stamp out a multi-billion dollar business backed by the Mafia,' I would say more power to them, that's courageous. I haven't heard any of them doing that" (Harpur, D3). "Let's stamp out violent pornography," I would argue, is one of the messages conveyed by *Bodily Harm*, a pro-censorship message that, while encapsulating Atwood's position on censorship and pornography in the early 1980s, was to change radically as that decade proceeded.

Atwood's considerably modulated attitude towards the censorship of pornography is most fully voiced in her next novel, *The Handmaid's Tale*, published four years after *Bodily Harm*. Before turning to the later novel, however, it is useful to consider an article Atwood wrote for *Chatelaine* magazine in 1983, precisely at the mid-point of the period between the two novels in question. The article, "Atwood on Pornography," is worth examining at some length as it explicitly recapitulates much of what Atwood says about censorship in *Bodily Harm*, while at the same time giving intimations of her changing position and the way in which it would manifest itself in *The Handmaid's Tale*.

The article is primarily an attack on pornography and echoes some of the concerns about its consequences that Atwood had raised in *Bodily Harm*. "When I was in Finland a few years ago for an international writers' conference," Atwood begins her article, "I had occasion to say a few paragraphs in public on the subject of pornography. The context was a discussion of political repression, and I was suggesting the possibility of a link between the two" (61). We have seen that establishing this link between political violence and pornography is one of Atwood's prime objectives in her antecedent novel. Indeed, as she explicitly states, the working definition of pornography in the article is fully informed by the research she conducted for *Bodily Harm*, which entailed viewing gruesome visual material expurgated by the Ontario Board of Film Censors (118). The kind of pornography she is talking about in this article, she says, is "the violent kind" (126). After defining her terms and outlining the positions of various parties to the debate, Atwood exhibits her familiarity with anti-pornography feminists of the early 1980s by asking a series of rhetorical questions about pornography's role in society: "Is today's pornography yet another indication of the hatred of the body, the deep mind-body split, which is supposed to pervade Western Christian society?" (126). This is the argument of feminists such as Susan Griffin, whose linkage of the mind-body split with pornography shows up so clearly in *Bodily Harm*. "Is pornography a power trip rather than a sex one?" (126), Atwood asks, echoing Andrea Dworkin (*Pornography*, 24–5) and reminding us of the power struggles enacted as playful pornographic encounters between Rennie and Jake.

If the definition and theorizing of pornography in the first half of the article clearly take shape from Atwood's work on *Bodily Harm*, so too do her judgment of and recommended action against pornography. For Atwood in this article the key issue relating to censorship and pornography is the same one I have identified as central to *Bodily Harm*: "This is obviously the central question: *What's the harm?*" (126). She immediately calls for the censorship of clearly harmful material such as child pornography: "there's a clear-cut case for banning ... movies, photos and videos that depict children engaging in sex with adults" (126). As for other violent pornography, Atwood draws comparisons between the pornography debate and three other areas of controversial legislation. She begins by discussing the regulation of hate literature. Legislation has been created against hate literature, she argues, for good reason: "whoever made the law thought that such material might incite real people to do real awful things to other real people. The human brain is to a certain extent a computer: garbage in, garbage out" (126). She suggests that we view pornography in the same way we do hate literature: "Those who find the idea of regulating pornographic materials repugnant ... should consider that Canada has made it illegal to disseminate material that may lead to hatred toward any group because of race or religion" (126). Her implication is that we should consider regulating pornography as we do hate literature.

In the next section Atwood considers sex education and observes that boys are increasingly learning about sex from pornographic sources. What "boys are being taught [is] that all women secretly like to be raped and that real men get high on scooping out women's digestive tracts" (128). Here she makes the case for the harmful effect of pornography on the attitudes of its male consumers (as she showed in *Bodily Harm* with Jake); she then links this effect to its negative impact on women: "In a society that advertises and glorifies rape or even implicitly condones it, more women get raped" (128). This assertion of the harmfulness of pornography rivals the strongest affirmation of this argument by feminists of the late 1970s and early 1980s (Andrea Dworkin, Griffin, Longino, etc.) who argued for the censorship of pornography.

Finally, Atwood turns to the subject of addiction in order to compare pornography to alcohol and drugs. The similarities she sees between them include "chemical changes in the body, which the user finds exciting and pleasurable"; their propensity "to attract a 'hard core' of habitual users"; and the fact that "tolerance develops, and a little is no longer enough ... Not only the quantity consumed but the quality of explicitness [of pornography] must be escalated which may account for the growing violence" (128). Her motive in drawing attention to these similarities is to suggest that we deal with pornography as we do with drugs and alcohol: by controlling it. Atwood acknowledges that society has not banned social drinking in order to counter alcoholism. "On the other hand," she writes, "we do have laws about drinking and driving, excessive drunkenness and other abuses of alcohol that may result in injury or death to others" (128). If, Atwood implies, we agree with banning the most damaging abuses of drugs and alcohol (and most Canadians reading her article in the early 1980s would have: it was then in Ontario that the great effort to stamp out drinking and driving began), then we should consider banning the more virulent forms of pornography.

Atwood's call for the censorship of pornography is not explicit in this article; it is implicit and hinges on the question of whether pornography produces measurably harmful effects in society. However, from her references to "Scandinavian studies that showed a connection between depictions of sexual violence and increased impulse toward it on the part of male viewers" (128) and from her comments about the connection between pornography and sex crimes involving rape and murder, Atwood's view in this article appears to admit the harmful effects of pornography. That the article is so intimately tied to what she was writing in *Bodily Harm*, which *depicts* the harm done by pornography, confirms this interpretation.

Nowhere, however, is Atwood explicit about the censorship of pornography, and towards the end of the article one paragraph sounds a note that dissents from the tone of the rest of the piece. In her penultimate paragraph she sets the stage for the quite different message about censorship that will be presented in *The Handmaid's Tale*. Atwood warns of the danger of regressing to an "age of official repression" and then adds: "Neither do we want to end up in George Orwell's *1984* in which pornography is turned out by the State to keep the proles in a state of torpor, sex itself is considered dirty and the approved practice it only for reproduction" (128). The intertextuality between *The Handmaid's Tale* and *Nineteen Eighty-four* has been widely observed, and the state that controls pornography and sex in the way described in this quotation closely resembles Gilead. It is almost as if, at the end of "Atwood on Pornography," the author is beginning to consider the full implications of the argument about censorship and pornography that she had made in *Bodily Harm*. She is not quite willing to let it go: to the above passage she adds, referring to the violent world promoted by pornographers, "But Rome under the emperors isn't such a good model either" (128). Nevertheless, although she does not mention the novel that would appear two years after the publication of this article, her concluding comments clearly show that Atwood had begun thinking about the changed position she would take on censorship in *The Handmaid's Tale*.[8]

The Handmaid's Tale extrapolates the encapsulated, tentative warning against censorship at the end of the *Chatelaine* piece into a full-blown dystopia that explores the complex causes and effects that censorship can have. The novel is most often compared to Bradbury's *Fahrenheit 451* and Orwell's *Nineteen Eighty-four* for their shared portrayal of a "near future where societal pressures enforce rigid limitations on individual freedom" (Wood, 131), but it is specifically the state control and suppression of discourse that is the essential feature they have in common. As Atwood has said (in this chapter's epigraph), "The attempt to censor is the attempt to establish a Utopia," but in *The Handmaid's Tale* she posits the futility of such an attempt by depicting, in Gilead, a dystopia that *results* from censorship. As Barbara Hill Rigney writes of the novel, "its principal subject is the suppression of language, especially language as used by women" (131). The novel implicitly presents four arguments against censorship, but these arguments are not presented without ambiguity. In fact, even as they demonstrate the dangers of censorship, these self-contradictory arguments demonstrate its necessity.

THE SUBJECTIVITY OF MEANING

One implicit argument that *The Handmaid's Tale* presents against censorship is that truth and meaning are subjective, that they can change over time. This is the argument that Mill uses when he claims that censorship may prematurely disqualify ideas that only later will come to be regarded as true. This tenet has no place in the world of Gilead, however, a society founded on religious absolutes. It has no place either in the object of Atwood's satirical attack, the conservative religious movement in the United States (Howells calls it the "American

'New Right'" [*Margaret Atwood*, 129]), which experienced increasing popularity in the early 1980s. While Atwood acknowledges that her depiction of Gilead draws on features of authoritarian regimes around the world, it is clearly meant to represent the fulfilled aspirations of these right-wing religious American forces. This is not the first time Atwood has voiced her concerns over the growth of conservative religion. In the interview with Tom Harpur in 1981 she says she "find[s] monolithic, rigid religions not only boring, but dangerous" (D1). But in that interview she also says she would not be against religious forces attempting to ban pornography ("If they said 'Let's stamp out violent pornography, let's stamp out a multi-billion-dollar business backed by the Mafia,' I would say more power to them, that's courageous" [D1]). By the time she comes to write *The Handmaid's Tale*, however, Atwood's concern about censorship by the Right has grown. A year after its publication she refers to the censorial tendencies of the Right to *justify* her novel: "Some people say that the power of the 'religious right' is on the wane. But you'll notice that Jerry Falwell [leader of the Moral Majority] just succeeded in getting 7-Eleven stores to stop selling Playboy and Penthouse" (quoted in Nichols, 3).

As it is for the American New Right, truth in Gilead is not subjective but is absolute and based on one authority: the Bible. And as with many censors, the rulers of Gilead are unsophisticated readers of texts, mistaking depiction for advocacy, biblical parable for God's command. At the heart of the handmaids' forced sexual servitude in Gilead is a literal (mis)reading of the story of Rachel and Jacob in Genesis 30:1–3 (one of the novel's epigraphs). To avoid competing readings that would suggest the subjectivity of interpretation, Gilead's rulers ban all writing except the Bible and keep that book under lock and key: thinks Offred, "It is an incendiary device: who knows what we'd make of it, if we ever got our hands on it?" (82). As Hilde Staels remarks, Gilead represents a society in which "the potential polysemy of discourse is replaced by absolutely homogeneous, univocal signs" (457).

Atwood conveys her argument against such univocal reading practices through Offred and the underground rebel movement in Gilead, with whom we are meant to sympathize. The censorship of discourse in favour of one authoritative reading is challenged by Offred's contextual approach to meaning and polysemous use of language. Marta Caminero-Santangelo writes that "Offred's early forms of 'resistance' constitute local and seemingly internal choices about meaning; Offred shifts from one context to another as a sheer demonstration that she can still draw on multiple discourses" (28). Offred recognizes that the Commander's "illicit" demand to play Scrabble would be ridiculous under normal circumstances, but that in Gilead, where words are strictly controlled, the request is truly subversive. Also, in Offred's justifiable uncertainty regarding the reliability of Ofglen (32) and the Eyes associated with Nick (275–7), Atwood shows that people's motivations and actions are open to multiple interpretations. As Offred says, "Context is all" (136; this phrase is repeated later on 180).

Not only are the significations of behaviour and Offred's surroundings contingent on circumstances; language is contextual for her as well. "Nolite te bastardes carborundorum" has been a desperate plea and directive of the handmaid who preceded her in the Commander's house. But its meaning changes when Offred reproduces it in the Commander's study: "Here, in this context, it's neither prayer nor command, but a sad graffito, scrawled once, abandoned" (174). Offred is aware of the rich and varied meanings of language. The novel is notable for her many meditations on the multiple meanings of words. She presents five interpretations of the word "chair" (104) and three for the word "job" (162). Staels points out Offred's constant use of similes, metonyms, and synaesthetic language, metaphorical techniques that highlight the multivalency of words: "In a society that censors aesthetic speech, Offred's poetic discourse reactivates the lost potential of language and the conditions for the production of meaning" (461). Even the underground dissident organization's password, "Mayday," for Offred is a pun (on the French "M'aidez" [42, 191]) that signals rebellion against Gilead's authoritative censoring of discourse.

There seems to be a strong vein of postmodern thinking coursing through *The Handmaid's Tale* that questions a denotative model of meaning and language. As Offred remarks, "It's impossible to say a thing exactly the way it was, because what you say can never be exact, you always have to leave something out" (126). Atwood's novel, as Caminero-Santangelo argues, can be classified as postmodern metafiction "through its suggestion that any narrative, even that which appears most immediate (or most objective) is inevitably a subjective reconstruction. 'Authenticity' is a concept challenged by postmodern fiction … and in *The Handmaid's Tale* nothing is ever authentic" (37). The constructed nature of reality and lack of authenticity and authority would seem to discredit the attempt of religious conservatives to institute censorship based on an absolute, God-given world-view. Yet Atwood warns of the danger of taking this postmodern conception of reality too far, to the point where it becomes a purely relativistic view of the world. She does this in the novel's epilogue through her satirical depiction of Professor Pieixoto, the sexist, callous Cambridge academic whose belief in the constructed nature of reality leads him to this comment: "in my opinion we must be cautious about passing moral judgment upon the Gileadeans. Surely we have learned by now that such judgments are of necessity culture-specific ... Our job is not to censure but to understand" (284). Atwood's warning is well noted by critics who are united in their condemnation of Pieixoto and his colleagues. Amin Malak says, "Atwood soberly demonstrates that when a critic or scholar (and by extension a reader) avoids, under the guise of scholarly objectivity, taking a moral or political stand about an issue of crucial magnitude such as totalitarianism, he or she will necessarily become an apologist for evil" (15), while Glenn Deer remarks that "the scholars are pompous cultural relativists" (125).

By attacking both the absolutist and relativist views of reality, Atwood critiques the most extreme positions on the censorship debate. An argument for the rigid control of discourse through censorship (made by the fundamentalists) must fail when confronted by the contextual nature of language and meaning. Yet if every utterance is contextual and no context can ever be fully known, then no utterance can ever be judged, let alone censored. The dilemma is summed up at the end of an article on *The Handmaid's Tale* in *Ms* magazine: "The answer, according to the gospel of Margaret Atwood, isn't to become rabidly intolerant of the intolerants ... and it isn't to become so tolerant that you cease to make distinctions about where you stand. 'You *have* to draw lines' [says Atwood]; 'otherwise you're a total jellyfish'" (Van Gelder, 90). Unfortunately, Atwood's appended injunction to "please, let's start drawing human lines," does not help us to understand *how* she would have the lines drawn. This is precisely the problem with *The Handmaid's Tale*: while it points to the untenability of both extremes, it offers no resolution to the question, no mechanism by which some truths can be deemed stable enough to be judged. The novelist surely means us to judge Gilead, but how can we when we "as readers can understand [Offred's] truth only as provisional" (Caminero-Santangelo, 38), because, Atwood reminds us throughout the novel, all Offred "can hope for is a reconstruction" (246).[9]

THE "SLIPPERY SLOPE"

A second critique of censorship suggested in the novel is what I have been calling the "slippery slope" argument. The idea is that while a particular practice may not be dangerous in itself, it could lead to practices that are. Most advocates of free speech, confronted with offensive material, oppose its censorship not because they condone the material but because they are afraid its censoring will lead to the censoring of other benign or worthwhile material. In Gilead one of the first acts of the new repressive regime is to eliminate pornography. "The Pornomarts were shut ... and there were no longer any Feels on Wheels vans and Bun-Dle Buggies circling the square" (163). At the time people do not protest its elimination: the narrator comments, "I wasn't sad to see them go. We all knew what a nuisance they'd been"; and the female vendor at the local newsstand says, "It's high time somebody did something ... Trying to get rid of it altogether is like trying to stamp out mice." The next day the vendor has disappeared, and the narrator's bank account has been frozen (163). This passage suggests that censorship of pornography is one of the first signs of the collapse of a democratic society into totalitarian rule. Furthermore, it warns that a passive reaction or, worse, a tacit consent to the censorship lends momentum to this collapse and will quickly rebound to result in the subversion of rights of those who do not oppose it.

One figure in the book who becomes trapped by her own assent to far-right religious values is Serena Joy, wife of the Commander for whom the narrator, Offred, is "handmaid" (sexual slave) during the course of the novel. Serena Joy's participation with the regime has been active rather than passive: she began as a celebrity on a gospel television show and went on to a public-speaking career in which she preached "about the sanctity of the home, about how women should stay home" (43). A number of critics have speculated that Atwood modelled Serena Joy on Phyllis Schlafly, an ultraconservative Republican who campaigned against the Equal Rights Amendment during the 1970s. As Wilson notes, "Atwood's Serena Joy appears to be based in part on Schlafly, who did extensive traveling, made speeches, and frequently appeared on television while saying that women's place is in the home" (*Atwood's Fairy-Tale Sexual Politics*, 383n16).[10] Schlafly may be a model for the second part of Serena Joy's career, but she was not a religious figure. In fact, the Serena Joy who appeared on the "Growing Souls Gospel Hour" (16) is based on one of the most popular television evangelists of the early 1980s: Tammy Faye Bakker.

Jim and Tammy Bakker rivalled the popularity of evangelists like Jerry Falwell until the demise of their PTL ("Praise the Lord") ministry in 1987.[11] Tammy Bakker was sincerely followed by millions of religious devotees, but she was even more popular with secular North Americans, who laughed at her extreme and well-timed emotional outbursts and outrageous make-up. This is the pre-Gilead incarnation of Serena Joy that Atwood's narrator and her husband

Luke witness on television: "We'd watch her sprayed hair and her hysteria, and the tears she could still produce at will, and the mascara blackening her cheeks. By that time she was wearing more makeup. We thought she was funny. Or Luke thought she was funny. I only pretended to think so. Really she was a little frightening. She was in earnest" (43–4). More evidence that Serena Joy is based on Tammy Faye Bakker appears in the epilogue to the novel, in which Professor Pieixoto tries to assign the true identity of Fred (Offred's Commander) to one of two Gileadean Commanders, Judd or Waterford, by comparing their wives. He tells us that Serena Joy was not Fred's wife's real name: "This [name] appears to have been a somewhat malicious invention by our author. Judd's wife's name was Bambi Mae, and Waterford's was Thelma" (291). I want to suggest that the possibility that Serena Joy's real name was Bambi Mae, a silly name that obviously rhymes with Tammy Faye, confirms the rather sly (though not, I think, malicious) invention by our author (keep in mind that Offred is not really an author, having recorded her story on cassette tapes, so Atwood is probably referring to herself).

Unlike Tammy Faye Bakker, Serena Joy sees her ideas for a perfect world twisted and exaggerated by a military coup into the society of Gilead. Women are forced to stay at home; their economic and political powers are taken away. One of the most important results of this transformation is that they are divested of their power to dissent, robbed of their freedom of speech. Atwood clearly manifests the ironic ramifications these changes have on Serena Joy: "She doesn't make speeches anymore. She has become speechless. She stays in her home, but it doesn't seem to agree with her. How furious she must be, now that she's been taken at her word" (44). Atwood warns that the assent (either active, like Serena Joy's, or passive, like Luke's purblind amusement at the evangelist's antics) to right-wing religious values, especially the tendency towards censorship, will come back to haunt the assentors and result in a loss of voice for all.

The slippery slope, the hypothetical extrapolation of current practices, is precisely what Atwood says *The Handmaid's Tale* is about: "A lot of what writers do is they play with hypotheses … It's a kind of 'if this, then that' type of thing. The original hypothesis would be some of the statements that are being made by the 'Evangelical fundamentalist right'" (quoted in Rothstein, c11). She stresses that the novel, which she labels "speculative fiction" (quoted in Cathy Davidson, 26), "takes certain positions – the tendencies now existing all over the world – and carries them to their logical conclusions" (quoted in Adachi, E1). According to David Cowart, Atwood's novel is warning that one such position susceptible to the slippery slope is the advocacy of censorship: "Once the logic of censorship has been accepted, one is defenseless against the less sensible but more powerful ideologue whose index one may – too late – find decidedly uncongenial" (111). This warning against censorship is part of the more general slippery-slope argument, which, writes Arnold Davidson, "portrays the advent of [Gilead] as an easy slide into 'final solutions' only slightly less brutal than those attempted in Nazi Germany" (113).

Davidson's comparison of Gilead with Nazi Germany is not gratuitous. There is clear evidence that Atwood wishes us to see in *The Handmaid's Tale* (written mostly in Berlin [Govier, 66]), "the nazification of the United States" (Larson, 496).[12] Like many prisoners of Hitler's camps, Offred is given a numerical tattoo by Gilead's authorities for identification purposes (60). On the one hand Offred is a victimized innocent bystander, reminiscent, as Atwood remarks, of "all the ordinary, apolitical people who ended up in concentration camps" (quoted in Van Gelder, 90). On the other, Offred is also portrayed as a passive accomplice whose inaction contributes to the fruition of the totalitarian regime. There is a lengthy passage in the "Night" chapter in the middle of the novel in which Offred reflects on a television documentary she saw as a child about the mistress of "a man who had supervised one of the camps where they put the Jews, before they killed them" (137). The details she concentrates on suggest that she sees the relationship in the film echoed by her collusive connection with Commander Fred. She focuses on the word "mistress," pausing to reflect that her mother had explained the word's meaning to her (137). Shortly afterward, thinking about the Commander, she says, "The fact is that I'm his mistress" and goes on to ponder the historical and personal significance of the term (153). She also tries to imagine how the Nazi's mistress could rationalize her relationship with a man who was "cruel and brutal," according to the film: "She did not believe he was a *monster*. He was not a *monster*, to her. Probably he had some endearing trait … How easy it is to invent a humanity, for anyone at all" (137; my italics). The last sentence of this citation is preceded and followed by sentences written in the past tense. The fact that it is in the present tense suggests that Offred shares with the Nazi's mistress the tendency to look for redeeming traits in a manifestly malevolent paramour. Indeed, Offred makes similar excuses for the Commander, even while he is sexually molesting her: "I remind myself that he is not an unkind man; that, under other circumstances, I even like him … He is not a *monster*, I think" (238; my italics). That the passage in which Offred recalls the film immediately follows her first illicit meeting with the Commander and her adoption of the role of Scrabble "mistress" confirms her identification, through her feeling of guilt, with the Nazi's mistress.[13]

Why does Atwood connect her futuristic society with Nazi Germany when totalitarian rule in Gilead is brutal enough to terrify any reader? The answer, I want to suggest, has to do with the credibility of Gilead and Atwood's use of the slippery-slope argument. Most commentators go along with Atwood's claim that Gilead is believable as the logical extension of current trends.[14] But some are more critical. "While we may imagine all kinds of negative worlds," writes Chinmoy Banerjee, "what is needed as a precondition of any critical force is that the imagined world be conceived as an extension of the historically existent world." The problem he finds with *The Handmaid's Tale* is that "the premise that Christian fundamentalism may lead to a theocracy in the United States is ... flimsy as a foundation for a dystopia" (78). Mary McCarthy's objections are even more specific: "I just can't see the intolerance of the far right, presently directed not only at abortion clinics and homosexuals but also at high school libraries and small-town schoolteachers, as leading to a superbiblical puritanism by which procreation will be insisted on and reading of any kind banned" (1). These comments point to the problem Atwood has in using the slippery-slope argument to warn against censorship and the fundamentalist right in general: she does not show the gradual steps on the slope between the United States in 1985 and Gilead. Where is the step-by-step movement towards the curtailment of individual rights? Gilead arrives in one fell swoop when right-wing insurgents "sho[o]t the President and machine-gun ... the Congress and the army declare[s] a state of emergency" (162). Where is the gradual encroachment on free speech from the censorship of pornography to erotica to women's magazines to the political content of newspapers? In Gilead newspapers and pornomarts are closed at the same time (163). In comparing *Fahrenheit 451* and *The Handmaid's Tale* Diane Wood traces the steps in the former novel by which "individual laziness precipitates a gradual erosion" of the right to own and read books (135), but in the latter this process is absent because it is a "revolution or *coup d'état* [that] brings about the loss of freedom" (134).

Based on the slippery-slope argument, Gilead has no credibility.[15] In order to make the society real to us, for it to be credible, then, Atwood must link it to a frightening society we do know, that is credible because it has happened. This is why she connects Gilead with Nazi Germany.[16] The identification has the effect of saying, if Nazi Germany can happen and Gilead is like Nazi Germany, then Gilead can happen as well. But this is a very different argument from the slippery-slope argument, which holds that Gilead is American fundamentalism writ large. The latter argument is the one Atwood says she is making in *The Handmaid's Tale*, but it is not backed up by events in the novel. It is not clearly illustrated in the novel, I would argue, because it is impossible to do so. As S. Morris Engel says of the slippery-slope argument in general, "the writer seems to imagine we are on a slippery slope and that if we take one step on it we will not be able to stop and will slide down the whole slope. But stop we often can, for most things are not like slippery slopes and do not lead to the envisioned dire consequences. Each new situation as it arises can be evaluated anew and decided on its merits" (160). Atwood does not show each "new situation," each discrete stage of censorship, because it would mean showing how each one would be evaluated anew, leading to a line eventually being drawn. This strategy of avoidance may not be conscious on Atwood's part, but *The Handmaid's Tale* is a good example of the way anti-censorship forces invoke the slippery-slope argument but inevitably fail to prove it.

Atwood uses the same fallacy to counter the other principal advocates of censorship in *The Handmaid's Tale*, radical feminists of the late 1970s and early 1980s, the very feminists she sided with in *Bodily Harm*. Most critics of *The Handmaid's Tale* find that, despite Atwood's protest to the contrary – she has said, "It would be quite wrong to interpret 'The Handmaid's Tale' as a book that is attacking feminists" (quoted in Nichols, 3) – the novel does critique the American feminist movement for its pro-censorship stance. Helen Buss argues that Atwood's "caution here is that if feminists seek fascist solutions they are ultimately condoning fascism" (quoted in Wood, 141n17), and Barbara Hill Rigney comments: "In *The Handmaid's Tale*, as in the actual and current situation [of religious groups instigating censorship in schools], some feminist groups exercise the same faulty judgement, thereby forfeiting their own freedom along with that of both the writers and the reading audience" (134). In the novel the representative of this feminist movement is the narrator's mother, "a quintessential feminist demonstrator" (Wood, 138), who, along with her cohort, is disparaged by the narrator: "They were talking too much, and too loudly. They ignored me, and I resented them. My mother and her rowdy friends" (169). Surely we are meant to identify with the narrator when, after witnessing the appalling circumstances of the parturition of the handmaid Janine, she affixes some of the blame for the state of affairs in Gilead to her mother's generation: "Mother, I think. Wherever you may be. Can you hear me? You wanted a women's culture. Well, now there is one. It isn't what you meant, but it exists. Be thankful for small mercies" (120). The implication in the novel is that feminist calls for the censorship of pornography will lead to widespread censorship that will eventually engulf the feminists themselves.

That this was Atwood's intent is confirmed in a 1986 interview with John Nichols in which Atwood discusses the novel's commentary on feminist censorship of pornography: "The problem with censoring pornography is that it gets people in the habit of censoring things. Usually the course of events is that pornography gets censored and then that extends to things like sex education and feminist writing would be on the line as well, once people started getting going with the scissors and bonfires. And the next thing that usually goes is political freedom" (3). As with the slippery-slope argument directed at the religious right, Atwood purports to be talking about what she portrays in *The Handmaid's Tale*, but the feminist slippery slope bears no resemblance to the novel. Feminists in the novel do censor pornography when they burn magazines, but this act hardly serves as the thin edge of the wedge: it has no relation to the sudden military coup that is the source of censorship of all discourse in Gilead. In *The Handmaid's Tale* Atwood puts forth the slippery-slope argument as a critique of calls for censorship by both the religious right and anti-pornography feminists without supporting the argument with credible evidence.

PORNOGRAPHY IS HARMLESS

A third way the novel opposes censorship is by questioning the argument put forward by some feminists – foremost among them Catharine MacKinnon – that pornography causes harm. In the interview with Nichols, Atwood acknowledges that "Pornography ... is bad for women" (3), the same observation she made in *Bodily Harm* and the *Chatelaine* article. But by the time of the interview, having written *The Handmaid's Tale*, she has shifted from supporting the censorship of pornography to seeing censorship as "a greater evil" (3).[17] The equivocation inherent in this view of pornography as the lesser of two evils shows up in the novel in several scenes that challenge the notion that pornography causes harm to women while, at the same time, furnishing evidence to the contrary.

One example in which we find a sceptical approach to the harmful effects of pornography is a scene that appears to be critical of what Howells calls "second wave North American feminism" (*Margaret Atwood*, 127). Offred flashes back to what was supposed to be a visit by her and her mother to the park to feed the ducks: "But there were some women burning books, that's what she was really there for. To see her friends; she'd lied to me, Saturdays were supposed to be my day" (36). From the beginning, by way of discrediting Offred's mother, Atwood portrays her as putting ideology before family, censorship above the needs of her child. The book-burning itself takes on a ceremonial quality, reminiscent of the practices of a cult:

Some of them were chanting; onlookers gathered.
   Their faces were happy, ecstatic almost. Fire can do that. Even my mother's face, usually pale, thinnish, looked ruddy and cheerful, like a Christmas card.   (36)

The reference to the Christmas card (and their chanting and ecstasy) reminds us that on this issue the feminists share the view of the religious fundamentalists, who, we have seen, are prime targets in the novel. There are in this scene other subtle ways by which Atwood attacks censorship by feminists. They are portrayed as having no qualms about co-opting children to their view before they are old enough to understand the ramifications of censorship: "You want to throw one on, honey? [one woman] said. How old was I?" (36). Once Offred is co-opted, her mother becomes patronizing: "Don't let her *see* it, said my mother. Here, she said to me, toss it in, quick" (36). Here Atwood levels the common complaint against censors: that they ban books without reading them. Atwood closes this scene with a particularly gruesome image, a striking rhetorical flourish: "I threw the magazine into the flames. It riffled open in the wind of its burning; big flakes of paper came loose, sailed into the air, still on fire, parts of women's bodies, turning to black ash, in the air, before my eyes" (36). By equating the burning of books with the burning of actual women's bodies, is Atwood implying that in censoring, feminists are defeating their own cause?
   The distrust of the conviction that pornography causes harm surfaces when the young narrator is handed a magazine to throw on the fire and, despite her mother's warnings, looks at one of its images: "It had a pretty woman on it, with no clothes on, hanging from the ceiling by a chain wound around her hands. I looked at it with interest. It didn't frighten me. I thought she was swinging, like Tarzan from a vine, on the TV" (36). The thoughts this image evokes in the narrator seem to point towards its harmlessness: it doesn't frighten her, nor does it appear to her all that different from other images she has encountered in popular culture. If, however, this reaction is meant to diminish the call for censoring pornography, it is certainly a weak attack. For, knowingly or not,[18] Atwood attaches to the narrator's reading of the image several cues indicating its naïveté. First

she reminds us that our reader is an innocent child: her description of the woman in the magazine not as "nude" or "naked" but as having "no clothes on" highlights the narrator's linguistic immaturity; her simple characterization of the woman as "pretty" indicates her ignorance of the patriarchal construction of female beauty, both in pornographic magazines (airbrushing) and in society. More importantly, her interpretation of the scene portrayed by the image is a misreading of startling simplicity. The narrator compares the woman to Tarzan, an icon of power noted for his freedom to swing through the jungle, to live independent of the strictures of a societally (patriarchally) constructed world. Yet a woman in chains on the cover of a men's magazine implies the male domination and enslavement of a female victim. The narrator's peculiar ability to see the bound woman as a figure of power and freedom undermines her claim for the harmlessness of the image and impairs, to a degree, Atwood's more general critique of the censorship of pornography in this section of the novel.

While Michele Lacombe points out that the novel criticizes the narrator's mother as "a radical lesbian, a participant in book-burnings as part of a misguided effort to curb pornography," she also sees that "Offred's mother is an ambivalent figure" (6). Indeed, several ideas typical of the narrator's mother's brand of feminism – including the idea that pornography is harmful – are supported by the novel. We are reminded of the violence against women, "the corpses in ditches or the woods, bludgeoned to death or mutilated, interfered with" (53), that the feminists' "Take Back the Night" marches (113) are meant to condemn. The offensiveness of pornography is emphasized by the films the handmaids are shown at the re-education centre, which depict the brutalization of women. The feminist objection is made by Aunt Lydia: "You see what things used to be like? That was what they thought of women, then" (112). Indeed, it is the Aunts who tout Gilead's liberation of women from violence and pornography: "There is more than one kind of freedom, said Aunt Lydia. Freedom to and freedom from. In the days of anarchy, it was freedom to. Now you are being given freedom from. Don't underrate it" (24). In this passage we hear an echo of feminists like Helen Longino who argue in favour of freedom from pornography: "The prohibition of such speech is justified by the need for protection from the injury (psychological as well as physical or economic) that results from [pornography]" (53). It is the sentiment behind Andrea Dworkin's comment, "We will know that we are free when the pornography no longer exists" (224).

The presentation of these feminist ideas in the novel is attended by ambiguity. Atwood genuinely seems to want to warn us about violence against women and pornography in our society. The grim explicitness of her descriptions testifies to her desire to pen "a crushing indictment of our own times" (Keith, 125). At the same time these warnings are almost always couched as rationales advanced by the despicable Aunts to justify the oppressive Gilead regime. Despite voicing the arguments of pre-Gileadean feminists, as Malak remarks, "Aunt Lydia functions, ironically, as the spokesperson of antifeminism; she urges the handmaids to renounce themselves and become non-persons" (12). On the one hand Atwood sees the merit of feminist ideas, especially the urge to censor pornography to prevent its harmful effects. On the other, by the time she writes *The Handmaid's Tale* she sees the misappropriation and intensification of the rationale behind censorship as a greater evil.

CENSORSHIP:
THE TABOO ON EXPRESSION

The last form of argument against censorship in *The Handmaid's Tale* that I want to explore involves Atwood's use of taboos, practices that society has deemed unacceptable. Two ideas found in the writing of Georges Bataille, a leading theorist on the subject, are particularly useful in establishing a theoretical frame for this analysis. The first is what I will call the "compression-explosion" model, which involves the dynamics and power of taboos; the second is Bataille's account of the motivating force behind taboos. When Bataille talks about the interdependence of taboo and transgression, he likens it to the dynamic of a compression followed by an explosion: "The compression is not subservient to the explosion, far from it; it gives it increased force" (65). The idea is that the more society works to suppress something, to make it taboo (the compression), the more power that thing will acquire, the more attractive the transgression (the explosion) of that taboo will be. This model can be applied to the suppression of discourse, for when censors outlaw some discourse, they are essentially making that material taboo.[19] Many advocates of free speech contend that, by making discourse taboo, censors are only making it more desirable, more powerful. As a result, they argue, censorship is counterproductive, resulting in the proliferation (usually through underground means) rather than the elimination of dangerous discourse (see Strossen, 263).

Atwood illustrates this dynamic in the novel by linking words and reading with sex, eating, and violence – all, to some degree, taboos in Western culture. Gilead is a society that devotes much of its energy to controlling an extremely wide array of social behaviour that it considers sinful; as a result, argues David Cowart, "The suppression of vice, of course, merely makes vice all the more inwardly canker-ous" (112). One such vice is sex. Bluntly put, "sex is evil in Gilead apart from procreation" (Rubenstein, "Nature and Nurture," 108), and procreation is carefully controlled through an official copulation ritual, called "the Ceremony," derived from Genesis 30:1–3, one of the novel's epigraphs. The key player in this ritual is the handmaid, whose allure is heightened because she is denied most men. A remark by Aunt Lydia about the handmaids, and therefore about sex in Gilead, depicts the workings of the taboo: "A thing is valued, she says, only if it is rare and hard to get" (107). The same idea is con-veyed when Offred thinks, "we are secret, forbidden, we excite them" (28). Like anything that gains in appeal because it is deemed a taboo, Atwood shows that sex goes underground in Gilead at Jezebel's, a brothel frequented by the hypocritical elite. The Com-mander's choice to take Offred as his companion to Jezebel's is espe-cially attractive to him because, as Moira explains, "they get a kick out of it. It's like screwing on the altar or something: your gang are supposed to be such chaste vessels" (228). The implication here, in language that appropriately invokes sacred and profane images, is that the stronger the taboo, the more attractive its transgression.

Atwood extends the compression-explosion model to censorship through the analogy drawn between the suppression of sex and that of discourse. This occurs during Offred's illicit visits to the Com-mander in his study: "Behind this particular door, taboo dissolved" (147). Only, to Offred's surprise, the taboo to be transgressed here involves words, in the form of outlawed magazines and the board-game Scrabble, which are substituted for sex: "What had I been expecting, behind that closed door, the first time? Something unspeakable, down on all fours perhaps, perversions, whips, muti-lations? At the very least some minor sexual manipulation, some bygone peccadillo now denied him, prohibited by law and punish-able by amputation. To be asked to play Scrabble ... seemed kinky in the extreme, a violation too in its own way" (145).[20] In terms very close to the Bataillean taboo of eroticism, Atwood has summed up this secret relationship, "the content of which is erotic but not sexual. It's erotic because he gives her access to forbidden words, to forbid-den printed pages, all these forbidden objects ... But as soon as you repress something, you eroticise it" (quoted in Matheson, 21). Offred recognizes the ridiculousness of making Scrabble (i.e., words, speech) taboo as has been done in Gilead, but she also recognizes the conse-quent power words acquire: "Now of course it's something different.

Now it's forbidden, for us. Now it's dangerous. Now it's indecent ...
Now it's desirable" (130).

The correspondence between discourse and sex is emphasized further by the fact that Atwood sets up the relationship between the Commander and Offred as analogous to one between prostitute and john. In this case the Commander acts the part of prostitute, offering Offred, who is "in the client position" (171), reading instead of sex. Nick, the Commander's chauffeur, takes on the role of pimp: "What does he get for it, his role as page boy? How does he feel, pimping in this ambiguous way for the Commander?" (170).[21] The description of Offred's meeting with the Commander sounds like an account of a nervous, inexperienced client's visit to a brothel: "I wish he [the Commander/prostitute] would turn his back, stroll around the room, read something himself. Then perhaps I could relax more, take my time. As it is, this illicit reading of mine seems a kind of performance." Offred feels exposed and, like a john, worries about the act happening too fast. The meeting continues with dialogue that could easily be from a stereotypical fictional scene in a bordello:

"I think I'd rather just talk," I say. I'm surprised to hear myself saying it.

He smiles again. He doesn't appear surprised. Possibly he's been expecting this, or something like it. "Oh?" he says. "What would you like to talk about?"

I falter. "Anything, I guess. Well, you, for instance."

"Me?" He continues to smile. "Oh, there's not much to say about me. I'm just an ordinary kind of guy."   (173)

The visiting hero, more sensitive than the average customer, tries to humanize the prostitute. The prostitute is unfazed and self-deprecating. Atwood sets up this scene, in which Offred reads, in terms of a visit to a prostitute in order to emphasize its transgressive nature. By doing so she suggests that just as sex (especially prostitution) becomes more powerful, more desirable when it is made taboo, words become more powerful when they are censored. As Staels writes, "From the point of view of Gilead, personal discourse is disallowed, because it is considered too dangerous. However, among the colonized individuals, the total suppression of personal desire and personal speech causes an irrepressible yearning for gratification" (459). This is an argument against censorship because it claims that banning offensive discourse does not eliminate it; rather, it increases people's fascination with it and merely causes it to emerge in unauthorized channels.

Sex is not the only taboo with which discourse and censorship are linked. Since her first novel, *The Edible Woman*, Atwood has been fascinated by the role food plays in people's lives. She has observed that for many women it has taken on the trappings of a taboo: "If you think of food as coming in various categories: sacred food, ceremonial food, everyday food, and things that are not to be eaten, forbidden food, dirty food, if you like – for the anorexic, all food is dirty food" (quoted in Lyons, 228). For Offred, denied free speech, letters take on the aura of some strictly regulated food, like sweets: "The [Scrabble] counters are like candies, made of peppermint, cool like that. Humbugs, those were called. I would like to put them into my mouth. They would taste also of lime. The letter C. Crisp, slightly acid on the tongue, delicious" (131). The opportunity to read in the Commander's study is like having the taboo on food (and concurrently sex) temporarily lifted: "On these occasions I read quickly, voraciously, almost skimming, trying to get as much into my head as possible before the next long starvation. If it were eating it would be the gluttony of the famished, if it were sex it would be a swift furtive stand-up in an alley somewhere" (172–3). The implication is, once again, that banning discourse is about as effective as denying food to the starving: it augments, rather than diminishes the appetite (for knowledge).

Finally I want to examine a scene in the novel that combines the taboo of censorship and the two taboos I have been discussing, those against sex and food, with one other, the taboo against mortal violence. Violence is another act outlawed in Gilead, like reading and sex, that makes its return in modified form. As we have seen, Gilead prides itself on making people safe from physical violence (212). The novel suggests, however, that, as with most taboos, violence reappears in this society not through underground channels but in the ritualized form of the sacrifice. Before turning to the scene of sacrifice in *The Handmaid's Tale*, it is useful to consider Bataille's interpretation of the role of sacrifice in society, in which he sees sacrifice as a form of eroticism. In defining eroticism, Bataille argues that when we are born we enter a state of profound separateness, of discontinuity, from everything else that exists: "We are discontinuous beings, individuals who perish in isolation in the midst of an incomprehensible adventure, but we yearn for our lost continuity. We find the state of affairs that binds us to our random and ephemeral individuality hard to bear" (15). Bataille defines erotic activity as anything that brings us close to returning to this continuity with "everything that is" (15). Because death is the ultimate fulfilment of that return to continuity, eroticism usually involves violence. Sacrifice is one kind of erotic violence that reveals the "continuity through the death of a discontinuous being to those who watch it as a solemn rite. A violent death disrupts the creature's discontinuity; what remains, what the tense onlookers experience in the succeeding silence, is the continuity of all existence with which the victim is now one" (Bataille, 22). Bataille sees the eroticism of sacrifice as analogous to that of sex – "In antiquity the destitution (or destruction) fundamental to eroticism ... justified linking the act of love with sacrifice" (18) – and eating – "The sacrifice links the act of eating with the truth of life revealed in death" (91).

The best example of sacrifice in Atwood's novel is the communal hanging, or "Salvaging," that Offred attends, which is followed by a "Particicution," the brutal dismemberment of a state-convicted rapist. These activities are supposed to be part of the justice system, but Atwood makes it clear they are really a ritualized, and therefore acceptable way for the handmaids to express their pent-up violence: in the Salvaging all the handmaids are expected to touch the rope in solidarity (260); in the Particicution they do the actual killing with their bare hands (262–3). Offred finds these actions repulsive, but she also reacts to the sacrifice with the exhilaration characteristic of a participant in eroticism:

But also I'm hungry. This is monstrous, but nevertheless it's true. Death makes me hungry. Maybe it's because I've been emptied; or maybe it's the body's way of seeing to it that I remain alive, continue to repeat its bedrock prayer: *I am, I am.* I am, still.

I want to go to bed, make love, right now.

I think of the word *relish*.

I could eat a horse.   (264)

In this passage the link between sacrificial killing and sex is clear. So, too, as Rubenstein points out, is "the link between eating and sacrifice" ("Nature and Nurture," 110). Offred's earlier report that, while the victim of the Particicution is being torn apart, she hears "A high scream ... like a horse in terror" (263), taken together with her remark that she "could eat a horse," as well as her pun on relish, suggests her erotic desire to partake fully in the return of the victim to continuity.

What does all this have to do with censorship? I want to suggest that Atwood views censorship as a kind of taboo analogous to those involving sex, eating, and violence and that Bataille's explanation of how taboos work constitutes an argument against censorship in *The Handmaid's Tale*. I have shown with other parts of the novel that Atwood links the taboos attached to sex and food to the prohibition against reading in Gilead. In the scene of sacrifice it is clear that

Atwood is aligning the taboos of violence, sex, and food. In that scene these taboos are also linked to reading. It is no coincidence that the site of the Salvaging and Particicution is "the wide lawn in front of what used to be the library" (256). The connection among the taboos is reinforced when Offred ponders what the Salvaging victims might have been convicted of: "reading? No, that's only a hand cut off, on the third conviction. Unchastity, or an attempt on the life of her Commander?" (259). Her speculation emphasizes the link between censorship ("reading") and the society's prohibitions against sex ("unchastity") and violence ("an attempt on the life of her Commander"). By linking censorship with these other taboos that breed underground or ritualized subversion, the novel implies that censorship is ultimately counterproductive.

This compression-explosion argument is reinforced by the fact that the novel illustrates Bataille's claim that the driving force behind the violation of taboos is the desire, on the part of the transgressor, to shed, however temporarily, profound existential isolation, to re-establish a sense of connectedness. Offred, in Gilead, suffers a particularly acute sense of discontinuity: cut off from friends, family, even her former occupation – that she was fired from *the library* bolsters the link between discontinuity and censorship – the hand-maid lives a life of utter isolation. She expresses her loneliness in a number of ways, but most poignantly when she reminds us how she has been cut off by censorship:

I don't know if the words are right. I can't remember. Such songs are not sung any more in public, especially the ones that use words like *free*. They are considered too dangerous. They belong to outlawed sects.

> I feel so lonely, baby,
> I feel so lonely, baby,
> I feel so lonely I could die.   (51)[22]

Offred is lonely, Atwood implies, because censorship, like other taboos, impedes her ability to feel a part of a collective, to have a sense of belonging. As Offred says of the story she is telling in *The Handmaid's Tale*, "You don't tell a story only to yourself. There's always someone else" (37). Atwood criticizes a regime like Gilead that tries to eliminate that "someone else" through censorship; and as the ultimate survival of Offred's testimony suggests, Atwood believes censorship will only make oppressed writers (and readers) more determined to speak out.

While I admire the intricacy with which Atwood formulates an argument against the designation of discourse as taboo, that censored expression will inevitably reappear through devious, underground means, I do not agree with it. First, the argument seems to be less about principle than it does about practicality. The argument that we cannot successfully ban harmful discourse is not a valid reason for not trying. Furthermore, despite advancing communication technologies like the Internet, which are hard to regulate, there is no evidence that as a society we cannot successfully control discourse. Atwood admits as much in *The Handmaid's Tale* in a passage that narrates how censorship of the young in Gilead *does* lead to the elimination of certain practices and ideas: "Are they old enough to remember anything of the time before, playing baseball, in jeans and sneakers, riding their bicycles? Reading books, all by themselves? Even though some of them are no more than fourteen – *Start them soon* is the policy, *there's not a moment to be lost* – still they'll remember. And the ones after them will, for three or four or five years; but after that they won't. They'll always have been in white, in groups of girls; they'll always have been silent" (205). The suppression here, of course, is of a detestable nature: Gilead eliminates fun, individuality, and expression among its women. The point, however, is that genuinely harmful discourse can be censored without leading to an even greater underground trade in that discourse.[23] I would argue, for example, that in Canada hate speech has been reduced, on balance, by the adoption of anti-hate-speech legislation.[24]

The Handmaid's Tale, then, implicitly conveys four arguments against censorship – the subjectivity of truth; the slippery slope; the harmlessness of pornography; and the compression-explosion model – that demonstrate a clear evolution in Atwood's thinking on the issue from the position she had taken at the beginning of the 1980s. At that time, as we see in *Bodily Harm*, Atwood was much more sympathetic to the idea that some of the clearly noxious discourse in our society should be censored. By the time she comes to write *The Handmaid's Tale*, however, Atwood is struggling to maintain a position nearer to that of some other writers such as Findley, who broadly opposes censorship; but like Findley, Atwood also provides evidence (albeit fictional) that undermines each of the arguments she employs to support that position. The ambivalence of these writers' works illustrates the difficulty of maintaining the neutralist liberal stance that opposes censorship on principle. What we will see in the next chapter, in the thoughts and work of Margaret Laurence, is a departure from this rigid and untenable position in favour of a view of censorship that is much more nuanced and, ultimately, more reasonable.

4 In Defence of Censorship: Margaret Laurence

> She was one of the most famous and beloved of Canadians.
> Still, during the last decade of her life, she had also been
> reviled, someone accused of being a pornographer. A deeply
> sensitive and private person, she had been terribly hurt by
> these accusations since she knew herself to be a truly righteous
> person, a writer dedicated to exploring human nature in all
> its various complexities.
>
> James King

> And yet I believe this is a question that citizens, Parliament
> and the legal profession must continue to grapple with.
> It is not enough for citizens to dismiss our obscenity laws
> as inadequate and outdated.
>
> Margaret Laurence

James King opens his biography of Margaret Laurence with two paragraphs that reveal the startling information that the esteemed Canadian author took her own life. These paragraphs are immediately followed by the comment reprinted above. That this comment on the effect of censorship controversies on Laurence figures so prominently in King's introductory remarks (and that he devotes a chapter to the incidents) testifies to the importance – only now emerging in public and critical consciousness – of censorship issues in Margaret Laurence's life, to the impact that opposition to her novels had on her writing and her psyche. Given this impact, it is particularly striking, then, that a writer such as Laurence, with even more at stake personally than other writers such as Findley or Atwood, should arrive at the position on censorship characterized by the statement quoted above in which she defends Canadian obscenity laws. How did she come to this position, and what reasons did she have to support it? The answers can be traced through her writing.

Most obviously, the censorship controversies forced Laurence to think deeply about her own position on censorship and its relation to another of her prime concerns, feminism.[1] These two subjects were issues of long-standing concern for Laurence,[2] and, as for Margaret Atwood, they came together most forcefully for Laurence in the debate over pornography. Like Atwood, too, Laurence chose to write about these issues in fiction (unsuccessfully in the case of an attempted novel) and in a magazine article. The main difference between the two writers is the very different conclusions that they reached. I have shown that Atwood began by sympathizing with the censorship of pornography but proceeded, through her *Chatelaine* article and *The Handmaid's Tale*, to a position in which she objected (I think mistakenly) to censorship on principle, even of pornography. Laurence, by contrast, began by experiencing censorship in a very personal way, the most significant example of which was the 1976 attack on *The Diviners* (in which her opponents accused Laurence of producing pornography). Laurence's response to this attack was to try to write a novel in which she aimed to retell the story of the *Diviners* controversy and work out her own feelings about censorship. This writing project, which I refer to as Dance Draft,[3] resulted in failure. After giving up on it, Laurence channelled some of her thoughts into the children's book *The Christmas Birthday Story*, but the principal expression of the position such an ardent and self-declared feminist as herself could take on the censorship of pornography found its fullest formulation in the article she wrote for *Toronto Life* in 1984 entitled "The Greater Evil." There Laurence arrived at a very different (and I believe more compelling) position on censorship than the one Atwood took in her dystopic novel a year later. There too, I will argue, Laurence set out a position that is both strongly feminist and strongly in favour of the state censorship of pornography.

THE FIRST *DIVINERS* CONTROVERSY

The first major censorship controversy to engulf Laurence occurred in 1976 in the Peterborough County town of Lakefield, where the author had been living since 1974. The attack was led by conservative religious Christians (I will refer to them as fundamentalists[4]) who wanted *The Diviners* banned from local high schools. The controversy came to centre on Lakefield High School, where the head of the English department, Robert Buchanan, refused to stop teaching the novel to his grade 13 classes. The dispute was taken to a textbook-review committee, which unanimously decided that the book was fit to teach. Then, at a raucous school board meeting characterized by fervid debate, the committee's decision was ratified by a vote of 10 to 6. The day after the meeting, however, the Reverend Sam Buick of the Dublin Street Pentecostal Church began circulating a petition "in defence of decency" (Goddard, B8), and displayed copies of *The Diviners* with offending passages highlighted in yellow. As King points out, these passages were of two kinds, containing either profanity or explicit sex (339–40).[5] In the end Buick took the petition to the board of education, but once again the board quashed his challenge.

From these events it is clear that the controversy over *The Diviners* was tailor-made to be fashioned into a tale by Laurence. In fact she recognized its adaptability as fiction early on. In June 1976, less than two weeks after the school board voted to retain *The Diviners*, she writes to Ernest Buckler: "How about all this, Ernie? If I'd made it all up, I couldn't have done better, eh?" (*A Very Large Soul*, 40). Central to this story is a Canadian small-town mentality – above all a sexual prudishness ruled by a religious priggery – of the kind Laurence was so adept at capturing in characters like Rachel Cameron's mother in *A Jest of God*. Present, too, in the figures of Buchanan and Laurence herself, are the heroes who, like the heroine in each of her Manawaka novels, attempt to break free of this limiting and parochial world-view. Given these similarities, it is not surprising that Laurence conceived the idea for a novel about censorship almost immediately after the *Diviners* controversy, and pursued the work assiduously over the following years.

FRUSTRATING FICTION

Before I turn to the draft of the novel that shows how Laurence attempted to recast her real-life censorship experience in fiction, I want to outline the evolution of this work and her ultimate decision to abandon it. The censorship débâcle in Lakefield took place between the beginning of February and the end of May 1976; as early as six months later Laurence had the idea for transforming the events into a novel. In a letter to Buckler dated 24 November 1976 she writes:

The problem, Ernie, is that as a political being (and yes, I'm that), I have to oppose the fundamentalists when they get into the political arena, which the School Board is definitely a part of, in my view, while, at the same time, as a fiction writer I have to try to understand their point of view, I mean really to try to make that leap of the imagination to get inside (to some extent) the minds and hearts of people like the Rev. Sam Buick of the Dublin Street Pentecostal Church. It is not easy, but in some way I feel it to be necessary. Maybe that whole thing, plus a whole lot of other things, is growing very very slowly and uncertainly into another novel – I don't know. We will see.   (*A Very Large Soul*, 40)

While this passage documents the proximity of Laurence's idea to write Dance Draft to the *Diviners* controversy, it also reveals something important about her approach: her attempt to put herself in the position of her opponents. Readers of Laurence are aware of her dictum to "write what you know," which, by Laurence's own estimation, accounts for the relative success of the Manawaka books (compared to, say, the African fiction).[6] Because characters are so important for Laurence, writing what she knows includes getting inside their heads, conveying "characters who – although they are fictional – are felt by writers to be as real as anyone we know" ("Ivory Tower," 17). This was especially true for her first Manawaka novel, *The Stone Angel*, which she describes as giving rise to "an enormous conviction of the authenticity of Hagar's voice" ("Gadgetry or Growing," 56).

When it came to writing about the fundamentalists, then, Laurence didn't want merely to depict them as ignorant, narrow-minded radicals. Nor did she want to portray them as evangelical hucksters. In the letter (of late November) to Buckler, referring to Sinclair Lewis's opportunistic preacher, she writes, "there is no way I could write about an Elmer Gantry." Rather, she wanted to understand her religious opponents and to convey the motivations behind what were obviously deeply held beliefs regarding morality and art: "My feeling," she continues to Buckler, "must be closer to what Joyce Cary did ... in THE CAPTIVE AND THE FREE, a novel which I don't think I dare re-read right now, although when I first read it (and it was his last – he literally kept himself alive until he had completed it) it seemed to me to be one of the most profound things I'd ever read" (*A Very Large Soul*, 40). Cary's novel is remarkable for its portrayal of the pernicious, immoral evangelist who is nevertheless, as Cary says in his "Prologue," a man of true pious faith, a "religious man who has sinned his way to God." If she was going to emulate Cary's work, Laurence would have to depict the fundamentalists as misguided in their deeds and pronouncements but, if not essentially good at heart, then at least human.[7]

Laurence probably found it difficult to derive anything good or reasonable from the fundamentalist position. Still, there were a few voices who opposed her in a rational way. Perhaps she caught a glimpse of this more judicious opposition in, for example, a letter to the editor of the *Globe and Mail*, which, in condoning the attack on *The Diviners*, made this argument: "Students in a classroom are a captive audience; they are required to be there. But they come from families with very diverse standards of language and behavior, standards which range from careless or habitual use of vulgar language to careful exclusion of all questionable expressions. With some families references to sexual practices are common; with others – the majority, I think – such references are generally shunned" (Woollard, 6). The letter writer goes on to argue that teachers avoid books that offend Jews and Blacks and asks why they would teach books that offend those who shun profanity and talk of sex. Finally, he asks why "good books ... of high literary merit by authors of repute – Conrad, Hardy, Galsworthy, E.M. Forster, Faulkner" – should not be taught instead. While none of these arguments constitutes a knock-down blow to the use of *The Diviners* in the classroom (for one, Faulkner's fiction contains potentially controversial sexuality, and Conrad's features arguably racist innuendo), they are at least presented in a sober, articulate way by someone who appears to be well read. They invite intelligent rebuttal, and it may be this kind of opposition that caused Laurence, in writing of the fundamentalists to Hugh MacLennan in 1979, to reflect: "Well, I think we have to fight the would-be oppressors, but we also have to know that the enemy is real, suffers pain, knows joy and discouragement – this is a difficult thing, more difficult than I ever realized until a few years ago, although it's a part of my faith, held for years. I would like some day to deal with some of this in a novel" (*A Very Large Soul*, 117). Laurence resented the religious conservatives for their authoritarian outlook, but clearly also wanted to find something sympathetic in her opponents, and to engage with their moral position in Dance Draft.

In reality, however, for the most part the attacks on *The Diviners* were petty, ignorant, and hurtful, offering little material on which Laurence could draw in order to depict a balanced, intelligent censorship debate in Dance Draft as, it appears, she wanted to do. It is possible that her inability to understand the uncongenial fundamentalists was what led to her ultimate failure to complete the novel. As Harold Horwood remarks: "Her principal characters were always people with whom she had a great deal of sympathy. She liked them. This was the first time that she tried to do one of those modern books about antiheroes in which, instead of liking the people you're writing about, you dislike them ... She was too sympathetic to people generally to be able to treat unsympathetic characters in a major way. I think this was one of her problems" (quoted in Wainwright, 100–1).[8] Indeed by 1982, six years after first conceiving the idea, Laurence had come to the conclusion that she would never understand or be understood by the religious would-be censors. In a letter to James Stark she comments on "trying to discuss my novel *The Diviners* with the fundamentalists who have tried to have it banned in this country." She continues: "I have avoided this kind of confrontation because I believe it to be fruitless. I certainly do not believe in speaking only to the converted, as it were, but there are persons with whom one cannot speak at all and indeed should not even try to do so."

It is possible that Laurence never came to sympathize and therefore fully engage with the characters (specifically the fundamentalists) because she never achieved the personal and critical distance from the events that she seemed to need to turn reality into fiction. King documents the difficulty Laurence had in writing *The Fire-Dwellers* while her experiences in Vancouver were still fresh in her psyche (191) and suggests that, for her writing to succeed, Laurence generally required "the strength the writer can draw from being absent from the landscape [both geographical and emotional, I would suggest] that inspires her and which can be the source of art only when one is removed from it" (307). Physical distance from her religious opponents was not an option, of course, unless she moved away from Lakefield, which she appeared not prepared to do. Emotional distance must have been elusive with the advent of further censorship attacks outside of Lakefield. In 1978, in King's County, Nova Scotia, a Baptist minister lobbied the local school board to remove *The Diviners* from the classroom, and in Etobicoke, Ontario, a school board trustee attempted to have *A Jest of God* banned from high schools (Birdsall, 53–4). Also that year a dramatic community meeting took place in Huron County in Ontario, where parents and religious groups demanded that three novels – one of which was *The Diviners* – be removed from the grade 13 curriculum (William French, 16). Although these attempts to ban Laurence's work were generally unsuccessful, they ensured that her troubling opponents remained fixed in her consciousness. It is not surprising, then, that in her 1979 letter to MacLennan, Laurence adds, "although I've been thinking of it for over a year, it's too close; I can't do it yet. Maybe it will not ever be given to me to explore that region; I can only wait and try to understand, as a novelist, the very people whom I am battling in my role as citizen" (*A Very Large Soul*, 117).

It appears that Laurence never did gain adequate distance from the censorship controversy, never achieved a workable perspective, so was never able to understand the characters she was trying to fictionalize. In 1984 she writes to MacLennan: "Things are well with me. I have found I was not meant to write the novel that I laboured on mightily for some years. That's okay. I'm taking other directions" (*A Very Large Soul*, 123). Her easygoing resignation to the failure of an intensely personal project that she had been thinking about and working on for almost eight years is deceptive; having to abort the novel represented a profound loss for Laurence.

THE UNFINISHED NOVEL

What is left of the project Laurence abandoned consists of a series of notebooks and folders, containing notes and draft fragments and historical and religious source material, acquired by the archives of

McMaster University Library and made available to scholars only since 1997.[9] From this material it is clear that Laurence meant to write a novel that portrays the experiences of two principal female characters. Mairi McDuff, born in Glasgow in 1900, is an orphan shipped from Britain to Canada as a Home Child. In Canada she is put to work by the brutal Sam Hogg, but soon leaves this hard life to marry Albert Price.[10] A large portion of the draft manuscript at McMaster, approximately seventy handwritten pages, describes Mairi's passage from England and early life in Canada. The other main character is Allie Price, the daughter of Mairi and Albert, born in 1922. At the age of twenty, Allie marries Steve Chorniuk, and they have a son together, Stephan. Allie becomes a high school teacher and, at the time she is telling her story, lives in Jordan's Landing, Ontario. While there are fewer written manuscript pages of Allie's narrative than of Mairi's, the copious accompanying research material on Christian fundamentalism and the detailed outline notes for Allie's story suggest that she was to be the focus. As King writes in his brief appendix, "Mairi would not have been the central character, that role being given to Mairi's daughter, Allie, a high-school teacher, whose remarks on Milton lead to a nasty confrontation with fundamentalist Christians" (397). It is certainly the attack by the fundamentalists that was to be the focus of Allie's tale.

Laurence set up the story of Allie's entanglement with fundamentalist would-be censors in a draft fragment that begins one day when Allie walks into her grade 13 classroom at Jordan's Landing District Secondary School: "'All right,' Allie says, smiling a little. 'We're going to talk about Satan'" ("Draft Ms"). What she wants to talk about is why Satan gets all the best lines in *Paradise Lost*, why Milton makes him the hero of the tale. By way of answering these questions she presents to her class two distinct approaches to interpreting the portrayal of Satan. The first, which Allie refers to as the Satanist argument, contends that Satan is the hero because Milton actually sympathized with him, that Milton was "of the Devil's party." In addition to this phrase from William Blake's *The Marriage of Heaven and Hell* (62), Allie marshals several other sources to support this view, revealing the depth of Laurence's research and interest in this interpretation of *Paradise Lost*. She cites H.A. Taine's *History of English Literature* (of which Laurence had an old copy) to her students: "The finest thing in connection with this Paradise is hell; and in this history of God, the chief part is taken by the devil. The ridiculous devil of the middle-age, a horned enchanter, a dirty jester, a petty and mischievous ape, band-leader to a rabble of old women, has become a giant and a hero" (1:450).[11] She also refers to the literary historian Emile Legouis, who wrote of Milton that, "In spite of himself, he was in deep sympathy with Satan, the great rebel of Heaven and the enemy of God" (581).

After explaining the Satanist view, Allie then presents the opposing argument, which she calls the anti-Satanist position. This argument holds that, while Milton may have depicted Satan as a hero, he did so on purpose: "he intended to show that evil can have a seductive power" ("Draft Ms"). She draws the class's attention to David Daiches' amplification of this idea: "Satan is a great figure, and he is meant to be: evil is not slight or trivial – nor, unfortunately, is it always unattractive. If evil were always obviously ugly, there would be no problem for men, and the task of recognizing and resisting it would be easy" (153). Though Milton depicts him with grandeur, Allie adds, Satan is still part of God's higher divine plan. In the end the depiction is profoundly devout.[12]

Following Allie's lecture there is some class discussion, and one thoughtful student asks whether these two views are mutually exclusive. Does Milton's sympathy for his rebel angel necessarily diminish the poet's religious integrity? Allie seizes on this duality, suggesting that it is possible that Milton was impeccably righteous while, at the same time, being such a consummate artist that he became engrossed in, and to some degree enamoured of, his hero. As this resolution to the dichotomy admits that Milton may have sympathized with Satan, Allie concludes by saying, "I suppose, in that way, I tend towards the so-called Satanist school of literary thought."

Though her choice of words may be somewhat infelicitous, Allie is subsequently shocked by the barrage they bring down upon her. Sitting in the back of the classroom are two students who have been silent to this point in the story. They are the twins Donno and Debbi, children of the local evangelist preacher, the Reverend Jake Flood. The youngsters sing and play the harp on their father's televised broadcast called "Paradise Path." On hearing Allie's last words about her view of Milton's relation to Satan, Donno interrupts to level an accusation: "You are talking blasphemy," he says. The interchange between Donno and Allie that follows is the initiation of the central conflict, that between Allie and the fundamentalists. Donno begins:

"How can the devil have anything good about him? That is blasphemy against our saviour. And – and – you said yourself – I heard you – and everybody heard you – you said you're a Satanist.

"Donno – that's not what I said at all. You haven't understood what I was saying.

"I heard all right," Donno Flood says. "You said you tend to be a Satanist, and Milton was possessed of the devil. That's what I distinctly heard you say. The devil took him over."

Allie asks him to stay after class, but "he does not reply. He is already halfway out of the room, as though pursued by all too imaginable demons."

There are a couple of other brief written fragments and extensive notes on the shape this part of Dance Draft would take, but for the most part the draft of Allie's story ends there. It is as if Laurence was able to set out the parameters of the conflict, who would be involved and what the subject of contention would be, but could not bring herself to depict the actual battle, with its accusations, pettiness, and hurt feelings. As King writes, "The novel *Dance on the Earth* [Laurence's original title] … was simply not a book that could be completed because in large part the process of writing it would have been too painful" (398). Despite its truncation, however, Dance Draft still reveals much about Laurence's mental and emotional positions in the years following her own censorship controversy. In the material we have we see many of the characteristics of the conflict that inundated Laurence in 1976, as well as the emergence of some ideas, including her interpretation of Milton, that had been brewing in her mind for some time. Finally, in Dance Draft we see some of the characteristics of her position on censorship beginning to coalesce.

AN ALLY IN ALLIE

One way Dance Draft can be seen to be a direct result of Laurence's own experience with censorship is the way she modelled her characters on participants in the 1976 controversy. Among these characters is the Reverend Jake Flood, whose children initiate the attack against Allie. Although Laurence does not provide much information about Flood in the draft manuscript for the novel, no doubt her encounter with the Reverend Sam Buick in Lakefield would have shaped this character. As well, given Flood's television show, "Paradise Path" ("Ms Notes"), she probably planned to use the popular television evangelist Billy Graham as a model. The draft material for the novel includes a large file of articles and clippings on evangelical Christianity ("Research Material") and a copy of "The Portable Canterbury," a review of books by and about Billy Graham that appeared in the *New York Review of Books* (16 Aug. 1979: 3–6) ("Notes").

The most important character in the story, of course, is Allie Price, who is an amalgam based on the two key players on the defending side of the real-life conflict: Robert Buchanan and Laurence herself. Like Buchanan, Allie is a high school teacher in a small town in Ontario who is attacked by fundamentalists for the content of her grade 13 class. The idea of having Allie get in trouble with the fundamentalists for teaching Milton may have come in part from

Buchanan's interest in and teaching about "echoes of the Bible and Milton" in *The Diviners* (Ayre, 9). Buchanan's views led to his being labelled "a disciple of Satan" by the fundamentalists, who eventually demanded (to no avail) that he be fired (Ayre, 9). As we have seen, the first accusation leveled at Allie by the fundamentalists is that she is an agent of Satanism, and as a result of the controversy she takes early retirement. A note by Laurence to herself among the draft material ("Check Bob Buchanan: 1. Retirement – 65? 2. Early retirement? 3. Union? 4. Milton – Gr 13?" ["Post-it Note"]) makes explicit some of the links between what happened to Buchanan and what happens to Allie.[13]

Of course the real model for Allie is Laurence herself. Initially this is suggested by the fact that Laurence makes her teacher female and that Allie, like Laurence (and her most autobiographical heroine, Morag), in the summer occupies a riverside cottage near her town of residence. More importantly, Allie and Laurence share many of the same concerns about Milton and his Satan. As Dance Draft shows, Allie is fascinated by the heroic stature and charismatic speeches Milton allows a character who epitomizes evil. Among Laurence's private papers is a sheaf of notes labelled "Morag's Notes on Paradise Lost – in margin of her copy of Milton's poems," which reveal that the Morag of *The Diviners* is struck by the same seeming contradiction. Although Laurence later excised them from the novel, an early draft ("Diviners Draft," 239–41) shows that she originally meant to include the "Notes" in the passage in which Morag is homesick and ill with the flu in Winnipeg and turns to Milton: "Reads *Paradise Lost*, sneezing" (*The Diviners*, 144). The "Notes" read:

Satan!   "Darken'd so, yet shone
Above them all the archangel: but his face
Deep scars of thunder had intrenched, and care
Sat on his faded cheek, but under brows
Of dauntless courage, and considerate pride
Waiting revenge."
Hell – heat & cold – note immensity – note power & force &
ferocity of descrip – extremes of darkness & terror
HORROR
vague but vivid
[...]
Light not as vivid as the darkness & powers of evil – (?) – Hardly an adequate Heaven – (?)
[...]
!!descrip! Milton does the darkness better than the brightness, nearly *always*.
(his Satan so much more interesting than his God, to me anyway).

[...]

N.b! Passion & ferocity of this! I hate what he's saying – but my God, the *way* he says it!   ("Notes and Research," 1–7)

That both Allie and Morag are clearly impressed by Milton's dark but loving portrayal of Satan suggests that Allie expresses a long-standing interest of Laurence herself.

In fact, Laurence became interested in this contradiction within Milton long before she literalized its expression through Allie – by conveying it in her own first Manawaka novel. Paul Comeau, who sees *Paradise Lost* as "one of the most influential books in Laurence's background" (11),[14] devotes an article to reading Hagar Shipley as Laurence's version of Satan. While it is difficult to accept Comeau's view that, at the end of the novel, "Hagar has become the embodiment of evil ... like her fallen prototype [Satan]" (18), his observation that Hagar's rebelliousness, self-deception, and pride remind us of Milton's archfiend (12) is compelling.[15] Furthermore, like Satan in *Paradise Lost*, as John Moss points out, "The indefatigable Hagar in *The Stone Angel* comes closest of Laurence's protagonists to heroic stature" (71). They are both, after all, tragic heroes in the classical sense. Laurence seems conscious, as she is of Milton's depiction of Satan, of the apparent contradiction of her sympathetic portrayal of the crusty old woman: "I feel ambiguous towards her, because I resent her authoritarian outlook, and yet I love her, too, for her battling" ("Ten Years' Sentences," 14). If, as her comment suggests, Laurence eventually came to see a correspondence between Milton (as the creator of Satan) and herself (as the creator of Hagar), then her depiction of the controversy over the work of Milton in Dance Draft is ultimately a portrayal of attacks against her own writing.

This correlation in Laurence's mind between Milton's work and her own is supported further by a passage in Dance Draft in which Allie voices her confidence in the ability of her students to deal with potentially controversial material. Before the class in which Milton becomes the focus of dispute, we learn that "[Allie] believes in discussion, in encouraging kids to express their own responses to literature." She goes on to reflect: "These aren't kids. They are young women and men. You can challenge them, push them a bit, make it almost like first year." After these thoughts, however, she cautions herself: "*Watch it*, she tells herself. Hubris. Spiritual pride. Downfall of Milton's Archangel" ("Draft Ms"). Here Allie obliquely compares herself to Satan. If Allie, like Hagar, represents Satan (remember she calls herself, albeit in a carefully qualified way, a Satanist), then Laurence is comparing herself to Milton in creating a character similar to his. In that case, once again, the fictional students' concerns regarding Milton most likely represent the real-life fundamentalist opposition to *The Diviners*. This claim is reinforced by the fact that Allie's rationalization of her subject-matter closely parallels Laurence's justification of *The Diviners* as teaching material. Like Allie, Laurence believed that high school students were mature enough to engage challenging material. In an open letter to teachers, following the controversy, Laurence writes: "I wish that the people who want to ban certain novels would talk to some of the many grade 12 and 13 students with whom I have discussed my writing. These students have read the novel they are studying – all of it, not just snippets here and there, and they have no difficulty, under the guidance of sensitive and informed teachers, of seeing that this work is an affirmation (and I think a serious and moral one) of faith in life and in humanity" ("A Letter from Margaret Laurence"). Thus, in Dance Draft, Laurence manages to represent herself in Allie[16] and her writing in the content of Allie's course in order to convey the circumstances of and her own reaction to the *Diviners* controversy.

Though Laurence was unable to continue Dance Draft, leaving untold the narration of the unfolding controversy as well as Allie's reaction to events, she did prepare notes that show that the shape the story was supposed to take resembles the *Diviners* controversy in several ways. Among these notes is an outline in which Laurence sets out the chronology of the story and traces the attack, which spans the school year: "Attack begins ... Attack escalates – (blasphemy, lewdness) ... lesbianism, communism ... feminism, 'abortion' – (and reactions of community) ... school board; principal; friends and neighbors ... Attack in abeyance – but – ... Upshot of attack – schoolbd, Colin (principal), Allie, kids ... Early retirement" ("Ms Notes"). The initial charges against Allie, of blasphemy and lewdness, were the principal accusations levelled at Laurence regarding *The Diviners*. In a letter to Ernest Buckler, Laurence writes: "[the fundamentalists] claim the novel is obscene, blasphemous, pornographic, etc." (*A Very Large Soul*, 39). This observation was prompted by detractors like Muriel White, who, at the time of the controversy, wrote: "The only purpose that this novel could serve in the field of education for students of any age would be for the promotion of degradation, the promotion of indecency and immorality, the knowledge of unsavory pornography and gutter language spawned in warped minds" (quoted in Ayre, 10). Indeed, as Patricia Morley puts it, the fundamentalists "appeared to see in the novel little but blasphemy, immorality, adultery, and fornication" (130).

While the allegations in Dance Draft of blasphemy and lewdness clearly have their origin in the attack on *The Diviners*, the charges of

lesbianism and communism are more tangentially related to the controversy. The reference to lesbianism seems connected to Laurence's
view of the attack as part of a larger fundamentalist conspiracy of
character assassination. In one file containing Dance Draft material
there is a prose fragment describing Allie and her sister-in-law dancing together, in joy and abandon, at Allie's cottage on the river (it is
this scene, most likely, that explains the novel's intended title, *Dance
on the Earth*). Accompanying this passage is this cryptic note: "Jake
Flood's spies – Attack – (lesbianism, communism, feminism, destroy-
ers of home and family)" ("Ms Notes"). The notion that somehow
Allie's antagonist in the novel has agents out gathering incriminating
information to be used against her is confirmed in another note in a
different file: it begins with Allie reflecting, charitably, "We've danced
only once since then, and heaven knows we've had our reasons not
to. I suppose the watcher didn't mean to betray us." But then her
thoughts turn more severe: "Of course he meant to … We thought
we were only closing [the cottage] for that winter. Little did we
know" ("Blue Notebook"). The implication, of course, is that one of
the Reverend Mr Flood's "spies" secretly watches this private dance,
which then gives rise to the fabrication that Allie is a lesbian.

The allegation of communism seems like one of those epithets
hurled by enemies desperate to affix any pejorative label they can
find, yet it too has its literary and biographical origins. The fundamentalists who insinuate that Allie is a communist probably get the
idea to do so from the fact that Allie's husband, Steve Chorniuk, was
"a communist of Ukrainian descent" (King, 394). But it is an incident
that occurred when Laurence was first starting out as a writer, which
connects communism and censorship, that may have given rise to
this accusation against Allie. In her memoirs Laurence records that
soon after she was married, she got a job as a reporter with the
Westerner, a Winnipeg communist newspaper. She had not joined the
paper for ideological reasons, but nor did she object to their left-wing
views of social justice. After the paper folded, she was hired by the
Winnipeg Citizen, but after a year she was summoned by its managing
editor and accused of being a communist. The editor's motives in
confronting Laurence in this way are not clear (she promptly
resigned), but it seems Laurence believed that any response other
than a fervent denial would have led to her firing, a ruthless imposition of censorship. Her last signed article for the *Citizen* is a defence
of freedom of speech in which she pleads for journalists at the CBC
"to be allowed to keep every iota of writing freedom and even to
extend and broaden it" ("In the Air"). In a critical essay that traces the
influence of Laurence's early newspaper work on her development

as a writer, Donez Xiques makes the connection between the charge of communism and later censorship controversies: "I wonder whether the pain brought on in Laurence's later years by the harsh distortions of book-banners and their efforts to vilify Laurence's novels was augmented by memories of these unsupported allegations when she was a young reporter for the *Winnipeg Citizen*" (206). If Xiques is right, then the charge of communism against Allie represents one more way in which Laurence expresses the pain she experienced during her own censorship dispute.[17]

In addition to reflecting some of the accusations made against Laurence during the *Diviners* controversy, Dance Draft also shows that Laurence planned to project her own emotional responses to the attack through Allie. In a note in the draft material Laurence outlines the evolution of Allie's feelings as the discord over her teaching deepens: "amusement ... surprise, disbelief ... hurt, bewilderment ... anger, fury" ("Ms Notes"). Like Allie, Laurence's first reaction to opposition to *The Diviners* was amusement. A full year before the conflict with the fundamentalists began, at a meeting of the Women's Art Association of Peterborough, where she was challenged for her use of profane language in *The Diviners*, Laurence, while responding to the charge, inadvertently set the tablecloth on fire with her cigarette. The resulting ruckus broke the serious tension in the room. As King points out, "This was one of the last – and very few – occasions she was able to laugh at the controversy regarding the language in *The Diviners*" (339). Initially as well, Laurence's response to the fundamentalist attack that began the next February was humour. At the end of February she sent a letter to Jack McClelland, jokingly suggesting that he market her forthcoming collection of essays, *Heart of a Stranger*, as a "great gift item" and sell it wrapped in tacky pink tissue paper and ribbon. Then she adds: "This village, you know, has numerous gift shops – perhaps I might start one myself, handling only two items ... this book plus THE DIVINERS. I would, of course, call the shop ... PORN 'N CORN" (quoted in King, 343). In the early stages, like Allie, Laurence seems to have been more surprised by the attack than hurt. Shortly after the controversy began, she wrote to David Watmough, "I'm not even wounded, although I was a bit shocked, at first" (*A Very Large Soul*, 202). But soon hurt and bewilderment set in. In March, Laurence told Gabrielle Roy, "I cannot help feeling hurt at having my work so vastly misunderstood" (*A Very Large Soul*, 175).[18] Three years after the controversy she was still feeling hurt, but was beginning to transform the pain into anger. In January 1979 she wrote a letter to Adele Wiseman in which, in an aside, a glimpse of her fury emerges: "(Incidentally, I think we should call

them something other than book 'banners' ... I like the word banners
in its other meaning too much to use it for those slobs!)" (quoted in
Lennox, 352). Nine days later, as a letter to Hugh MacLennan shows,
her anger seemed to be spurring her towards action: "Anyway, I have
found all these ignorant attacks very hurtful indeed, but feeling hurt
isn't going to achieve one damn thing. Now I am prepared to give
battle, in whatever way I can" (*A Very Large Soul*, 116–17).

One active response, which Laurence pursued and which she has
Allie follow, as a result of their respective controversies, is an investigation of the place of women with respect to the Church. Like
Laurence's other female heroines, Allie, even before being confronted
by the fundamentalists, is interested in feminism. In fact, as Laurence's notes indicate, this interest probably accounts for the epithet
"feminist" pejoratively hurled by the fundamentalists: "They disap-
prove of *Allie* for questioning M[ilton]'s view of the inferiority of
women. Women *should* be submissive and inferior. It *was* woman's
fault – *The Fall*" ("Draft Ms"). The anti-feminist criticism enhances,
rather than extinguishes, her interest in the subject: "Allie becomes
more + more involved in her own views of women and the Holy
Spirit Church. Male-oriented hymns." This interest further arouses
the ire of the fundamentalists, who "view as *blasphemy* her views on
the female principle in the Holy Spirit."

Allie's newfound interest in a feminist approach to religion no
doubt reflects Laurence's own questioning after her conflict with the
fundamentalists. King notes that "Margaret's religious sensibility
[was] reawakened following her brush with the fundamentalists"
(353), a sensibility that "included at its centre the notion of female
power" (354). In 1979 Laurence spoke at a United Church service in
Kingston in which she expressed her feelings on the subject: "After
centuries of thinking of God in strictly male, rather authoritarian
terms, it seems to me that there has to be some recognition of the
female principle in God ... I think many women nowadays, and
many men, feel the need to incorporate that sense of both the moth-
erhood and fatherhood in the Holy Spirit" (quoted in King, 354). In
August of that year Laurence wrote to William Ready asking him to
procure for her a Roman Catholic prayer book. In explaining her
request, she writes: "I find myself increasingly wondering why it is
that the various Protestant churches give so little recognition to the
female principle in life" (*A Very Large Soul*, 165). At the time Laurence
was probably gathering resource material for Dance Draft and
planned to turn her perusal of the prayer book into Allie's investigation of "male-oriented hymns."

Another incident occurred in that eventful year, 1979, that reinforced Laurence's thinking about the female principle in Christian faith and shaped her construction of Dance Draft. A controversy erupted in Toronto over the temporary installation at Bloor Street United Church of the sculpture *Crucified Woman* by Almuth Lutkenhaus. The sculpture shows a naked, slender female figure with arms outstretched, reminiscent of a crucified Christ. Laurence connected this work of art with the female principle in divinity, for, at the end of a lengthy section in her memoir on women's role in religion, she presents the sculpture as an example of the expression of "so many of us now, both inside the churches and outside, [who] feel that the recognition of the female principle in faith, in art, in all of life must come about much more fully than it has done" (*Dance on the Earth*, 15). Laurence goes on in the memoir to defend the sculpture against "fundamentalists [who] were outraged, and stormed around crying ... 'Heresy!' and so on" (16). Clearly this anti-feminist attack by fundamentalists on a "heretical" work of art hit close to home for Laurence: as King remarks, "Of course the disapproval heaped on Lutkenhaus reminded [Laurence] of her own difficulties with *The Diviners*" (446n). The Lutkenhaus censorship controversy also influenced her work on the design of Dance Draft. Her description of the sculpture – "'Crucified Woman' is almost dancing, on the earth, the life dance of pain and love" (*Dance on the Earth*, 17) – contains the title she was planning to use for her novel. She even received permission from the sculptor to use a photograph of *Crucified Woman* on the cover of the novel ("Third Ts"). Thus the Lutkenhaus affair both reflected her own trouble with fundamentalist censors and fuelled her desire to respond to them through the novel she was working on.

LITTLE LADY JESUS

Of course the novel was never completed, frustrating Laurence's attempts to convey her increasing concern with the female principle in Christian faith. She did, however, find other channels for this idea. She wrote at length on the subject in her memoir (which came to bear the title of the novel she abandoned). Another vehicle for these ideas was her children's book, *The Christmas Birthday Story*, published in 1980. The book retells the Nativity story in secular rather than religious terms, and injects a feminist perspective into the tale. Most striking are Mary and Joseph's feelings about the sex of their impending baby: "They didn't mind at all whether it turned out to be a boy or a girl. Either kind would be fine with them." As Laurence observes in her memoir, "Those few, and as it turned out, controversial sentences express much of my own life view and my faith, with its need to recognize both the female and male principles in the Holy Spirit" (221). Laurence was aware that by encoding the female principle within the retelling of the Bible story she was challenging the fundamentalists who had attacked her. In August 1980 she wrote to Jack McClelland: "The little book may be condemned by the same rednecks who condemned *The Diviners*, as blasphemous, because Mary and Joseph don't care whether their child turns out to be a girl or a boy" (quoted in King, 361).

That the children's book was a response to the *Diviners* censorship controversy is emphasized by the juxtaposition of Laurence's thoughts in a letter to her friend Budge Wilson. The letter, written two years after the controversy, begins, "I'm doing a lot of reading … a whole pile of fundamentalist literature (I use the word 'literature' very loosely here!) Golly! Some of the latter is so hate-filled it scares me" (*A Very Large Soul*, 212). Obviously, motivated by her conflict with would-be censors, Laurence was gathering information on the fundamentalists to mould into a written response. Indeed, her next thought in the letter refers to Dance Draft: "At last my mind seems to want to come to grips with a new novel in a practical way … I mean, I'm thinking story and people, not just vague areas. Pray for me and it." Her plea for Wilson's benedictions sounds a note of desperation, and, as we know, Laurence was struggling with the novel; perhaps she turned to the children's story as a substitute vehicle for her ideas on the female principle. In the letter to Wilson she quickly moves from the novel to her children's book: "I've realized that a lot of Christians will hate my re-telling of the Christmas story … Of course to the fundamentalists the story would be blasphemy, I daresay, in my re-telling, but then, if it is ever published, it sure ain't aimed at them!" (*A Very Large Soul*, 212–13). That Wainwright, the editor of the collection to which this letter belongs, saw fit to follow this comment with Wilson's own observations on the censorship controversy's negative impact on Laurence, strengthens, despite Laurence's own disavowal, the contention that *The Christmas Birthday Story* was a charged response to the fundamentalists who attacked *The Diviners*.

I have shown that Dance Draft and *The Christmas Birthday Story* were both sparked by the *Diviners* censorship controversy and were Laurence's means of responding to it. The novel was abandoned, however, and the children's story addressed only a limited area of her concern with the fundamentalists (namely, the female principle in religion). She had yet to respond fully, publicly, and in print to the controversy. At about the time she abandoned her work on Dance Draft, Laurence turned to non-fiction, a discourse in which she did not have to try to understand or sympathize with characters who represented her treacherous censoring adversaries, and was finally able to set out her extensive ideas on censorship. Most people know these ideas in the shape of her article "The Greater Evil," which appeared in the September 1984 issue of *Toronto Life* and was republished at the end of her memoir. Certainly this article is important, as Laurence's remarks in a draft of her memoir make clear: "I have written about this subject, after a great deal of thought and research and soul-searching, in an article which appeared in *Toronto Life* magazine, and which I append to this memoir. It expresses my very strongly held views and my deep beliefs in this whole area" ("First Ts"). But few people know that this article is an abridged version of an appreciably longer speech she gave before Ontario provincial judges and their wives on 2 June 1983 in Peterborough, Ontario. The issues she broaches in the article are explored more deeply in the speech, and her position emerges more clearly. I will be arguing that what the magazine article shows, and what the omitted sections of the speech emphasize, is that, despite her experience with the censors – in fact, I would argue, *because* of her experience with the censors – Laurence came to a position that, though not unequivocal, ultimately favoured some forms of censorship. This position is quite different from what one would expect, given the painful and angry response Laurence exhibited upon first being attacked.

Laurence begins her article by saying that her position on censorship is one of ambiguity: "I have a troubled feeling that I may be capable of doublethink, the ability to hold two opposing beliefs simultaneously. In the matter of censorship, doublethink seems, alas, appropriate" ("Greater Evil," 265). While she appears to be using the word "doublethink" in a common, general sense to communicate her mixed feelings,[19] we cannot help thinking of the novel that, more than almost any other work, has had an impact on twentieth-century thinking about censorship. In George Orwell's *Nineteen Eighty-four* doublethink means more than mere mixed feelings. As Philip Rahv explains, doublethink is a technique "which consists of the willingness to assert that black is white when the Party demands it, and even to believe that black is white, while at the same time knowing very well that nothing of the sort can be true" (182). "Freedom is Slavery" is Big Brother's most powerful doublethink motto in defending censorship. For Orwell doublethink is hypocrisy. When Laurence invokes the term, is she suggesting that there is an absolutist party line that she is being asked to toe? As her next words in the article suggest, the party to which she belonged, and from which she is, for this article, temporarily withdrawing, is the one consisting of writers: "As a writer, my response to censorship of any kind is that I am totally opposed to it. But when I consider some of the vile material that is being peddled freely, I want to see some kind of control. I don't think I am being hypocritical. I have a sense of honest bewilderment" (265). Laurence knew that some of the points she was about to make in favour of censorship would go against the "tribe" she was supposed to speak for.[20] By subtly linking the institution of creative writing with Orwell's authoritarian regime, she frees herself to depart from its absolutist stance against censorship. In doing so, however, like the doublethinking citizens of Oceania, she opens herself to the charge of hypocrisy. But her modest denial of this charge pre-empts and forestalls it. Rhetorically she has cleared the ground to argue for "some kind of control."

CENSORSHIP: AN "EVIL"

First, however, Laurence outlines her reasons for being against censorship on principle, reasons that have emotional validity but little rational force. The first is personal. "I have good reason to mistrust and fear censorship," she writes. "I have been burned by the would-be book censors" ("Greater Evil," 265). It is usually books that are burned by censors, but Laurence conveys the feeling that she herself was consumed by the flames. What sets Laurence apart from other Canadian authors like Atwood and Findley with respect to censorship is that the attacks on Laurence were much more immediate (coming from her adopted home town), more wide-ranging (garnering national media attention), and much more personal. As Laurence notes, "Some awful things were said about the book and about me personally, mostly by people who had not read the book or met me … One person confidently stated that 'Margaret Laurence's aim in life is to destroy the home and the family'" (265–6).

While Laurence admits in this part of the article that the controversy over *The Diviners* left her "scorched mentally and emotionally" (a phrase that picks up the burning motif), the bulk of her portrayal focuses on the humorous aspects of the altercation. She recalls the fundamentalist minister who complained to a reporter of an obscene passage in the novel: "The reporter asked if the fundamentalist minister himself had found the scene sexually stimulating. 'Oh no,' was the reply. 'I'm a happily married man.'" Another detractor of the novel rose at a public meeting to announce "that he spoke for a

delegation of seven: himself, his wife, their children – and God."
Finally, she tells of the bachelor pharmacist who "claimed that young
people should not be given any information about sex until they are
physically mature – 'at about the age of 21.' I hope [Laurence adds]
his knowledge of pharmacy was greater than his knowledge of biol-
ogy" (266). It appears that, by 1984, Laurence had distanced herself
sufficiently from the censorship attack that she could regain a more
objective perspective on it, sometimes even perceiving its humour.
Perhaps this is what allowed her finally to write about it directly in
this article. In any case, rhetorically, Laurence's choice to play up the
emotional hyperbole and comical nature of the attack may be an
effective way of putting her opponents – the "self-appointed groups
of vigilantes" – in their place, but it is not a particularly strong argument against censorship. It appeals more to the readers' sympathy
for Laurence's painful encounter with the fundamentalists than to
their logical considerations of any flaws in censorship itself.

Laurence quickly moves away from her personal interest in censorship to the main purpose of the article, a philosophical working
through of the issue. Initially she adopts an anti-censorship position,
quickly piling up five arguments in a kind of rhetorical barrage that
neither flows logically nor is supported by evidence. First she attacks
the claim, made by some advocates of censorship, that certain representations (like pornography), being apolitical, can be censored without threatening social democracy. Artists are political, Laurence
argues, merely by "portraying life as they honestly [see] it." She
continues: "Artistic suppression and political suppression go hand in
hand, and always have. I would not advocate the banning of even
such an evil and obscene book as Hitler's *Mein Kampf*. I think we
must learn to recognize our enemies, to counter inhuman ranting
with human and humane beliefs and practices. With censorship, the
really bad stuff would tend to go underground and flourish covertly
… I worry that censorship of any kind might lead to the suppression
of anyone who speaks out against anything in our society" (266–7).
There is a break in the logical sequence of ideas between the first and
second sentences of this passage: what Laurence's tolerance for Hitler's doctrinal tract has to do with her view of art as inherently
political is not clear in the article.[21] To a degree it relates to her next
and second point in the passage, which is the argument that offensive
speech should be challenged, not buried, but she leaves herself little
space to develop this idea. In quick succession she voices a third
standard critique of censorship, namely that outlawed discourse will
go underground (this is the "compression-explosion" argument that
I traced in Atwood's *The Handmaid's Tale*). Then comes her fourth

point, the "slippery-slope" argument, in which it is presumed that a little censorship will result in the censorship of all. Finally, to the string of propositions in the above passage Laurence adds a fifth and last rhetorical thrust, an appeal to the authority of F.R. Scott, who quotes John Stuart Mill: "The time, it is to be hoped, has gone by ... when any defence would be necessary of the principle of freedom of speech" (267).

At this stage in the article Laurence's reasoning against censorship is unconvincing. Despite her earlier distancing from the institutionalized stance of the writer, her arguments consist of platitudes that could be any writers' union manifesto. Her manner of listing these platitudes, their seemingly arbitrary juxtaposition, which results in at least one non sequitur (namely, the logical lacuna between the first two sentences of the passage above), and their presentation without supporting evidence weakens her discussion. She turns to Scott and Mill at the end, not to invoke any of their theoretical arguments but merely to cite them as important thinkers against censorship. This appeal to authority is a common logical fallacy. Furthermore, examination of the longer speech that Laurence wrote prior to the article shows that the author had little more to say there by way of arguing against censorship: the one-paragraph argument is as schematic in the speech as it is in the article. In both Laurence's conviction on this side of the argument seems strangely hollow.

PORNOGRAPHY: "THE GREATER EVIL"

Precisely because her arguments seem inadequate, perhaps, Laurence turns quickly in the article to the other side of the censorship debate, offering a charged and compelling opposition to pornography – "The Greater Evil." To make it clear that the constraint of discourse she will be sanctioning is limited, she begins by outlining what she would not censor: "I do not object to books or films or anything else that deals with sex, if those scenes are between two adults who are entering into this relationship of their own free will" (267). Sensitive to the danger of making generalizations, she challenges her own categorization of acceptable discourse by citing Vladimir Nabokov's *Lolita*, which portrays a sexual relationship involving a minor, as a book she would *not* ban. Her explanation? "Ambiguity" (267). Despite this proffered explanation, I am certain that, if we were able to question Laurence on this exception, she would argue, and be able to present evidence to the effect, that *Lolita* is, as Donald Morton puts it, "more than either a case study of sexual perversion or pornographic titillation," that "Lolita fulfills the highest standards of artistic perfection in the organic fusion of its fable and its form" (66).[22] In other words, what Laurence gives as a troubling exception to her "rule" is actually an example of the precision-enhancing process (promoted in this study) that comes from being sensitive to the context of the work in question. Rather than making her position more ambiguous, this sensitivity makes her position more flexible and, therefore, ultimately more reasonable. The comment on Nabokov is an example of the way Laurence's experience with censorship caused her to get past the posturing of blanket anti-censorship arguments to grapple with the more difficult but more rewarding politics of censorial context.

Another exception to her principle that acceptable discourse on sex must depict consenting adults is "the portrayal of social injustice, of terrible things done to one human by another or by governments or groups of whatever kind, as long as it is shown for what it is" (267). Whereas the Nabokov exception relied on artistic merit, the exception here, which would apply to films such as *Not a Love Story* (to which Laurence refers in the speech), rests on Laurence's belief in the audience's ability to derive intent from a representation. "As long as it is shown for what it is" implies a real difference between two films, say *Deep Throat* and *Not a Love Story*, both of which contain scenes of the violent sexual degradation of women: the intent behind the former is to glorify this kind of behaviour, while the intent behind the latter is to show it as unacceptable. Later in the article, in discussing obscenity laws, Laurence questions the ability to distinguish this intent: "how are we to enshrine in our laws the idea that the degradation and coercion of women and children, of anyone, is dreadful, without putting into jeopardy the portrayal of social injustice seen as injustice?" (270–1). Her distrust of the law's ability to make this distinction is justified, but it does not cause her to take a stand against all censorship. Rather, Laurence feels courts and judges are the proper arbitrators for determining which works would propagate and which would curb social injustice. Laurence's intuition is correct. In many areas of jurisprudence, from libel law to murder, the intent of a perpetrator must be interpreted by judge or jury. If we trust a person's *life* to this interpretive ability, surely we should have few qualms about trusting *representations* to the same faculty.

Once she has qualified her stand in favour of the censorship of pornography, Laurence turns to the kind of representations to which she does object: "films and photographs, *making use of real live women and children*, that portray horrifying violence, whether associated with sex or simply violence on its own, as being acceptable, onturning, a thrill a minute" (267–8). This is the kind of material Laurence defines as pornography, and part of her opposition to it, as indicated by her use of italics, is that "these films and photographs make use of living women and children ... [which is] a degradation of them" (268). The first kind of harm Laurence identifies in pornography is the harm done to the women and children who are involved in the making of it. While this claim appears to be unexplained and unsupported in the article, this is not the case in the speech. There she explains that the degradation of the women involved in pornography lies in their coercion: "It is always said, of course, that in films and photographs using adult women (and 'using' is an apt word), the women themselves make this decision. I wonder how 'free' that decision frequently is, how much pressure and intimidation and threat and sheer monetary need are operative here" ("On Censorship," 9). To support her allegation she cites Michelle Landsberg, who writes, in her book *Women and Children First*, "It is useless for porn users to protest, as they always do, that 'it's only fantasy.' Real fantasy exists in the mind. Modern pornography uses and abuses millions of very real women and children ... The horror is that you can't make kiddie porn without real live kiddies. For them, it is not a harmless daydream" (Landsberg, 85). As further evidence Laurence refers to the anti-pornography film *Not a Love Story*, which, through interviews with actors who appear in pornography, conveys "the true extent of coercion, bondage and violence ... [and] the extent of the use and abuse of women in this lucrative business" ("On Censorship," 12).

The use of real women and children in pornographic photos and films is objectionable to Laurence not just because of the coercion of those participants but because of the message it conveys to viewers: "That violence against women and children, real persons, is acceptable" ("Greater Evil," 268). I discuss below Laurence's formulation of the classic anti-pornography argument that pornography has harmful effects on its consumers, but here Laurence is making the subtle point that pornographic photos and films do not *represent* violent sex (in that they stand for or symbolize the action) but that they *re-present* it (that is, viewers see real violent sex happening to real women and children). This point, taken together with the fact of the coercion of the subjects of pornographic photos and films, for Laurence marks a distinction between print and visual pornography: "I have to say," she writes, "that I consider visual material to be more dangerous than any printed verbal material" (268). This is an important distinction because it reminds us that pornography has changed. When pornography mainly consisted of writing or drawings, no real women were harmed in its making, and the portrayal of real women was always mediated through abstracting print. Free-speech laws formulated at this time did not have to worry about the vitiating effects of visual pornography (for amplification of this idea, see MacKinnon, 8–9). Laurence recognizes that pornography has evolved while free-speech advocacy has remained largely static when she turns from her criticism of pornography to what at first appears to be an argument against censorship: "But is censorship, in any of the media involved, the answer? I think of John Milton's *Areopagitica*." She goes on to quote Milton's famous line about the importance of being able to consider vice with all her baits and pleasures, but then adds, "Obviously, Milton was not thinking of the sort of video films that anyone can now show at home, where any passing boy child can perhaps get the message that cruelty is OK and fun, and any passing girl child may wonder if that is what will be expected of her, to be a victim." She demurs at the end, "All the same, we forget Milton's words at our peril" (269), but the warning does not address Milton's anachronicity and sounds like a half-hearted sop to free-speech advocates.

In the speech, though not in the article, Laurence presents another difference between written and visual pornography, one that relates to the harm the latter may effect in society through its viewers: "unlike written material, a film or photograph need only be looked at, and its image imprinted on the mind and emotions. No effort is required, merely a passive taking in of images that are far from passive ... an incitement to violence, in fact" ("On Censorship," 11). While her distinction between print and visual media may stem more from her bias as a writer than from actual evidence, the comment nevertheless shows that Laurence held the view that pornography is an incitement for men, in real life, to carry out violence against women, a prime argument of anti-pornography feminists. In the article Laurence finds in violent pornography "a strong suggestion to the viewer that violence against women ... is acceptable," and that pornography teaches that "women actually enjoy being the subject of insanely brutal treatment, actually enjoy being chained, beaten, mutilated and even killed" ("Greater Evil," 268). Despite these observations, in the article her opinion on the link between pornography and violence is ambiguous: "The effect of this material is a matter of some dispute, and nothing can be proved either way," but, she adds, "many people believe that such scenes have been frighteningly re-enacted in real life in one way or another" (268–9).

In the speech, however, Laurence's conviction that there is a direct causal relationship between pornography and harm is much stronger. In fairness to detractors of this argument she cites Jill Abson, who summarizes several studies that "apparently [Laurence's qualifier] found that 'the only action directly tied to erotica is not sexual coercion or violence, but masturbation'" ("On Censorship," 11). But Laurence immediately undercuts Abson when she adds: "[Abson] believes that no real difference can be made between the erotic and the pornographic." For Laurence is clear, in defining her terms in both the article and the speech, that "the distinction must be made between erotic and pornographic" ("Greater Evil," 268). Moreover, she explicitly undermines Abson's reliance on research that found pornography to be harmless by quoting Lynn McDonald, who discounts the studies as being years out of date. The mostly Scandinavian research, McDonald writes, "that showed a decline in sex offenses after the liberation of pornography laws has now been thoroughly discredited'" (quoted in "On Censorship," 11). The evidence Laurence cites that pornography does cause harm is much more extensive in the speech. She refers to a study by historian Barbara Roberts suggesting that rapists and wife-beaters are habitual consumers of pornography (11). Furthermore, she writes that Michelle Landsberg – in giving the example of Clifford Olson and citing a study that found that after watching pornography, men felt rape was more acceptable – shows that "porn has a real and proven connection with incest, rape and violence" (11).

What should be emerging from my discussion so far is a picture of Laurence's position on pornography that shows her to have been, with good reason, much more concerned with the troubling aspects of pornography than with the dangers of censoring it. Examination of the speech, in contrast to the more ambivalent article, shows that Laurence's arguments against pornography are more logical and thorough than those against censorship. Even the space she gives to each side of the debate is telling. Her warnings against censorship in the first half of the article (before she turns to Canadian law) are nearly the same in both the article and the speech, consisting of one paragraph. She gives two paragraphs to her arguments in favour of regulating pornography in the article ("Greater Evil," 268–9), but these are drawn from a critique of pornography of over five pages (seven paragraphs) in the speech ("On Censorship," 7–12). Evidently she feels more distraught about pornography than about censorship. In fact, the emotional dimension of this debate, for Laurence, clearly plays a more central role when she is criticizing pornography, for it is then that Laurence becomes impassioned. She speaks of her "feelings of fear, anger and outrage at this material" and says she could "weep in grief and rage" when she thinks of the attitudes it promotes ("Greater Evil," 268). In the speech she reports her reaction upon seeing clips from pornographic films and photos from magazines in

Not a Love Story: "I felt, as I imagine many women must have felt when viewing this film, at times that I was literally choking, being choked, held powerless, violated. I felt an overwhelming sense of outrage" ("On Censorship," 12). Although Laurence's use of the fire metaphor to describe her personal "trial by fire" at the hand of the censors is a strong reaction, it pales beside her emotional, even physical reaction to violent pornography.

THE SOLUTION: CENSOR WITH CARE

According to Laurence, then, in concrete terms, what is to be done about this pornography? In the second half of her article she turns to contemporary Canadian law and argues, essentially, that legislation designed to censor obscenity, including violent pornography, while difficult to formulate, is necessary for a just society. She argues against censorship boards, seeing their mandate as vague, their accountability insufficient, but she still feels the courts have a central role to play in regulating pornography. In addressing specific obscenity provisions contained in Section 159 of the Criminal Code, she writes, "My impression of federal law in this area is that its intentions are certainly right, its aims are toward justice, and it is indeed in some ways woefully outdated and in need of clarification" ("Greater Evil," 270). One area in which she feels the law needs to be improved is in dealing with violence: "I think that violence itself, shown as desirable, must be dealt with in some way in this law" (271).[23] In a related concern, Laurence suggests (in her speech) that discourse communicated through new visual technologies, characterized frequently by violent content, also needs to be controlled: "in our age of sophisticated technology, with video films, video games and much more, it does seem to me that the New Brutality, as it is sometimes called, should be dealt with in law more specifically" ("On Censorship," 18). Although she sees problems with current legislation aimed at controlling pornography – it strikes her as archaic, with too much concern for depictions of sex and not enough for depictions of violence – Laurence ultimately argues that "in cases of obscenity, test cases have to be brought before the courts and tried openly in accordance with our federal laws" ("Greater Evil," 270).

In addition to the general philosophical reasons outlined above, Laurence draws on a couple of sophisticated theoretical justifications in favour of state regulation of pornography. One such justification is the argument that pornography should be seen as an action, as opposed to the pure expression of ideas, and therefore be ineligible for absolute protection by free-speech legislation. This argument is invoked by pro-censorship feminists such as Catharine MacKinnon: it is one of the main thrusts of MacKinnon's book *Only Words* (and is alluded to by the ironic title), in which she argues: "Speech acts ... In the context of social inequality, so-called speech can be an exercise of power which constructs the social reality in which people live, from objectification to genocide" (30–1).[24] In her speech Laurence again cites Michelle Landsberg, who compares pornography and murder by way of defending legal regulation of the former: "All law is an attempt to enforce morality. Murder has always been with us, and law won't eradicate it. But laws there must be, as an expression of society's definition of what is human and right" (quoted in "On Censorship," 14). Laurence echoes Landsberg's sentiments in her article, where she sees pornography as a means of damaging people:

> We must, however, have some societal agreement as to what is acceptable in the widest frame of reference possible, but still within the basic concept that *damaging people is wrong*. Murder is not acceptable, and neither is the abasement, demeanment and exploitation of human persons, whatever their race, religion, age or gender. Not all of this can be enshrined in law ... What the law *can* do is attempt to curb, by open process in public courts, the worst excesses of humankind's always-in-some-way-present inhumanity to humankind.   ("Greater Evil," 273)

Here Laurence challenges the notion that pornography is the expression of ideas and therefore eligible for special protection. Rather, her characterization of pornography as abasement, demeanment, and exploitation suggests that pornography is an action and, as such, is subject to judgment of its moral content in the same way that other actions, like murder, are. Notice that Laurence qualifies her argument by maintaining that "the widest frame of reference possible" should be used in judging pornography[25] and that laws will never be able fully to protect members of society. While remaining sensitive to the dangers of state censorship, she nevertheless argues for its necessity.

The other powerful argument in favour of limited censorship on which Laurence draws consists in interpreting freedom positively as well as negatively. This dual conception of freedom distinguishes between "freedom as ability and freedom as immunity ... 'freedom to *do* what?' and 'freedom *from* what?'" (Schauer, 114). A strictly negative conception of freedom (common among some liberals), which prohibits state interference in the lives of its citizens, tends to favour an absolutist pro-free-speech position because it does not acknowledge that the overall freedom of those citizens can be enhanced by the positive intervention of the state in other areas, such as ensuring the equality of all citizens. When the dissemination of one idea interferes with the speech rights of others, as Fiss writes, "the state ban on [that] speech does not restrict or impoverish public debate, but paradoxically enough, broadens it, for it allows all voices to be heard" (84).

Laurence recognizes that in the argument over censoring pornography, a more comprehensive definition of freedom must be used: "I think again of F.R. Scott's words ... 'Freedom is a habit that must be kept alive by use.' Freedom, however, means responsibility, and concern toward others. It does not mean that some few unscrupulous and inhumane persons are permitted to exploit, demean and coerce others, and instead of being brought to justice, are permitted to make huge and to my mind immoral financial profits, while the poor, the underprivileged, the disabled, the minorities, and women and children, continue to suffer and pay the price" ("On Censorship," 19–20). Ironically, Laurence uses the words of F.R. Scott, the liberal authority she invoked earlier in her half-hearted attack on censorship, to show that the pornography debate is not just about whether pornographers have the right to protection of their work as speech; it is also about whether that right should displace the right of less powerful members of society to equality. In this debate she sides with the woman lawyer (whom she does not name) who argues that "there's no doubt – the real obscenity things should be prosecuted. The long-term way will be to equalize the position of women" (16). Laurence rejects the neutralist liberal approach to free speech, which relies solely on the negative conception of liberty. Rather, she sees censorship of pornography as leading to *more* freedom, in the sense of greater equality for society, especially for women.

Given that, in her writing, Laurence supports the ideological thrust of the obscenity provisions of the Criminal Code and frames the pornography debate with a more sophisticated definition of freedom than those who favour an absolute anti-censorship position, had she lived longer to see the significant role the Charter of Rights and Freedoms would come to play in Canadian law, she probably would have supported the 1992 Supreme Court decision in the Butler case. In this landmark case against a distributor of hard-core pornography, the court ruled that, although the distributor's Charter rights of free speech were violated, this violation was justified. The court gave a number of reasons for this justification, including the argument for the harmfulness of pornography, but it also argued: "If true equality between male and female persons is to be achieved, we cannot ignore the threat to equality resulting from exposing audiences to certain types of violent and degrading material" (Robertson, 7). In her

speech Laurence even goes so far as to acknowledge that she would
be willing to have her own work submitted to the kinds of tests that
were later administered in the Butler case: "I would be prepared, if
need be, to defend my work as being as true as I can make it, to
human life with its complexity, its suffering, its injustice, its joys"
("On Censorship," 20). Thus Laurence demonstrates that she is open
to the application of a well-thought-out and carefully worded criminal censorship statute in a court that is sensitive to the intent, context, and effect of the material that comes before it.

Thankfully Laurence never had to undertake the defence of her work
in the kind of legal procedure she advocates – given the obvious
artistic merit of her work, such a process would have been a farce –
but she did have to experience one more serious censorship controversy. In 1985 Robert Buchanan was again attacked for teaching *The
Diviners* to his senior high school students in Lakefield. This time the
attack was led by Helen Trotter, a municipal councillor from nearby
Burleigh-Anstruther, and her husband, who called the book "disgusting" and "morally degrading" (quoted in Contenta, A1). The Trotters
were supported by the Concerned Citizens for Bible-Centred Religious Education for Our Schools. Like Reverend Buick and company
in 1976, those attacking *The Diviners* in 1985 based their opposition
on the profanities and sex in the novel. Robert Buchanan threatened
to resign as head of Lakefield's English department if the fundamentalists had their way, and vowed to keep teaching the book. He was
backed by several members of the community – one of whom circu-
lated a petition opposing the proposal to ban the book – and students
at the Lakefield high school. National media once again got hold of
the story and defended Laurence's writing. At a meeting in January
1985 the school board decided to reject Trotter's request for a special
committee to review the book and reaffirmed the review process that
had been in place since 1976. The board decided it would send Mrs
Trotter a form on which she could register her complaints and try to
work out a specific agreement for her children (Susan Scott, 23). The
board then considered the matter closed.

By 1985 Laurence had learned that more could be gained by engaging her opponents over the issue of censorship than by remaining
quiet, so in this round she came out swinging. Her principal thrust
was not that she was against censorship but that she was against the
censorship of the kind of book she and other serious writers produced, which had been condemned as pornography: "People who
want to condemn my books show remarkably little concern for other
social issues, for the suffering, for the poor and oppressed and for

the enormous violence in our media. My books are highly moral books which show a concern for the individual" (quoted in "Angry Author," A3). In this comment Laurence hints that she views the attacks on her work as diverting attention away from *real* pornography, which she sees as the proper target of censors. "I am very much against pornography," she says. "I think this attack is ridiculous because we're not writing pornography at all … In the books of serious Canadian writers, you don't find that at all" (A3). Laurence's concern is spelled out in a letter of support she received and kept in her private papers, a letter written by Lynn McDonald (whom she quoted in her speech to judges) to the chairman of the Peterborough Board of Education during this latest *Diviners* controversy: "The pornography charge is pernicious as well for the damage it does to the anti-pornography movement. There is a serious and growing problem of violent pornography in Canada with women and children the prime victims. The credibility of all of us who are working for stronger controls on this genuine threat is impugned with these preposterous charges against Margaret Laurence." Despite this latest ordeal Laurence still felt, like McDonald, that there was a place for the censorship of socially repugnant material. In an interview with Peter Gzowski on CBC radio during the 1985 *Diviners* controversy Laurence reiterated her call for the trial of pornography in "open court."[26]

The evolution of Laurence's thinking, then, regarding censorship is very different from Margaret Atwood's, another feminist Canadian writer concerned with pornography, who moved from a position of anti-pornography in *Bodily Harm* to one of anti-censorship at the time of her writing *The Handmaid's Tale*. Laurence's experience originates in a very personal episode, the 1976 controversy, which would shape her writing until her death just over ten years later. Her immediate response to the controversy was to try to write a novel in which the events that engulfed her were recast as fiction. Unable genuinely to understand the thinking of her antagonists, a prerequisite for Laurence to creating convincing characters, she abandoned the project after years of struggle with it, leaving material in draft form that shows she had meant to model the plot on the *Diviners* controversy and the protagonist on herself.[27] After abandoning this project, Laurence turned to other forms of writing to work through many of the issues the controversy had raised. In her children's story, *The Christmas Birthday Story*, she was able to express her increasingly strong belief in the female principle in Christianity, an idea she had found her fundamentalist opponents strongly resisted.

However, it was finally in her non-fiction article "The Greater Evil" that Laurence was able to convey her thoughts on censorship in a methodical and thorough way. When we examine that article closely and compare it to its original version as a speech Laurence delivered to judges in Ontario, we find that her urge to ban violent pornography is considerably stronger than her fear of the evils of censorship. For Laurence, pornography is "the greater evil." Her arguments in support of this position are subtle but compelling, and draw largely on the store of feminist reasoning (formulated by writers such as Catharine MacKinnon) of the early 1980s. She points out differences between the print and visual media and argues that pornography conveyed in the latter format does damage not only to those who participate in its making but also to women who are subjected to the degrading attitudes absorbed by men who watch it. While she expresses some misgivings about how to control pornography without jeopardizing discourse that is not harmful, she maintains the importance of obscenity laws aimed at regulating the most repugnant pornographic representations. To support this opinion she suggests we view these representations less as speech and more as actions whose moral content is open to judgment and control through legislation. She also argues that free speech cannot be the *sine qua non* of liberty in our society as long as it allows pornography, which erodes the equality of many citizens, therefore limiting *their* liberty. The important message here is that censorship is not to be dismissed as an absolute evil. Rather representations that pose the potential to do harm in society should be examined in a court that considers their context and their effect, and ultimately judges whether that potential is sufficiently threatening to curb the very important rights each citizen has to freedom of speech.

5 The Inevitability of Censorship: Beatrice Culleton and Marlene Nourbese Philip

As I have argued in the introduction to this book, censorship is not only the heavy-handed, often legally sanctioned, direct suppression of discourse by an authorized agent. In this chapter I discuss "socio-cultural censorship," which is the exclusion of some discourse as a result of the competition of social groups in the cultural marketplace. I present examples of this type of exclusion of and in Canadian literature, and point to discussions of this literature by critics and the writers themselves to show that it makes sense to see this exclusionary practice *as* censorship.[1] This being the case, the debate over whether or not censorship is *acceptable* in democratic, capitalist societies is a red herring. It is *inevitable*. The competitive cultural marketplace is woven into the very fabric of these societies; censorship is a practice that occurs in many sectors, at many levels of society on a continual basis. Therefore, rather than debating whether or not we should strive to eliminate censorship, which is as impossible as eliminating competition among social groups, we should accept the inevitability of censorship's presence and strive to make it as just, reasonable, and beneficial to members of our society as we can (I will present some suggestions in the Conclusion of this study for making our censoring practices more constructive).

The most striking examples of socio-cultural censorship of and in Canadian literature occur at sites where members of Canada's marginalized – that is, disadvantaged economically, politically, etc. – groups have been prevented from making their voices heard. In an article in which he decries the idealization of free speech at the cost of cultural pluralism in Canada, John Marriott asks: "can we speak of free speech and censorship without addressing the contextual, political issues of class, gender, race, sexual orientation, faith, etc.? ... After all, art, culture, and censorship are words for the same impulse, aren't they?" (164). Marriott's two questions are integrally related: in the second he implies that our society's practice of granting something the status of art or culture is a practice of censorship in which something else is denied that status; as his first question points out, it is the disadvantaged (by class, gender, race, etc.) segments of society that usually experience this censorship. Marriott argues that this censorship occurs "when the representations of one culture are imposed on other cultures ... These struggles for and against social visibility amount to culture as a censorship shell-game" (167). As Marriott points out, it is possible to investigate this kind of censorship from the point of view of any disadvantaged group. I choose to focus on race[2] as a site of marginalization that, coinciding with the ascendancy of Canadian literature beginning in the 1960s, has emerged as one of the most blatant areas of socio-cultural censorship in our society. There are many races that could be discussed here, but I will focus on literature by Native and Black writers since members of both groups are particularly concerned with the silencing of their voices in Canada and because they admirably illustrate the different forms of socio-cultural censorship I wish to examine.[3]

THE FACES OF SOCIO-CULTURAL CENSORSHIP

There are four main ways in which these marginalized writers have been subjected to socio-cultural censorship in Canada.[4] One way is through educational policies. Mariott makes the case that censorship results from government underfunding of higher education: "There is nothing free about speech in Canada when the most insidious and ruthless form of censorship is being systematically implemented along class lines, by eroding and restricting education and the emancipation that is made possible through it" (167). It is true that visible minorities, who have traditionally constituted a disproportionately large segment of the lower class, will have less opportunity for post-secondary education as tuition fees skyrocket.[5] Probably fewer Native and Black poets, playwrights, and novelists will emerge as a result. Still, reduced access to higher education has not been a key aspect of socio-cultural censorship decried by marginalized writers in their fiction or non-fiction writing. Instead, these authors, especially from the Native and Black communities, have complained of the censorship imposed through educational policies in public schools regarding the teaching of language and history. They argue that, by imposing Standard English and colonial versions of history on their students, Canadian educators are in effect censoring their marginalized students, their values and perspectives. In so far as these students may become writers, they are censoring marginalized writers as well.

A second way in which marginalized writers are censored is through what I want to call cultural gatekeepers,[6] agents who mediate between writers and readers and who, to a degree, decide what texts achieve currency in the culture. These agents include publishers, critics, anthologists, award-granting bodies, and, in as much as they determine which writing is acceptable or desirable, readers themselves. In his article "Uncompromising Positions: Anti-censorship, Anti-racism, and the Visual Arts" Richard Fung gives some examples of how cultural gatekeepers act as censors:

While this article focuses on the campaigns advocating or opposing state censorship, the circulation of ideas and images in countries such as Canada and the United States is far more dependent on less obvious systemic factors, such as (the often narrow, often Eurocentric) notions of "innovation" or "excellence" when it comes to arts funding and curating, or marketability and audience in mass culture venues. So while it is rare for a piece of art to be banned by the government, it is normal that a film or video be refused distribution or airing because its audience is too "specific," it is not "objective," or it is in poor taste.   (138)

While Fung discusses mainly the visual arts, his argument holds true for literature as well. For Native and Black writers in particular, cultural gatekeepers have been very real sources of censorship in Canada.

Marginalized writers identify a third form of censorship in what is commonly referred to as cultural appropriation. This is a practice in which White[7] authors write in the voice or from the perspective of non-White characters. Many Native and Black writers claim that cultural appropriation in effect censors their own voices and demand that White writers refrain from writing in this manner. In response to these demands some White writers claim in turn that they are being censored by those who would limit their artistic purview. The issue is complex: there are various positions within both the dominant and minority cultures on the aptness of seeing cultural appropriation as a censorship issue and on whether or not it is acceptable.

The fourth and perhaps most complex form of socio-cultural censorship is that practised by the marginalized writers themselves. Self-censorship occurs when members of a minority culture have internalized the values of the dominant culture to such a degree that they suppress, either consciously or not, the discourse they would naturally express in favour of a discourse that is acceptable in the society. As Fung writes, "The regulation of expression is accomplished by the everyday practices of thousands of decision-makers, from petty to powerful, simply doing their jobs. This includes the self-censorship of cultural producers themselves. It is ironic, therefore, that the relatively few incidences of state intervention in the capitalist liberal democracies are used to convey an image of a 'free' world" (138). Fung's comment places self-censorship in context by depicting it as one cog in the machinery of socio-cultural censorship. It also reminds us of the central point of this study, that the absence of censorship in a society in which groups compete (that is, in capitalist societies) is impossible. To accumulate evidence of the systemic nature of this socio-cultural censorship I now turn to a more detailed examination of the four kinds of censorship I have identified above, in relation to the work of Native and Black writers in Canada. I will use this evidence to argue that censorship is unavoidable in our society and that, rather than arguing over its merits as a practice, we should be scrutinizing the way in which it is carried out.

The official, state-sponsored censorship of Native culture in Canada has been well documented. As John Marriott explains, "past Canadian law is patterned with formative statutes drafted and enforced so as to silence and eliminate the expression and survival of native cultures. From the assimilationist Indian Act of 1874, which banned celebration of the potlatch, to statutes of Canada in 1926–1927, which outlawed the sundance, native speech and identity have been defined as criminal" (164–5). He goes on to show, however, that the more insidious silencing of Native voices has been the less direct though no less ubiquitous forms of socio-cultural censorship. As Native writers have emerged in recent years, their primary message has been that they have been voiceless previously not because they haven't wanted to write or been capable of writing; as Emma LaRocque argues, "it cannot be said that we have been wordless from lack of skill or effort. Yet, we have been silenced in numerous and ingenious ways. In effect, we have been censored" (xxii). LaRocque is talking about censorship through educational policy, by cultural gatekeepers, by other writers appropriating Native culture, and the self-censorship of Natives themselves. All four of these forms of socio-cultural censorship are reflected in Beatrice Culleton's *In Search of April Raintree*,[8] either in the experiences of the main characters or in the writing of the autobiographical novel itself,[9] and hence I choose it for detailed examination here.

CENSORING NATIVE LANGUAGE AND HISTORY

Socio-cultural censorship of Native Canadians has occurred through education when Native children, attending Canadian schools, have been forced to give up their own languages and distinct histories. Greg Young-Ing reports on the "devastating impact the Canadian residential school system has had and continues to have on First Nations and Aboriginal people" who were "punished for speaking their language" (180). Basil Johnston, documenting the actual violence used to prevent Native children from communicating in their mother tongue, records that "if a boot or a fist were not administered, then a lash or a yardstick was plied until the 'Indian' language was beaten out" (15). The principal character of Maria Campbell's novel *Halfbreed* was still experiencing this linguistic suppression when she went to school in the late 1940s: "We weren't allowed to speak Cree, only French and English, and for disobeying this, I was pushed into a small closet with no windows or light and locked in for what seemed like hours" (47). By the time April Raintree, the narrator of Culleton's novel, and her sister Cheryl grow up in the 1960s, any Native language has already been eliminated in their family. When the children are taken from their parents and placed in foster homes, their chances of learning a Native tongue from other members of the Native community are much reduced, so the schools they attend have little resistance, in the form of a Native mother tongue, to suppress, and English easily becomes the language that censors their ability to express their ancestral culture.

The kind of educational censorship that does become a site of struggle in Culleton's novel is the censorship of Native history. Coomi Vevaina finds that, in fiction by Campbell, Culleton, and Jeannette Armstrong, "structural or institutionalized racism [that] is backed up by the entire social system" manifests itself in the suppression of Native history in school (62). In Armstrong's novel *Slash* the Native narrator thinks about "all the history books and stuff at school and in movies. How it was all like that, a fake, while really the white people wished we would all either be just like them or stay out of sight" (36). In *In Search of April Raintree* Cheryl is the character who resists the Eurocentric view of the past that the dominant culture attempts to foist on its history students. During a lesson on early relations between Native people and colonial powers in which the former are depicted as bloodthirsty savages, Cheryl objects: "This is all a bunch of lies!" (57). The teacher, in a manner symbolic of the mainstream culture's attitude towards Native voices, responds, "I'm going to pretend I didn't hear that." After Cheryl protests again, the teacher appeals to the "objective" nature of history: "They're not lies; this is history. These things happened whether you like it or not" (57). Cheryl rejects this argument, citing evidence of Native historical experience that would contradict the teacher's version. She refuses to back down even when confronted by the principal of the school, who demands she apologize to the teacher and the class. Despite the principal's corporal punishment, Cheryl refuses, but finally gives in when her foster mother threatens to cut her off forever from her sister. Forced to choose between the truth and maintaining her only tie with her Métis culture, she chooses the latter (58).

Cheryl's capitulation in the altercation with her history teacher underscores the fact that the presentation of the dominant culture's historical "truths" ultimately tends to erase those of the marginalized culture. As Dawn Thompson writes of this episode, Cheryl "demonstrates that written memory does in fact 'forget' facts that are not useful to those writing the history books; forgetting is actually a common practice of colonizers" (99). This "forgetting" is a form of censorship. Cheryl too, of course, is censored in this scene, by those who have power over her. Though she bows to the pressure of the authorities in school, however, Cheryl later tells April in a letter of her plans to counter this repression: "history should be an unbiased representation of the facts. And if they show one side, they ought to show the other side equally. Anyways, that's why I'm writing the Métis side of things. I don't know what I'm going to do with it but it makes me feel good" (84–5). Here she asserts a theory of history that counters her teacher's univocal approach to the subject (which the teacher attempts to disguise as unbiased), and offers hope that both her voice and the voices of Native historical truth may eventually overcome the restrictions imposed by socio-cultural censorship through education. Without a doubt, one of Culleton's goals in writing *In Search of April Raintree* was to disseminate a Métis version of history, and her adaptation of the novel for schools underlines how important it is to her to mitigate the censorship practised by the teaching of mainstream history.

"KEEPING" OUT NATIVE CULTURE

Another way Native literature is censored in Canada is through the power exercised by cultural gatekeepers, those agents who decide what writing eventually reaches the public. These agents control the means of communication in our society and, as early investigators of post-colonial literature recognized, "the key feature of colonial oppression [is] the control over the *means of communication* rather than the control over life and property or even language itself" (Ashcroft, 79). The importance of the means of communication in Culleton's novel is symbolized by the special status afforded the typewriter that April gives Cheryl for her birthday. To Cheryl, who is proud of her culture and searches for ways to express that pride, "That [typewriter] was something she could appreciate" (124). Although Cheryl never seems to use it, she keeps it even in the most dire financial circumstances: "We're always broke. I sell all the furniture, except the typewriter. I wonder why April gave it to me? She's the one with the writing talent" (223). The answer to Cheryl's question is that April recognizes Cheryl as a guardian of Métis culture and sees writing as the necessary means to exercising that role. Cheryl must recognize this role on some level as well, since she treasures the typewriter above all her other possessions. Certainly other members of the Métis community, who regard Cheryl as their standard-bearer, see the potential that writing holds for them. As April remarks of Cheryl's friend Nancy and her family: "Imagine that, they're so poor and yet they kept that typewriter for Cheryl all that time, when they could have sold it" (211). Despite this recognition of the importance of writing Métis literature and the possession of the immediate means of communication represented by the typewriter, Cheryl never manages to have her voice publicly heard – one reason being that the major means of communication are controlled by mainstream cultural gatekeepers. For many potential writers, marginalized like Cheryl, these gatekeepers have included publishers, critics, and anthologists.

Publishers are the cultural gatekeepers who are most frequently accused of censorship by Canadian Native writers. Lee Maracle, for example, when asked about a solution to discrimination in Canadian publishing, calls for "the development of our own presses and our own publishing houses ... A non-discriminatory kind of access. Usually what happens is only the people with a certain politic gain access to money, which acts as a kind of censorship" (quoted in Williamson, 171). One form this kind of censorship takes is the obstruction of Native writing from being published at all. As Margaret Harry writes, "Until recently, it was virtually impossible for a native writer to find a publisher; and, despite the recent proliferation of periodicals produced by the Indians and Inuit themselves ... there are still proportionately very few books ... Most Canadian publishers, especially the larger firms with facilities for extensive promotion and distribution, do not publish works of native writers. One can only assume that such works are thought to be not commercially viable: white readers are indifferent to them" (146–7).[10]

Harry puts her finger on an interesting problem: is the refusal to publish Native writing the decision of publishers alone, or do they merely take their cue from their readers, whose tastes determine which manuscripts publishers buy? LaRocque notes that "the interplay between audience reception and publishing cannot be minimized ... On another level, we [are] again rendered voiceless no matter how articulate we [are]" (xvi). Yet LaRocque also places control with the publishers themselves, who have preconceived notions of Native writing that would exclude the work of many Native writers. She contends that this is what happened with some of her poems that publishers rejected: "Now they could be bad poems, I don't know. Maybe I need to revise them, but I think it is because white publishers and editors want something that fits into their stereotype of an 'Indian poet'" (quoted in Lutz, 194).

A second form that censorship takes in publishing is the altering of Native texts to suit the demands of the dominant culture. As Anne Cameron explains, "Native groups have long insisted communication, publication and education are loaded against them. They have also insisted the truth can't be fully or properly told unless native writers are given publication and distribution WITHOUT being edited to death by Anglo academics who are part of and thus support the dominant ideology" ("Métis Heart," 164–5). One must be careful, of course, to recognize the difference between editing for aesthetic reasons and censorship, but these groups maintain they "can make a distinction between editing as craft and editing as ideology" (LaRocque, xxvi). Maria Campbell makes this distinction when she recounts her experience in the publication of *Halfbreed*.[11] According to Campbell, the original manuscript consisted of more than 2,000 pages. Naturally the publisher decided to reduce it to a publishable length, and Campbell acknowledges that "part of the decision not to publish all of it was a good one." "However," she adds, "a whole section was taken out of the book that was really important, and I had insisted it stay there. And that was something incriminating the RCMP ... The decision was made by the publisher – without consulting me" (quoted in Lutz, 42). This is a fairly blatant example of censorship by a publisher; usually a publisher will insist that changes to a manuscript are necessary to ensure a book of "good quality." But I concur with Barbara Godard, who questions the neutrality of even these motives for altering a marginalized writer's work, challenging the notion of "that 'good' book that merits publication" and arguing that aesthetic "quality" is itself a product of hegemonic ideological forces ("Politics," 186). As I argued in the Introduction, when a publisher makes the decision to exclude or alter some work on ideological grounds, it is censorship.

Beatrice Culleton is one Métis writer who has had her work successfully published, in the case of *In Search of April Raintree*, by a small publishing company specializing in Métis literature. The novel has been widely acclaimed, was reprinted ten times in the eight years after its publication, and is frequently used in high schools and universities.[12] One might conclude that the novel would have been accepted by a mainstream publisher had that been Culleton's wish, but the author questions this assumption: "If I hadn't been published by Pemmican, which is a Métis publishing house, would I ever have been published? I still have doubts about that and no matter how many readers of my books reassure me, I still wonder" (quoted in Barton, 14). Culleton's remark suggests that, were it not for alternative publishing houses, her novel, despite its obvious importance, in effect would have been censored. Perhaps this feeling informed Culleton's shaping of her character Cheryl, who is not as fortunate as her creator in her search for an outlet for her discourse on Métis culture. Cheryl prefaces her recital of the most extensive and passionate example of this discourse with a comment on its censorship: "I wrote this one piece in university but they wouldn't publish it because they said it was too controversial. I still know it by heart. Want to hear it?" (168). The piece she recites from memory[13] is a speech on the plight of the Métis that begins with a comment on the silencing of the Métis voice: "White Man, to you my voice is like the unheard call in the wilderness. It is there, though you do not hear" (168). If this voice is ignored by being banished to the wilderness, it is censored as that wilderness is being destroyed: "You do not stop at confining us to small pieces of rock and muskeg. Where are the animals of the wilderness to go when there is no more wilderness?" (169). Thus Culleton places the censorship by publishers of Cheryl's speech in the broader context of the socio-cultural censorship of Native voices.

I have presented these examples of Native and Métis writers who have spoken in interviews and written in fiction of the restrictive practices of publishers in order to suggest that these practices constitute a form of socio-cultural censorship. This line of reasoning leads to some startling conclusions, as Lee Maracle discovers when she follows a similar intellectual path in her playful essay "Native Myths: Trickster Alive and Crowing." In that stylized piece, the autobiographical narrator addresses her ruminations on the relationship between publishing and censorship to the Trickster, Raven: "Censorship; Noah Webster jumps off the shelf, heavy with his unabridgedness, tattered by fifty years of life, and spills the meaning of censorship into the vortex of my confusion: 'Anyone empowered to

suppress a publication' ... Publisher: 'Anyone who arranges the publication of a work'" (183). Maracle juxtaposes the definitions to show
their similarity. This leads to the narrator's "embarrassing discovery":

> "the publishers have the right to choose what they publish. 'Letters to the
> Sun are edited for brevity and good taste.' ... 'your work has been rejected
> because ... ' Perfectly just, given that the publisher is responsible for making
> the work public. My dilemma is that the publisher is ipso facto absolved of
> any accusations regarding censorship, given her right to choose. Censorship
> requires a third party official."
>
> Raven just disappears, leaving me with the nagging suspicion that it is not
> just intellectual confusion that tears at my nocturnal wanderings.   (183)

This equation of publishing and censorship poses a dilemma for
Maracle because, as she says, the publisher's choice of one text over
another is "perfectly just"; yet censorship is something that traditionally has been seen as a societal evil. Indeed, it is not intellectual confusion that afflicts Maracle's narrator but the problem of a received
definition of censorship. Once we see that censorship is inherent in
any society in which ideas and cultures compete, that censorship *is*
the choice that a cultural gatekeeper, like publishers, must make, we
will stop arguing about the good or evil of censorship and start arguing about how to practise it in a responsible, humane way.

Other cultural gatekeepers shape the literary canon, determining
which works are widely read and endure, thereby exercising the
same kind of censoring power over Native culture as do publishers.
"For the canon," as Arnold Krupat writes, "like all cultural production, is never an innocent selection of the best that has been thought
and said; rather, it is the institutionalization of those particular verbal
artifacts that appear best to convey and sustain the dominant social
order" ("Native American Literature and the Canon," 146).[14] One
cultural gatekeeper who helps to shape the canon is the literary critic.
Margaret Harry maintains that "The lack of commitment by publishers and readers to the works of native writers is reinforced by the
generally negative attitude of Canadian critics. Perhaps 'non-atti-
tude' would be a better word, since most Indian and Inuit works are
not criticized negatively, but rather not criticized at all" (147). The
lack of critical attention to Native works certainly contributes to their
relegation to obscurity, but what is probably an even greater factor
in their effacement is criticism that judges Native literature according
to colonial stereotypes. As Agnes Grant asks, "Are conventional critical judgments depriving readers of access to a potentially moving
literature? What we say and do as critics and teachers will influence

who will be publishing in the future. Are we perpetuating voids?" (126). These voids, created partly by critics who dismiss Native literature that features Native content (myth, history, belief, humour) and Native form (language, tropes, influences of oral story-telling), are the spaces where Native writing is censored from the Western literary canon. A similar power is exercised by anthologists of Canadian literature. Terry Goldie observes that "the power of such anthologies in establishing the canon is hard to deny" (377); yet, writing in 1991, Goldie asserts, "Today, Canadian anthologies are as lacking in Native material as are the American" (378).[15]

As the 1990s have progressed, of course, Native writing has become increasingly visible. Native prose and poetry have been included more frequently in anthologies of Canadian literature,[16] and a number of anthologies of Native writing have emerged (for a list of these anthologies, see the Bibliography). Critics have begun paying more attention to various forms of Native expression as well (the *Canadian Literature* special issue on Native writers is a good early example). While Culleton has benefited from this opening up of the literary canon, from both increased sales of and heightened critical attention to *In Search of April Raintree,* the characters of her novel do not. For Cheryl especially, whose discourse, produced in the early 1970s, is censored by publishers even before it can reach the potential anthologist or critic, this progress comes too late.

APPROPRIATING NATIVE VOICES

A third form of socio-cultural censorship that Native authors discuss is the appropriation of their voice by non-Native writers. Leonore Keeshig-Tobias asserts that, for White Canadian writers, "to continue telling Native stories, writing Native stories, is to continue speaking for Native people and paraphrasing Native people – censoring the Native voice" ("The Magic of Others," 174). Appropriation has a censoring effect because there is a limited space for the dissemination of discourse in our society and, as Jeannette Armstrong points out, "every time a space is taken up in the publishing world and the reading community, it means that a Native person isn't being heard and that has great impact" (quoted in Williamson, 22). This kind of censorship is typical in societies featuring a marketplace of cultural competition. In this marketplace it is the dominant culture that determines the nature of the cultural goods consumed. In Canada, according to Barbara Godard, White writers who adopt a Native perspective "create a 'market' for Indian material. If the Indians themselves do not interpret their tradition in the same way, then they

cannot sell their work. The Indian view will never be known" ("Talking about Ourselves," 62).

Appropriation is not only a source of censorship in literary writing
(e.g., fiction, poetry, and drama) but is practised by non-Native writers in the academy as well: "by creating a recognized school of experts
who are a relatively 'low risk' to publishers, and by saturating the
market with a wave of books about Aboriginal peoples, this wave of
academic writing has the effect of ultimately blocking-out the Aboriginal Voice" (Young-Ing, 182). An example of this kind of appropriation
in Culleton's novel is represented in the incident that follows a series
of insulting comments directed at Cheryl at the Radcliffe New Year's
party in Toronto: "Then two men came over and one asked Cheryl
what it was like being an Indian. Before she could reply, the other
man voiced his opinion and the two soon walked away, discussing
their concepts of native life without having allowed Cheryl to say one
thing" (116–17). Though the appropriation is probably not conscious
on the part of these men, as Margery Fee observes, the passage nevertheless illustrates the "process [that] goes on in academic writing,
as various 'experts' carry on discussing their ideas without reference
to the ideas, opinions and feelings of their 'subject(s)'" (178). This
process, which ultimately renders Cheryl silent, demonstrates the
censorship that occurs through the appropriation of the Native voice.

Many Native writers respond to this form of censorship by invoking the concept of Native copyright, whereby "a storyteller can't use
the story of another person unless an exchange has been made, and
then this story must always be identified as coming from that person" (Godard, "Talking About Ourselves," 66). One of the reasons
Native copyright rules were established, according to Penny Petrone,
was to maintain control of narratives by selected caretakers of the
culture: "This secrecy meant that only a limited few – certain initiated
elders – had knowledge of them. Only they had the right to tell or
hear them, or to perform the associated rituals. Restricted access to
certain kinds of knowledge helped to ensure their power and authority" (11). Though Native copyright mainly militates against the
appropriation of intact, discrete narratives, some Native writers have
interpreted the rule more broadly to apply to non-Native writers
dealing with any aspect of Native culture. Godard reports that, at a
conference she attended in 1983, it was this principle that was relied
on when "again and again ... the native women insisted that non-
Indians not write about Indian things without their permission"
("Talking about Ourselves," 66).

Not surprisingly, the attempt by Native writers to gain some control over the dissemination of their cultural practices by calling for

the cessation of cultural appropriation is interpreted by some non-Native writers as an attempt at censorship. Coomi Vevaina reports that "non-Native writers like George Bowering, Timothy Findley, Lynn Andrews and Darlene Barry Quaife, to name only a few, label the viewpoint of the Natives as 'fascist' and cry out against 'Native censorship'" (58).[17] But Native writers have an answer to this accusation. Jeannette Armstrong asks her readers to imagine themselves in the position of the oppressed Native writer: "Imagine yourselves in this condition and imagine the writer of that dominating culture berating you for speaking out about appropriation of cultural voice and using the words 'freedom of speech' to condone further systemic violence, in the form of entertainment literature about your culture and your values and all the while, yourself being disempowered and rendered voiceless through such 'freedoms'" ("The Disempowerment," 209). Here Armstrong insightfully alludes to the rhetorical gesture non-Native writers make when they complain of censorship. Because censorship is considered a universal evil, by invoking it White writers are able to take the moral high road and shift the debate away from their discursive practices to one over free speech, which they cannot lose. Of course Native writers are doing the same thing when they appeal for freedom of speech, when what they are really arguing for is more space in the cultural arena. When taken to an extreme, their assertion amounts to the untenable claim that, regardless of their quality or size relative to other cultural producers, the principle of free speech should give marginalized voices equal preponderance. Both sides will continue to talk past one another until they recognize that censorship is a systemic feature of our culturally competitive society, and that to make that society more "just" entails discovering where that censorship is appropriate and where it is not.

NATIVE SELF-CENSORSHIP

The last form of censorship of Native discourse can be called self-censorship: this is when Native writers, in response to pressure from a predominantly non-Native literary world, refrain from writing or alter some work they might otherwise produce. Sometimes these writers accede to this pressure knowingly, as in the case of Rita Joe, who, recalling the advice she received from a Native editor, describes her conscious acquiescence to self-censorship: "And I remember he gave me advice a long time ago: 'When you write something, don't step on toes!' And then he would explain to me which toes: the band council, the chief, Department of Indian Affairs officials, and secretary of state, or whatever, or prime minister, you know. 'Don't say unkind things!' And I never did, I followed his advice. That was back in 1969" (quoted in Lutz, 243). For others, self-censorship is a more unconscious process whereby colonial values are gradually internalized and reproduced in cultural discourse. As Marilyn Dumont argues, "These colonial images we have of ourselves inform me that internalized colonialism is alive and well in the art we generate and which gets transferred by media into the popular images which are supported by the art buying public (read: white patrons) ... I would argue that the misrepresentation of me makes me doubt my experience, devalue my reality and tempts me to collude in an image which in the end disempowers me" (48). This self-censorship can affect the content of Native discourse, as in Rita Joe's case, or the form of that discourse. Formal self-censorship of Native writing means that some writers are pressured to use certain genres like autobiography despite the fact that many Native writers find this genre uncomfortably self-aggrandizing (Harry, 149) and that it is "not a traditional form among Native peoples but the consequence of contact with the white invader-settlers" (Krupat, *For Those Who Come After*, xi). Self-censorship also results in the transition from oral to written storytelling: "The written format ... in effect violates traditional givens regarding telling stories" (Salat, 76), as it precludes many features of oral narration, such as the importance of teller-audience interaction (Frey, xiv), the fluidity of meaning with each telling (Ruppert, 107), and the very subversiveness that oral practices offer against exclusionary Western written forms (Emberley, 93; Donovan, 43–67).[18]

Culleton depicts self-censorship in both principal characters of *In Search of April Raintree*. From very early in her life Cheryl wants to disseminate her own view of Métis culture, but she soon learns, from a dominant non-Native society indifferent to this view, to keep her discourse to herself: "I think my fellow-classmates might not be able to hack another speech on Métis people. I was going to deliver this speech but now I've decided I will keep it among my papers on the history of the Métis people" (77). Cheryl must also censor her feelings from her sister because April does not sympathize with her cultural views. After Cheryl disappears, April reflects on the isolation Cheryl must have felt after discovering the truth about their parents: "I'm sure she never told me all of the things she discovered ... She carried that around with her all alone, not wanting to share her problems" (204). This self-silencing, on both the public and personal levels, and its resultant isolation, may have led to Cheryl's ultimate self-censoring act: suicide.

If Cheryl's self-censorship consists of keeping her Métis expression to herself, April's is the effacement of even those thoughts that could be considered expressive of a Métis viewpoint. April's self-censorship is much more complete because she has internalized[19] a White mentality that denigrates Métis culture. As Margery Fee writes, "April has been through the process of internalizing both the oppressor role and that of the oppressed ... she becomes her own best oppressor, or in terms of ideology, she internalizes the belief in her own 'Native' nature as inferior in a way that maintains and reproduces the power of the dominant elite" (176). A prime example of this internalization is April's attitude towards Métis history. When Cheryl gives her a book on Louis Riel, April "crinkle[s her] nose in distaste" (44) and proceeds mentally to recite pat colonialist history lessons using words such as "rebel" and "crazy half-breed" to describe Riel and "treason" and "folly" to describe his actions. She concludes her reflections with the self-hating statement, "So, anything to do with Indians, I despised" (44–5). Thus, despite the fact that "She's the one with the writing talent" (223), April's internalization of White prejudice effectively censors any Métis voice she might possess. Only towards the end of the novel, after leaving a marriage ruled by her racist mother-in-law and being brutally raped, does April realize that she will never escape her Métis heritage. Sadly, it takes Cheryl's suicide for April finally to stop censoring the Métis part of her: in the end she "used the words 'MY PEOPLE, OUR PEOPLE' and meant them. The denial had been lifted from [her] spirit" (228).

Culleton herself exhibits self-censorship in the revised version of *In Search of April Raintree*, simply entitled *April Raintree*, which she produced in 1984 to be used in Manitoba schools. Critic Dawn Thompson correctly sees this revision as a kind of censorship when she writes: "*April Raintree* is revised, vocabulary simplified and censored in order to render it more appropriate for a young audience" (100).[20] In an interview with Stephanie McKenzie, Culleton explains how this second text came into being:

When *In Search of April Raintree* was first published, I had intended the novel to be read by an older audience. However, children, as young as nine years old, became interested in and related to the text. I hadn't thought of this possibility. The Native Education Board of Manitoba then asked me to revise the novel for use in the school system (both native and non-native). The revisions were made so that teachers of grade seven, as well as of the upper grades (ten, eleven and twelve) could use the book. I primarily focused on the rape scene and Cheryl's language (she swore a lot in the original).

Culleton's self-censorship of the content of her novel is conscious, but it illustrates the influence that a social authority, such as the school system, can bring to bear on a writer's work. As Helen Hoy remarks, "The revision acts as a reminder, at the level of dissemination, of precisely the social, economic, and institutional (specifically educational) constraints on what can be said and heard, on how it can be said, that Culleton conveys within the novel. We can observe 'specific effects of power,' which Foucault describes as working to certify 'truth,' being bestowed on one version of the story in preference to another" (169–70).

Though she ended up acquiescing to institutional constraints and censored her material in order to gain access to a student readership, Culleton is remarkably at ease with these alterations: "I agree wholeheartedly with the Native School Board's proposal," she says. "I'm a mother, and it is important to me that kids retain their childlike innocence as long as possible. Such innocence is still important to maintain" (quoted in Stephanie McKenzie). This line of reasoning is substantially different from that used by most writers who hold to the sanctity of freedom of speech. It is difficult to imagine a writer like Timothy Findley, whose novel *The Wars* was attacked in schools for precisely the same reasons that Culleton altered her text, agreeing with any such changes. The reason for this contrast is that these two writers approach the notion of censorship from very different directions. For Findley it is always inappropriate (even though he practises it himself). For Culleton, coming from a background of oral culture in which context – author's intent, content and form of discourse, nature of audience – determines the suitability of the storytelling (Godard, "Talking About Ourselves," 58–60), sometimes censorship is appropriate. It is this pragmatic approach to censorship, in which context determines how we judge a particular work, that should, I argue, replace arguments on principle about the desirability of censorship.

Although Black writers in Canada share many of the concerns of their Native colleagues regarding censorship, one of the major differences is the broadening of an issue that Native writers see mainly in terms of race to include feminist considerations. As Sunanda Pal writes of Claire Harris, a prominent Canadian Black poet, "The silence of oppressed women, whose words and sentences remain unuttered or emerge in faintly audible songs, is a major concern of women writers today" (135). Indeed, unlike the Native writing community, the silencing of the Black voice is an issue, is *the* issue, almost exclusively for Black *women* writers. Harris is one of the three most prominent of these Black writers in Canada; the others are Dionne Brand and Marlene Nourbese Philip. I will focus on Philip because, as Leslie Sanders observes, "she is probably the best known African Canadian writer" (135),[21] her work has received the most critical attention, and most importantly because, more than any other writer, she is concerned with the silencing imposed on Black discourse by dominant cultural forces in Canada. Philip sees this silencing as different not in kind but only in degree from the censorship imposed by authoritarian governments: "There is often, in fact, a direct link between the power structure that supports the privileged position of white writers in countries like Canada, the circumstances of their own writers of colour, and the existence of regimes which imprison writers in other countries" (*Frontiers*, 151). That the silencing of Black voices is the most important theme in Philip's writing is, superficially, demonstrated by the sheer number of times the word "silence" (or some variant of the idea, such as "wounded word") appears in the titles of critical articles on Philip's writing.[22] More telling is the title of her central poetic work, *She Tries Her Tongue, Her Silence Softly Breaks*. I will examine ways in which this book of poetry and her novel *Harriet's Daughter* – which shares a number of the concerns highlighted in Beatrice Culleton's book – comment on socio-cultural censorship of Blacks in Canada.

"A FOREIGN ANGUISH / IS ENGLISH"

While some Native writers see the suppression of Native language mainly as a function of the dominant culture's educational policy, Philip sees Black dispossession of language as fundamental to Black Canadians' disempowerment and as affecting every aspect of their lives. Philip sees herself in the role of Other, in a position of difference; and, as Godard points out, "The official explanation of her difference in Canada is cultural, yet she poses it as linguistic" ("Marlene Nourbese," 152). Indeed, as Philip herself writes, "Language itself – [is] symbol of death and life for me" ("Journal Entries," 73).

Philip portrays linguistic suppression as a form of censorship in her poetry. In *She Tries Her Tongue* the narrator suggests that the success of colonialism depends on the eradication of minority languages. Philip conveys this idea in the poem "Discourse on the Logic of Language" by reproducing official "edicts" next to the central portion of the poem in which the narrator questions her relationship to the English language. The first edict calls for the mixing of slaves from as many linguistic groups as possible to limit their ability to communicate with one another (56). Edict II is even more severe: "Every slave caught speaking his native language shall be severely punished. Where necessary, removal of the tongue is recommended.

The offending organ, when removed, should be hung on high in a central place, so that all may see and tremble" (58). While this passage documents the origins of the colonial slave trade in the physical censoring of Blacks, it also represents the effect that the imposition of Standard English has had on Black culture. As Brenda Carr observes, "Philip's mimicry of fact-based discourse is used to recast rather than to authorize history, to interrogate the paralegal codes that delegitimate free speech. The excised tongue also signifies enforced language loss and, by extension, loss of culture and history" (74). The representation of the censored voice in the amputated tongue echoes in the last, title poem of the volume. The "blackened stump of a tongue / torn / out" (92) is the plight of a people for whom the narrator acts as a latter-day "Philomela" (98). The mythological allusion is apt. Philomela was first raped by her brother-in-law, Tereus, who then cut off her tongue so she could not speak against him. She turns to her loom to depict the atrocity in tapestry and brings the perpetrator to justice. The narrator's self-identification with Philomela posits Philip's poem as a counter to the cultural rape enacted upon Blacks through the suppression of their language.[23]

Indeed, for Philip the control of language and the control of the body are one and the same, and she figures the censorship of the Black voice in the ultimate control of Black women's bodies: rape.[24] Godard locates the trope of "the stealing of the mother tongue as rape" ("Marlene Nourbese," 160) at the thematic centre of *She Tries Her Tongue*. This trope is clear in the excerpt Philip appends to the end of the poem "Universal Grammar," taken from the imaginary work *"Mother's Recipes on How to Make a Language Yours or How Not to Get Raped"*:

Slip mouth over the syllable; moisten with tongue the word.
Suck Slide Play Caress Blow – Love it, but if the word gags, does not nourish, bite it off – at its source –
Spit it out
Start again.   (67)

Philip writes that "I was suggesting in this excerpt ... the link between linguistic rape and physical rape," but adds that the poem ultimately rejects subjugation through "an attempt to place woman's body center stage again as actor and not as the acted upon" ("Managing the Unmanageable," 299). Despite its gesture towards resistance, the overriding message of the poem is the colonial regulation of Black bodies and Black texts. As Carr puts it, "New World settings may be read as a theatre for the cruel enactment of regulated bodies: unnaming and renaming, censoring, and managing those inscribed as corporeal commodity" (88). For Philip, the censoring that is represented by the act of rape is first and foremost a censoring of language.

"KEEPING" OUT BLACK CULTURE

If the denial of language is at the heart of the censoring of the Black voice in Canada, among the agents of that censorship are cultural gatekeepers who obstruct the dissemination of Black writing. Philip quotes the Marxist critic Raymond Williams, who argues that in the case of art, "no work is in any full practical sense produced until it is also received" (quoted in *Frontiers*, 30). Like Williams, Philip sees the marketplace, where cultural gatekeepers operate, as the site that determines whether the texts of Black writers are received by the public: "While the Black writer, for instance, may have to deal with funding agencies, she also has to deal with the marketplace and the censorship of the marketplace that occurs through racism" (*Frontiers*, 225). One of the key cultural gatekeepers who practices censorship because of racism, according to Black writers, is the Canadian publisher. Of a politics of Canadian publishing characterized by the disinclination to publish Black texts, Claire Harris says: "The effect is the censorship of a new vision of Canada ... one that includes all its people as full and legitimate citizens" (quoted in Williamson, 116). Philip, too, sees publishers as censors, agreeing with Russian poet Joseph Brodsky that they can be more dangerous than book burners: "'Burning books,' ... Brodsky writes, is 'after all ... just a gesture; not publishing them is a falsification of time ... precisely the goal of the system,' intent on issuing 'its own version of the future.' This 'falsification of time' which results from the failure to publish writers is as characteristic of the dominant culture in Canada as in the Soviet Union" ("The Disappearing Debate," 102).

Philip documents the various ways publishers deny access to Black writers in her essay "Publish + Be Damned." She touches on many of the same points that Native writers raise in their discussions of publishing restrictions. In response to the argument that publishers merely cater to the demands of their readers (shifting censoring responsibilities from themselves to the audience), Philip argues that the Canadian publishing industry receives substantial government grants, freeing them from the pocketbooks, and therefore tastes, of their readers (160). Furthermore, she calls the assumption that the work of marginalized writers will only appeal to marginalized readers "erroneous, narrow-minded, and even racist" (161), a point supported by bestsellers such as Culleton's novel. She also broaches the subject of literary quality or merit, terms that publishers often cite as the criteria for their publishing decisions. Many Black writers see these terms as smokescreens for the ideologically biased attempt by publishers to get authors "writing right." As Godard points out, "The strait-jacket of writing right has been eloquently described by Himani Bannerji and Makeda Silvera as a form of censorship" ("Writing Resistance," 107–8). Philip sees "writing right," or the production of "good" literature, not as an objective aesthetic criterion; rather, "the assessment of value and quality of a work is a judgment that is all of a piece with wider political, cultural and social values" ("Publish," 163). These values, for Philip, are predominantly White and mainstream, and she calls for "a more comprehensive definition of quality, and not one that is predominantly European" (166).

Although she does not comment on censorship by cultural gatekeepers directly in her poetry or fiction, for Philip, as for Culleton, censorship by publishers played a role in the reception of her novel *Harriet's Daughter*. Merit does not seem to have been an issue with the novel. Philip reports that the book readily found a publisher in England, and was runner-up for the Canadian Library Association's Book of the Year for Children award ("Racism in the Book Business," D7). Indeed, in 1997 Leslie Sanders wrote, "Now it has probably been read by half the adolescents in Toronto and appears on university courses as well" (134). Philip believes the book was rejected by Canadian publishers because of the nature of its content: "McClelland and Stewart was among three Canadian publishing houses that turned down a manuscript of mine on grounds of race of the characters – they were African Canadians" ("Racism in the Book Business," D7). Godard sees this incident as another example of a publisher demanding a Black author "write right," and then, when she refuses to do so, refusing to publish her work: "In Canada, Philip is subject to the literary institution's systemic 'white washing,' which seeks to exclude the representations of her racial alterity from Canadian discourse" ("Marlene Nourbese," 156). This exclusion of Black writers' representations by publishers is a form of socio-cultural censorship.

Black writers identify other cultural gatekeepers who act as censors by preventing their voices from being heard. Some even see the suppression of free speech in the very groups created to fight *against* censorship. Godard writes that the power relations that lead to censorship "are produced and reproduced in those very institutions aiming to promote freedom of speech and aid writers economically, namely PEN International and the Writers' Union of Canada" ("Marlene Nourbese," 159). One example involving the latter organization took place in 1988, when some members resigned over a debate about cultural appropriation and the splinter group Vision 21 was formed.

Philip writes that, at that time, "the Union censored the resignation statement of a female member relating to the presence of sexism within the Union membership, by disallowing publication of this statement in the Union newsletter" (*Frontiers*, 148–9). The controversy involving PEN resulted from a verbal attack allegedly directed by June Callwood against Vision 21 members demonstrating outside the 1989 PEN Congress. In this case Philip reprimanded the media as much as the free-speech lobby group: "The media have, in fact, effectively censored the expression of our views concerning the composition of the Canadian delegation to the 54th Congress, as well as the events that took place outside Roy Thomson Hall. Whether or not this was intentional is irrelevant" (*Frontiers*, 142).

In addition to lobby groups and the media, some Black writers also see socio-cultural censorship among government award- and grant-funding bodies. Dionne Brand's book of poetry *No Language is Neutral* was nominated for the Governor General's award in 1992. It did not win, writes Brand, because of the nature of Canadian society: "I know where I live. I live in a white-dominated society. They are not about to let anybody of colour, at this moment, get any closer to the prizes and accolades at the very heart of their national discourse. They are not about to let anybody like me or you do that yet. They have complete control at this point over all those things. But I think it's more than keeping people of colour out; I think it is keeping their master discourse going, a discourse of white supremacy" (369). Philip applies the same rationale to the distribution of government grants. Failure to communicate news of funding programs to marginalized groups and a dismissal of the legitimacy of their cultural idioms leads to underfunding of Black artists: "At present, many artists – Black artists – believe that it is futile for them to apply for funding; they do not believe their applications will be considered fairly. And they are right" (*Frontiers*, 130). To be sure, minority groups are sometimes passed over for practical reasons (for example, if they lack an institutional affiliation). But all these agencies – free-speech groups, the media, award and funding bodies – like all agencies that deal with writers and their work, at times act as cultural gatekeepers. The result of their decisions is the promotion of certain discourses over others, and, whether intending to or not, they act as agents of socio-cultural censorship.

INAPPROPRIATE APPROPRIATION?

Like Native artists, Black writers see a third form of socio-cultural censorship in the appropriation of their voice by White writers. While many White writers feel they have a right to exercise their imagination in any way they choose, Philip argues that "the 'right' to use the voice of the Other has, however, been bought at great price – the silencing of the Other; it is, in fact, neatly posited on that very silence" ("The Disappearing Debate," 101). She makes this claim based on the contention that, given limited access to audiences because of finite resources of cultural gatekeepers such as publishers, mainstream artists will be promoted before marginalized ones: White writers "must understand how their privilege as white people, writing about another culture, rather than out of it, virtually guarantees that their work will, in a racist society, be received more readily than the work of writers coming from that very culture" (106). The conclusion she draws is that cultural appropriation, for Blacks, amounts to the restriction or censorship of artistic freedom: "For some, artistic freedom appears to be alive and well in Canada; these writers, however, pay not the slightest heed to the fact that the wider context includes many who, because of racism, cannot fully exercise that artistic freedom. In Canada, that wider context is, in fact, very narrowly drawn around the artistic freedom of white writers" (107).

The theme of the silencing effects of appropriation emerges in her poem "African Majesty" in *She Tries Her Tongue*, in which Philip comments on an exhibit of African art held at the Art Gallery of Ontario in 1981. I want to offer a reading of the poem that sees in it the depiction of the creativity and dynamism of Western art forms, in particular those of the French formalists of the early twentieth century, as being derived from African art, while at the same time being predicated on the destruction of that art. The African resources used by Western artists ("rainfall/magic/power") are "depth-charged" (48): they are both charged with deep meaning and subject to explosion through Western appropriation. Philip describes African art as belonging to "a culture mined / to abstraction," where "mined" evokes both the sense of a culture replete with richness and one that is, again, subject to being blown up; "abstraction" reminds us of the school of art that exploited African cultures as well as the mental agony suffered by members of those cultures. When she writes, "corbeaux circle / circles of plexiglass / death" she is portraying the French formalists "Braque, Picasso, Brancusi" (whom she mentions later in the poem) as ravens ("corbeaux" is the French plural noun meaning "ravens" or "crows"); ravens (a symbol of death) circle over the corpses of African cultures looking to scavenge material for their art (the plasticized circles of cubism). Ultimately, to practise this kind of production of high art, "to adorn the word with meaning," is "to mourn the meaning in loss" (49). For Philip the African Majesty exhibit is representative of a dominant culture in the West that appropriates Black artistic work for its own success and in so doing erases or censors the authors of that work themselves.

As with Native writers and the appropriation issue, Black writers' demand that their White counterparts stop using their voices arouses various responses. Some, like Margaret Hollingsworth, counter with the accusation that the anti-appropriation stand is itself a kind of censorship (143). Others, such as Bronwen Wallace, disagree: "It's about who gets published and who doesn't. I don't see it as censorship; we're being asked to stand in solidarity with Women of Colour" (quoted in Williamson, 288). Philip agrees with Wallace that being against cultural appropriation means being against racism, not in favour of censorship. In her essay "The Disappearing Debate; or, How the Discussion of Racism Has Been Taken Over by the Censorship Issue," Philip sees censorship as a red herring: "The quantum leap from racism to censorship is neither random nor unexpected, since the issue of censorship is central to the dominant cultures of liberal democracies like Canada. In these cultures, censorship becomes a significant and talismanic cultural icon around which all debates about the 'individual freedom of man' swirl. It is the cultural and political barometer which these societies use to measure their freedoms" (98). It is true, as Philip argues, that White writers seize on the "talismanic" quality of the word "censorship," holding it as an impenetrable shield before anyone who wishes to question the limitlessness of free speech. This rhetorical use of the term is precisely what I have been arguing is characteristic of the neutralist liberal approach as a whole. But just because the word "censorship" – as a result of the way those who use it currently define it – tends to deflect debate away from some of the key issues at stake (such as racism), it does not follow that censorship is not what is being advocated by Black writers. This point is made cogently by the Black social philosopher Glenn C. Loury, who observes that, in discussion of certain sensitive issues, only certain people have "cover" to comment. An example he gives is the inadmissibility of a news story on the problem of skin-colour prejudice when reported by a White journalist. "The censorship in these cases is partial," Loury writes; "those who have 'cover' express themselves freely, whereas those who lack it must be silent" (173). In the debate over cultural appropriation, in effect, each side is trying to censor the other in order to advance its own political and aesthetic agenda.

CENSORSHIP FROM WITHIN

Loury's chapter "Self-Censorship in Public Discourse: A Theory of Political Correctness and Related Phenomena" sheds considerable light on the causes and mechanics of self-censorship (the fourth form of socio-cultural censorship that I identify) in the Black community.

Here Loury argues that "self-censorship is the hidden face of political correctness. For every act of aberrant speech seen to be punished by 'thought police,' there are countless other critical arguments, dissents from received truth, unpleasant factual reports, or nonconformist deviation of thought that go unexpressed (or whose expression is distorted) because potential speakers rightly fear the consequences of a candid exposition of their views" (157–8). The potential speakers to whom Loury refers are usually members of some group, and it is that membership, which is often constitutive of their identity or crucial to their social progress, that would be threatened were they to express their dissenting views (147). Loury acknowledges that the self-censorship that arises from political correctness is not of the same magnitude as systematic, state-sponsored censorship, but they are similar in that "conventions of self-censorship are sustained by the utilitarian acquiescence of each community member in an order that, at some level, denies the whole truth. By calculating that the losses from deviation outweigh the gains, individuals are led to conform. Yet by doing so they yield something of their individuality and their dignity to 'the system'" (181). When it comes to self-censorship, whether in a totalitarian state or in a democracy like Canada, as Loury concludes, "The same calculus is at work in every case" (181).

Philip shows the struggle of one young woman to resist this yielding, through self-censorship, of her individuality and dignity to "the system" in her novel *Harriet's Daughter*. The system she is resisting can be characterized in two ways, and Philip represents both characteristics in Harriet's father, Cuthbert. We have remarked in her poetry that Philip sees censorship of Black voices as a gender issue (the most striking example of this being the poet's portrayal of the censorship of Black language as rape). Accordingly, in keeping with many Black writers' particular emphasis on feminist issues, Philip portrays Cuthbert as an intransigent, sexist character. As Margaret complains, "My father … is a male chauvinist pig, no doubt about that" (14). More than merely an incidental example of controlling misogyny, however, Cuthbert is clearly depicted as representative of an oppressive patriarchal authority. Colonialism is one patriarchal institution to which he is linked. When Margaret, in disobedience of her father, stays late at the library, her thoughts are like those of a runaway slave: "I had been running, I was tired, and I was late … and I was sick and tired of being scared of my father and his power" (31). It is at this moment that she conceives the idea for the Underground Railroad game. Her psychological association subtly links Cuthbert and slave owners, whom, as propagators of colonialism, Philip sees as agents of a primarily patriarchal order. Cuthbert also resembles the rigid Old

Testament God, a traditionally patriarchal figure. This resemblance is clear not only in Cuthbert's authoritarian behaviour but also from the terms in which Margaret thinks of her father ("or HE as I call HIM") and herself (as a sinner) (6). It is made explicit when Margaret, who wants to wear a T-shirt to church, is told by her mother to "Have a little respect for the house of the Lord," and Margaret thinks, "I was really tempted to say I thought I lived in the house of the Lord" (38).

The other cultural force depicted as trying to shape Margaret is an inflexible, traditional Black ethos, also embodied in the figure of her father. Cuthbert tries to mask this conservatism by criticizing his wife for being "primitive" because of her distrust of banks (among other things), but he betrays his own attachment to traditional West Indian behaviour in his devotion to playing dominoes with his compatriots. As Margaret comments, "That's why I say he's a phoney. He's not leaving *his* past behind him, but he wants her to. And he's *so* concerned about being coloured, which as far as I can see means being stuffy and boring and not liking anything worth liking" (17). Thus, as the source of struggle for the protagonist, Margaret, Cuthbert is depicted, unflatteringly, as a representative of the patriarchy and of an old-fashioned Black value-system. As her friend Bertha Billings says to Margaret, "Cuthbert may play good dominoes, and think he's God but he can act real foolish sometimes, which is how he's been acting over you" (146).

The foolish way Cuthbert acts involves the rigid control he exerts over members of his family, especially Margaret and her mother. The form that this control takes that particularly interests me here is the self-censorship he causes these other characters to impose on themselves. One reason Cuthbert wants them to censor themselves is his concern over what White people will think. Loury explains that it is common for members of a cultural group, such as Blacks, to stifle their own members for fear of what outsiders will think:

sometimes it is insiders, not outsiders, who are specifically forbidden to voice certain opinions or address certain issues in mixed company. "Washing dirty linen in public" refers to injudicious speech by an insider that is taboo in mixed company but would be appropriate if no outsiders were present … The taboo may derive from a concern that outsiders will misinterpret the information, a fear that the insider's words will be exploited by outsiders against the group's interest, or a worry that outsiders will feel legitimized in their own criticism of the group once an insider has confirmed it. (174)

Cuthbert uses precisely this rationale when he grounds Margaret in punishment for her tardy return from the library (a punishment designed not only to restrict her actions but ultimately to cause her to censor the expression of her interests and desires): "He made the gross sound in his throat and began on The Importance of Coloured People Being on Time – I began to tune him out. The last words I heard were, 'People think that all Coloured People are always late'" (33). Another example in which Cuthbert, conscious of what others will think, urges his daughter to circumscribe the expression of her sense of identity is when he condemns her Underground Railroad game. His justification is that Margaret's way of expressing herself will reinforce stereotypes of Blacks: "The first thing they're going to say is 'There they go again, those Coloured People – always causing trouble.' How many times do I have to tell you that you have to be careful, people are very quick to believe the worst about us" (89). Thus Cuthbert's fear that Margaret is washing the dirty linen of the Black community in public causes him to pressure her to censor herself.

The self-censorship that Cuthbert imposes on his family takes several forms. We have seen that language is an important area in which Black writers feel censored. It is an area in which Philip shows that Margaret and her mother, Tina, experience self-censorship as well. Tina is originally from Jamaica and has a noticeable accent when she speaks English. In a conversation Margaret has with her friend Zulma[25] we learn that Tina only allows her accent to surface in a supportive atmosphere:

"Sometimes I hear my mother on the phone with her Jamaican friends; when they get going I can hardly understand them."
"Your mother talk dialect?"
"Yep, but she likes to pretend she doesn't know how to; she thinks it's better to sound like a Canadian"   (10).

It is possible that the source of this self-censorship is a Canadian society that values a homogeneous "Canadian" accent and discourages difference, but it seems that Cuthbert is largely responsible for it as well. Shortly after the exchange with Zulma, Margaret reflects, "A lot of the time I feel sorry for my mum; she lets my father push her around too much. She fights back sometimes but not often enough ... I'm sure she would pretend she had never heard of Bob Marley" (13–14). It is Tina's awareness of her husband's intolerance for anything (including reggae music) that does not fit with his conception of Black culture and, more importantly, of his sensitivity to how others see that culture that causes her to suppress the natural patterns of her speech.

Cuthbert exerts pressure on his daughter to censor the way she uses language as well. Margaret is aware that she is constantly in danger of invoking the wrath of her father through her speech: "Me, he says, my mouth will get me in trouble" (16). Frequently her use of language summons her father's disapproval when she is rude: "So I got grounded again for – 'Rudeness to Your Parents' – which has got to be one of the worst, if not the worst sin in my house" (6). A more important way Margaret feels her language is controlled is in her choice of name for herself. As she begins to explore her cultural identity through research and the Underground Railroad game, Margaret decides she would like to change her name to Harriet, in tribute to both the Black American abolitionist leader Harriet Tubman and Harriet Blewchamp, a Holocaust survivor. This name change becomes of paramount significance for Margaret, who lists it among things she "would most like to see changed" in her life: "My name. I want a name that means something – important?" (25–6). Her father, of course, opposes the name change: "And what's all this nonsense about changing your name? Isn't Margaret good enough for you?" (90). As Heather Zwicker observes, "She has been named by her father, an oppressive patriarch, for his mother, whom Margaret has never met … She is named, essentially, within the patriarchy" (146). In fact the imposition of this name is Cuthbert's attempt at fixing Margaret's identity. This forced identification places her among those who, according to Himani Bannerji, "suffering from denials, erasures, dis- or misidentification, evince a passion for naming themselves" (21).

Margaret's desire to escape her given name and the role it implies is dramatized in a dream featuring the image of Harriet Tubman's face: "I stood against a wall facing a firing squad except that there weren't any soldiers: just my parents, Zulma's parents and Ti-cush's mother. They didn't have guns but each was holding a piece of paper with my name written on it. I screamed at them: 'My name is not Margaret, it's …' but each time I tried to say my name nothing came out, and I would have to start all over again, screaming: 'My name's not Margaret, it's …'" (36). In this dream Margaret censors herself each time she tries to speak her chosen name, Harriet. It is clear that the dream is about her fear of having to suppress her expression of her identity to please her parents (I would suggest particularly to please her father). Godard links this fixing of identity with the censorship of Natives: "Synecdochially, this [imposition of names] connects with the political situation of Canadian indigenous peoples subject to the imperialism of occupation and organized forgetting, to a politics of the erasure of representation" ("Marlene Nourbese," 156). In the case of *Harriet's Daughter*, the pressure for Margaret to censor her self-naming represents the pressure that a young, Black woman feels to suppress the expression of her culture in a hostile society.

Language is not the only area in which Cuthbert causes Margaret to censor herself. Her father also discourages her from expressing her views on aspects of Black culture that challenge his old-fashioned ideas. When he discovers she is planning to do a school project on Rastafarian culture and reggae music, Cuthbert objects: "He went on and on about how Rastas were criminal, and how they gave decent, hardworking Coloured People ... a bad name; how they smoked dope, and how their music was primitive" (40). While Cuthbert may feel his traditional conceptions are threatened by this new wave of Black culture, his objections are typical of what a White Eurocentric critic might say about this culture, especially in calling its music primitive (as we have seen in her poem "African Majesty," Philip rejects this reductionist epithet applied to Black art). It is as if, once again, his sensitivity to how White society views Blacks has caused him to imbibe its stereotypes. The result of Cuthbert's intransigence is Margaret's self-censorship: "Never mind Dad, I'm not going to do the project" (41). This incident in the novel is about more than just the quashing of a school project, however. Dub poet Lillian Allen writes extensively about the importance of reggae music as a tool for the liberation of expression in Jamaica: "It subverted the complex and subtle structure of censorship under capitalism, a structure maintained by the imposition of class-based and racially-based standards for expression. These 'standards' conspire to negate, exclude and limit the possibilities for expression" (254). This role for reggae music is not limited to Jamaica. It has the same liberating powers for Blacks in Canada as well. As Allen adds, "Those of us working in Toronto ... although thousands of miles from the source, discovered that our artistic responses were similar" (258). The subtle structure of free-speech restrictions Allen is talking about refers to the forms of socio-cultural censorship I have been discussing in this chapter. Margaret's self-censorship with regard to her project on reggae, a powerful tool with which to counter this censorship, represents the diminishment of Black discourse in Canadian society.

It should be noted that, despite the various ways Margaret and her mother are shown to censor themselves, by the end of the novel, through their own determination and the help of their neighbour Bertha, they manage to have their voices heard and their opinions taken seriously. Margaret's mother stands up to Cuthbert in their final confrontation; she insists he allow her to speak and does so in her naturally inflected English: "'You let me talk Cuthbert Cruickshank.' I couldn't believe this was my mother – she who would let my father go on and on. 'You let me talk. I sick and tired of listening to you carry on about what *you* know'" (137). She wins the argument, which allows Margaret to go to Tobago with her friend Zulma, whom Margaret has been trying to help return home throughout the novel. Seeing her plans realized, her mother liberated, and her father put in his place gives Margaret a sense of efficacy, a sense that she now has the power to speak and act. She no longer feels the need to be someone else, no longer feels the need to be Harriet, who had the power to speak out against repression; she reclaims her name, Margaret (though, with a nod to her newfound sense of African identity, foresees taking an African name in the future) (130). By ending the novel on a triumphant note, Philip suggests that, though many Blacks are still subject to self-censorship because of old-fashioned and racist currents in our society, there is hope that they will gain their voices in the future.

THE INEVITABILITY OF CENSORSHIP

The study of literature by Native and Black Canadian writers reveals that these writers and critics of their work identify several forms of socio-cultural censorship that serve to silence their voices. The education they receive in this country tends to erase their links to their culture, most notably in the areas of history and language. Native and Black writers trying to disseminate their work find impediments in cultural gatekeepers such as publishers, editors of anthologies, and award-granting and arts-funding bodies. They also feel they are censored when White writers appropriate their culture by producing writing about or from the perspective of Native or Black characters that displaces their own writing from the literary marketplace. Finally, Native and Black writers censor themselves. Sometimes this self-censorship is performed in deference to the demands of other members of the minority group itself. More often, though, it is the intentional or unconsciously internalized adoption of mainstream values that leads marginalized writers to alter the form or content of, or even fully suppress, the expression of their views.

My goal in identifying these forms of socio-cultural censorship is to confirm my contention that, in a liberal, capitalist society in which competition plays a paramount role, censorship is inevitable. Now it may be argued that the forms of socio-cultural censorship I have identified are products of racism and sexism, and that these evils should not be accepted as unavoidable in our society. This is true, and I am certainly not arguing that the censorship of Native and Black writers that occurs for these reasons is acceptable. I used the comments and texts of marginalized writers merely to show that these forms of censorship exist. If we accept that they do, then we must acknowledge that eliminating racism or sexism will not do away with socio-cultural censorship. For censorship is the act of exclusion of some discourse, not the racism or sexism that causes such an exclusionary act. A publisher who is able to put aside the racism that is the reason behind his refusal to publish a Native writer may still decide not to publish that writer on other grounds, such as "merit," or the fact that his particular readership will not buy the book. As Philip reminds us, both of these rationales take their substance from the ideologies to which the publisher or readership ascribes. While ideologies can shift or be changed, while mainstream publishers can institute affirmative-action plans or alternative publishers gain more power in the marketplace, ideologically based choices about what is published – and therefore what is not published – will never disappear.[26] The same argument pertains to discrimination among discourses in education. It also applies to self-censorship, which would continue regardless of the presence of racism or sexism because there will always be some discourse that will be ideologically unfashionable (even if, in a profoundly liberal society, it was one that decried tolerance).

So if these various kinds of socio-cultural suppression are indeed kinds of censorship and are integral to the workings of our society, then there is little point in arguing about whether or not censorship, as a principle, is acceptable or desirable. There is also little point in condemning all instances of censorship: no teaching would get done and no books would be published were these condemnations acted upon. More realistic is the position that acknowledges the inevitability of censorship and grapples with the ideologies, the contexts, motivating various instances of censorship in an attempt to distinguish between the reasonable and the unreasonable. So while a publisher who rejects a Native manuscript without even glancing at it most probably merits our disapprobation, the publisher who reads the manuscript and rejects it on other grounds must be considered more carefully, together with the context of that rejection. If the manuscript is dismissed on grounds of quality, what is the standard against which it is being measured? How much can that standard be said to be objective, and how much does it rely on dominant cultural forces? What is the relative weighting of the value of publishing high-quality texts compared to the importance of reserving a forum for Native writers? This last question entails consideration of how much the publishing company is simply a money-making enterprise and how much of a responsibility it owes to writers and readers; it also calls for an analysis of what other publishing vehicles would be available for this writer (for example, small or alternative presses). All these questions would need to be answered before judgment could be passed on whether this instance of publishing censorship was justified or not.

I do not believe that the kind of socio-cultural censorship practised by publishers or educators or White writers who write from a Black perspective is different in kind from the censorship of a pornographic movie by a film board or the banning of a novel in a high school. In all these cases people make ideologically motivated choices to prevent the dissemination of some discourse. In fact, belief systems are at play whenever a decision to censor something is made. Thus, just as we would not condemn outright, without looking at the context of the situation, a publisher who decides not to publish a particular book or a teacher who chooses not to teach a particular novel or a particular history lesson, we should not prejudge any case involving censorship by automatically invoking the sanctity of free speech. In every case of censorship, context is crucial. Exactly what is entailed in establishing this context and who should be entrusted with establishing it are the subjects of the Conclusion of this book.

6 Conclusion: Towards a More "Just" Judgment

In the course of examining censorship issues raised, both explicitly and implicitly, in English Canadian literature, I have identified several different arguments that Canadian writers make against censorship and have tried to show that their flaws render them incapable of sustaining a position that opposes censorship on principle. Two of these arguments, which Findley makes implicitly in *Headhunter*, are the non-consequentialist and consequentialist arguments for free speech. The non-consequentialist argument claims that free speech has intrinsic worth for society and that censorship, which infringes on free speech, is therefore detrimental. The problem with this argument is that whenever its proponents attempt to explain why free speech is *inherently* good, they inevitably do so by describing what free speech is good *for* (it furthers democracy, gives rise to "truth," etc.). In other words, the non-consequentialist position consistently slides into a consequentialist one, in which censorship is attacked on the grounds of its preventing the potential benefits of free speech in society. This consequentialist argument is presented in *Headhunter* as well, but is weakened by the novel's illustration that speech can lead to extremely destructive ends as well as to beneficial ones.

We see the very destructive ends of some discourse in *Headhunter* in the effect that Slade's paintings have on Kurtz and, through him, on the abused children in the novel; but we see it even more strikingly in *Bodily Harm* in the damage that pornography does to women. In that novel Atwood traces the effects of pornography from its influence on pornographic "art" to its connection to male fantasy and violence, to its instigation of violence in general. Laurence, too, contends that pornography is a "greater evil" than censorship, that it does harm both to the women (and children) involved in its making and to women who are demeaned and subjected to violence by the men who consume it. I take the position that it is admirable to protect speech that is beneficial to society, but that we should consider censorship of speech that clearly does harm.

It is all very well to want to protect "good" speech and censor "bad," but where does one draw the line? This is the slippery-slope argument, which both Findley and Atwood invoke in their fiction: once a society begins to regulate discourse, there is no natural place to stop, and the end result is tyranny. I reject this argument because I see it more as an exercise in abstract rhetoric than as a description of the way decision-making unfolds in practice. In reality we do draw lines (or use judgment) in deciding what is acceptable and what is unacceptable. When one human being kills another, for example, we condemn it as murder if it is done with cold-blooded intent. If, however, it is done through negligence, we call it manslaughter and impose a milder punishment. Both self-defence and insanity are considered valid reasons for a killer to be found "innocent" of a capital crime, though a killing has taken place. We do not refrain from imposing heavy penalties on murderers out of a fear of sliding down a slippery slope to a point where we will feel obliged to impose the same penalties on those who kill in self-defence. Judgment allows us to discriminate among the different contexts of different cases. By the same token, we should not be afraid that practising some censorship will lead to the indiscriminate censorship of any (or of all) discourse.

Moreover, in warning us not to *start* practising censorship, the slippery-slope argument assumes that we do not *already* practise censorship. The fact is that censorship occurs in many areas of our society in many forms that we would not want or would not be able to eradicate. The makers of the film version of *The Wars* censored Findley's work when they cut key scenes from the movie; but it would be absurd to advocate the removal of their right to practise such censorship. The demands of the capitalist marketplace end up censoring Rennie, in *Bodily Harm*, by making it difficult for her to sell her socially conscientious journalism; but, short of the complete abolition of the capitalist system, this kind of censorship is an ineluctable element of our society. The same can be said of socio-cultural censorship, which I explored at length in my last chapter in order to show that censorship takes place when educators exclude certain languages and histories; when cultural gatekeepers prevent the dissemination of discourse; when mainstream artists appropriate the voices of marginalized artists; and when artists suppress their own voices. As long as competition among social groups is a feature of our society (and it always will be as long as we retain democratic principles), socio-cultural censorship will occur.

Once we acknowledge that we *do* practise censorship and that it is an inevitable part of our relations with one another, the debate over whether we should eliminate it gives way to the question of *how* to practise censorship in the most constructive way. Throughout this book I have stressed the importance of making censorship judgments more "just." I would like now to specify what I mean by "justice" within this context and offer some suggestions towards applying the concept to censorship disputes.

"JUSTICE"

When I say that we must strive to resolve censorship disputes in a "just" manner, I mean that we should aim for carefully considered deliberation that leads to the "best" decisions possible, for it is often a lack of such informed decision-making that results in injustice. An example of the kind of justice I am describing is the judgment process a jury is supposed to undertake in a court of law. In that process the jury is expected to be fair and equitable (indeed, those considered unable to be reasonable are eliminated early on in the selection procedure), which means that each party to the dispute is given an adequate opportunity to present reasons for its beliefs, and these reasons are considered without prejudice (in so far as that is realistically possible). I believe judgments in censorship disputes should be characterized by their aspirations towards the same kind of fairness and equity. More importantly, a jury tries to render verdicts that are consistent with a consensus among its members concerning what is morally right. In making their decisions, jury members may concede the non-existence of any moral absolutes, but this does not deter them from making judgments that, in their eyes, are the best ones possible. I believe that there are "best" decisions to be made in censorship conflicts as well. There will never be an absolute, objective standard or principle against which we can measure discourse to determine if it is acceptable. But that does not mean that we must rule out judging altogether and allow all manner of discourse; for some judgments are better than others. How can we undertake to make the best or most just censorship judgments possible? What follows are a few suggestions.

SET THE BAR HIGH

First, I want to make it clear that, in rejecting the position of those who stand against censorship on principle, I am not diminishing the importance of free speech. As with all aspects of human endeavour,

I believe society should step in to regulate people's activities only when it is truly necessary to do so. The accused in a criminal court of law is considered innocent until proven guilty and can be convicted only if the evidence against him is beyond a shadow of a doubt. The same stringent tests should have to be satisfied in censorship cases before any discourse is banned. (The Canadian Charter of Rights and Freedoms echoes this approach as it guarantees the "freedom of thought, belief, opinion and expression," making them "subject only to such reasonable limits prescribed by law as can be demonstrably justified in a free and democratic society.")[1] Rather than devaluing free speech, I believe this attitude towards censorship actually gives expression a more prized place in our constellation of values; for a society that admits that it censors but strives to do so openly and only when absolutely necessary will have a more credible position on free speech than one that pretends it is against *all* censorship, but allows it to happen willy-nilly.

CONTEXT IS CRUCIAL

In addition to setting the bar high when contemplating whether to censor some discourse, careful consideration must be given to the context surrounding that discourse. Just as there are many circumstances of legal cases – the reliability of evidence; the intent of the accused; the disposition of the victim, to name only a few – that are central to the adjudication of these cases, there are also a large number of contextual factors that are key to the successful settlement of censorship controversies. I will not attempt to enumerate all of these factors here – in fact, there are probably as many as there are censorship controversies – but I do want to discuss a few of the more critical ones. One is the composition of the audience that receives the discourse under dispute. The impact or influence of the discourse may vary according to different audiences, making censorship appropriate in some cases, inappropriate in others. The British government, for example, allows Orangemen to march in Protestant areas of Northern Ireland to express their anti-republican views, but has recently stepped in to prevent marches in Catholic areas, knowing that, before a Catholic audience, the Orangemen's message is an incitement to violence. This is appropriate censorship.[2] Censorship will also often be appropriate when the audience is children. That we go to considerable lengths to protect children from discourse that is openly available to adults suggests that the composition of the audience is an important factor in censorship disputes.[3]

In addition to considering who is *receiving* certain discourse, we should also pay attention to who is *producing* it. The position of a speaker in society – whether the speaker is a member of a mainstream or a marginalized group, for instance – can be relevant in resolving questions about censorship. It is acceptable for a Black comedian to poke fun at the Black community (as Loury says, he has "cover"), but a White comedian knows it is unacceptable for him to make such jokes and will now usually censor himself. The "identity politics" involved in deciding who is allowed to speak on certain issues are obviously complex, but consideration of the identity of the speaker as a contextual factor is justified by the different histories and access to power possessed by different speakers. Another example that illustrates the importance of *who* is speaking is the "Son of Sam" legislation, a law passed by the Canadian Parliament but quashed by the Senate in the spring of 1998 ("Pulp Fiction," D6). This law held that profits from the sale of writing by violent criminals are to be seized and held by a public trustee; this money would be used to pay damages to the victims of these criminals should they decide to sue. While it is true that the law was poorly worded and overly broad, its primary goal, to prevent serial murderers and rapists from profiting from their crimes, is admirable and an example of censorship that is justified by the identity of the producer of discourse.[4]

A third contextual factor that should be considered when it is relevant is the harm a particular discourse is likely to cause. Unlike criminal court cases, however, in which there is a clear victim, when it comes to the effects of a certain discourse it is not always easy to determine whether members of society suffer from the dissemination of that discourse. Studies are most often cited by both sides in the censorship dispute over pornography. I have not relied on this scientific research because, so far, it has proved to be contradictory and inconclusive.[5] But as practitioners of social science develop more precise tools and a more reliable body of evidence is accumulated in this relatively young field of research, scientific study of the effects of discourses such as pornography may play a larger role in determining which forms of expression should be excluded from society.

The most important contextual factor in censorship controversies is the nature of the discourse in question. Our society rightly values certain kinds of speech over others. Political discourse, for example – narrowly defined as the public exchange of ideas about the management of the state – is considered to be deserving of a higher degree of protection than non-political discourse. One of the most vigorous formulations of this idea is by First Amendment scholar Alexander Meiklejohn: "The guarantee given by the First Amendment ... is assured only to speech which bears, directly or indirectly, upon issues with which voters have to deal – only, therefore, to the consideration of matters of public interest. Private speech, or private interest in speech, on the other hand, has no claim whatever to the protection of the First Amendment" (94). Meiklejohn's contention that non-political speech has *no* claim to protection is rather extreme, but his distinction between different levels of speech is correct. False advertising, threats, private libel, and shouting "fire" in a crowded theatre are examples of non-political speech we do not (and should not) have any qualms about censoring. In fact there are many distinctions we can make when it comes to classifying forms of expression. A pornographic film, such as *Deep Throat*, is distinct from both a documentary film about the pornography industry, such as *Not a Love Story*, and a collection of erotic drawings, such as those produced by Toronto artist Eli Langer (and, for that matter, from novels such as *The Wars* and *The Diviners*). The latter distinction, namely that between pornography and art, is not always an easy one, but I believe it can usually be made. My last recommendation for improving censorship judgments is a suggestion for making the process of distinguishing among different discourses more reliable.

EMPLOY EXPERTISE

The single most useful change we could effect in the way we deal with censorship disputes would be to make use of the expertise possessed by those trained in interpreting discourse. I would invoke the courtroom analogy once again to point out that many of the key players in any legal trial are experts in their field: the lawyers are skilled in reading law and making arguments; expert witnesses are frequently called to testify about some aspect of the trial; and the judge is trained in the parsing and application of legal arguments and the fair proceeding of the trial. When it comes to judging some text, who would qualify as an expert in a case of potential censorship? Anyone who has appreciable experience and knowledge in dealing with texts would be a valuable contributor. Among other things, this person should be able to recognize when a text is being ironic; he or she should be able to tell when certain passages in a work (such as sex scenes) are integral parts of a larger whole (as in *The Diviners*) and when they are the *raison d'être* of the work (as in erotica); and he or she should be familiar with characteristics of literature – complexity of character, theme, style, etc. – that set it apart from other forms of discourse, such as pornography. These abilities are all skills practised and taught in English departments at universities across the country. Graduate students and English professors are too often accused of inhabiting an ivory tower, of being out of touch with the practical realities of our society; I believe that censorship disputes offer them the perfect opportunity to apply the skills they have acquired and, in so doing, contribute to censorship judgments that are more just.

I would like to end by showing how the suggestions I have made in this Conclusion could be applied in real censorship controversies. The two cases I have chosen are substantially different from one another. The first, involving Little Sister's Bookstore, is an example of censorship of a traditional nature – that is, the overt and intentional prevention of the dissemination of discourse by government authorities. The second case, involving Lynn Crosbie's book *Paul's Case*, illustrates the kind of opposition to free speech that may not fall within the narrow purview of the traditional definition but that is, I have been arguing, a more pervasive, frequently as controversial, and above all very real form of censorship. Despite their differences, these two cases show that attention to context and expertise can help to mitigate censorship "stand-offs" that are often drawn-out and painful to both sides, and can aid in achieving more fair solutions.

LITTLE SISTER'S

In the fall of 1994 the British Columbia Supreme Court began hearing a trial in which Vancouver's Little Sister's Bookstore challenged the power of Canada Customs to seize and destroy books at the border. According to *Restricted Entry: Censorship on Trial*, a book that makes the case for Little Sister's, the bookstore based its challenge on two arguments: first, that Canada Customs practised its censorship unfairly, singling out gay and lesbian bookstores for harassment; and second, that censorship of any sort practised at the border was wrong because it violated Canadians' right to freedom of speech (Fuller, 15). In January 1996 the court agreed with the first argument and ordered Canada Customs to make its screening procedure more equitable; the court rejected the second argument, however, maintaining that, while the powers of seizure violated the right to free speech spelled out in the Charter of Rights and Freedoms, this violation was justified. This ruling was upheld by the BC Court of Appeal in June 1998 and by the Supreme Court of Canada in December 2000.

The court rulings were correct. The complainants in the case were able to demonstrate that Canada Customs discriminated against gay and lesbian publications and against particular gay and lesbian bookstores – an example given at the trial was that Canada Customs regularly detained gay political newspapers and magazines such as *New York Native* and *The Advocate*, "but only in shipments to Little Sister's and Glad Day. Other Canadian newsstands and bookstores imported the same materials with impunity" (Fuller, 12). That Canada Customs was biased, however, proved only that the way it censored was faulty, not that border censorship itself was wrong. Little Sister's decided to make the latter argument, that border censorship should be eliminated altogether, by taking an absolutist anti-censorship stand: participants in the trial committed to the Little Sister's side claimed that they were "passionately opposed to censorship" (Fuller, xvi). As I have argued, however, the position against censorship on principle is very difficult to maintain: there will always be exceptions to such a stance. The owners of Little Sister's Bookstore, for example, "drew their own, very strict line by refusing to stock child pornography of any sort, as well as materials depicting violence against women" (Fuller, 13). The courts recognized that advocates for Little Sister's were using freedom of speech as a broad shield to try to protect the particular speech in which they were interested, and correctly ruled that gay and lesbian expression could be protected without having to allow all publications, including the truly noxious ones, into the country.

While I agree with the court rulings, I believe that the many years of acrimonious wrangling between gay and lesbian bookstores and Canada Customs and the numerous and costly court challenges – Little Sister's first took Canada Customs to court in 1990, ten years before the final decision by the Supreme Court – could have been avoided had some of the recommendations I have made above been in place. First, expert readers, not Customs officials, should decide which texts are allowed to enter Canada. Customs officials generally do not have the formal interpretive training and experience necessary to judge texts. They will not be aware of the many contextual factors – the intended audience of the text, the background of its producer, its potential harm, and, most importantly, the clues that determine the nature of the text (whether it is pornography or art, for example) – that must be considered in contemplating censorship. One of the Customs officials testifying in the Little Sister's case, Frank Lorito, admitted as much when he related his experience with Kathy Acker's novel *Empire of the Senseless*. The book had been detained at the border, but Lorito, in charge of hearing appeals, was sent scholarly commentaries and reviews of the novel by the owner of a gay and lesbian bookshop in Montreal. Lorito testified that he was impressed by this material (he eventually released the book) because he did not feel he was "really well versed in literary [matters], but when someone tells you that it has literary merit and they're experts in the field, then I think you pay attention to what they say" (quoted in Fuller, 131).

Had textual experts been in charge when the publications destined for Little Sister's came to the border, they would likely have recognized the contextual factors that render these publications acceptable in Canada. They would have read the signs that distinguish a book such as *Empire of the Senseless*, which depicts sexual abuse of women in order to combat it, from pornographic works that advocate sexual abuse. Being cognizant of the importance of *who* produces certain discourse and *for whom*, they would have realized that, because of history, the portrayal of violence and of domination and submission in gay and lesbian publications is very different from their portrayal in "straight" pornography. In the latter the violence is almost always perpetrated by men against women. This material frequently, if implicitly, reaffirms the view of women as subordinate objects to be used and abused. There is a justified fear that it contributes to harm against women in real life. No such fear arises from the dissemination of sexually explicit gay and lesbian publications.

With the Little Sister's material, experts of the sort I am calling for would have set the bar high before censoring any discourse. Certainly they would not have literally judged a book by its cover or censored it based on a few racy passages taken out of context (as some Customs officials were known to do: Fuller, 129). They would have been well aware of the defences open to controversial publications based on claims of artistic or political significance, and they would have had the tools to substantiate or dispel those claims. At the same time, they would have been familiar with which kinds of discourse have been found to have harmful effects on society and which have not, and would have weighted this factor accordingly in the overall evaluation of each publication under examination. In the end, I suspect, expert readers would have banned very little, if any, of the material in question in the Little Sister's controversy. Their decisions would have been more dependable than those of Customs officials because of their expertise, and more defendable than the arguments offered by Little Sister's, because their decisions would have relied on judgments of individual concrete texts rather than the broad, abstract, and ultimately untenable principle of free speech.

CROSBIE'S CASE

As this is a study of censorship of and in Canadian *literature*, I think it is fitting to conclude with a case that, like Laurence's ordeal with

The Diviners, represents the myriad of ways in which Canadian writers are constantly being involved in censorship controversies across the country. On 22 April 1999 in Toronto, at a fund-raising event for PEN Canada, an organization that promotes freedom of expression – the irony of this case has been lost on no one – a reading from Lynn Crosbie's *Paul's Case* became the locus of debate over censorship. The passages read from Crosbie's 1997 work – a literary exploration of the crimes of Paul Bernardo and Karla Homolka – evoked several oppositional responses among the audience. While we cannot necessarily attribute censorious motivations to those who left the hall in protest during the reading (Kelly, A7), those members of the audience who called out "Enough!" (Stoffman, D14) were clearly voicing a censoring impulse, as was the person who said afterward that "he thought the book should not have been read" (Saunders, C1). In fact, according to journalist Doug Saunders, "some organizers had tried to cancel the reading, until other performers threatened to withdraw" (C1), a point confirmed by the author. Thus, while no censorship actually took place in the reading of passages from *Paul's Case*, an attempt was made, and, more important, the articles and letters that made up the discussion of the controversy after the fact took the form of a debate about censorship.

I emphasize that the resulting debate was about censorship and not really about *Paul's Case*. It often happens with censorship controversies that, with little regard for specifics of the case, for its context, a dispute over some discourse quickly becomes abstracted to a debate over the broadly opposing principles of free speech and censorship. Doug Saunders led the charge in this debate by defending the reading of Crosbie's book on the (neutralist) grounds – on which we have also seen Findley rely – that free speech should be absolute: "True supporters of free speech," he writes, "after all, must support most staunchly those works that they most detest. The principles are meaningless if they apply only to forms of expression you find agreeable" (C1). Interestingly, Saunders takes his absolutist argument to its extreme logical ends when he suggests that the Crosbie reading serve merely as a jumping-off point, arguing: "each year, the PEN organizers should offer a reading from a work likely to offend its audience, perhaps by a person who is widely detested. Ernst Zundel should read from *Mein Kampf*. Phillippe Rushton should read from his noxious theories on race and brain size. Child-porn advocate John Robin Sharpe should read a few of his favourite tales" (C1). These examples are usually cited by critics of the absolutist stance as the absurd ends to which this position leads, but Saunders puts forth his ideas without the least sense of irony. Few, of course, would take Saunders' provocative ideas seriously (even Sandra Martin, PEN's incoming president at the time, dismisses them [c1]), but they illustrate how far from the discourse in question (here *Paul's Case*) censorship debates often stray.

   The letters written in response to Saunders' column were no more relevant to Crosbie's work. In defending the book, its editor, Michael Holmes, contends that because the author earlier had been subject to attack – he cites threats of physical violence and lawsuits – the reading was appropriate (c1). In essence he takes the neutralist position that ignores the actual content of the material in question, instead arguing, like Saunders, that the absolute nature of free speech is best demonstrated by the defence of expression that someone finds offensive. At the same time, the only letter taking the opposing view, written by one of the offended audience members, also relies on a discourse of "rights" and "freedoms," terms usually indicative of an argument based on principles rather than specifics. The letter states: "We were a captive audience who paid to support writers' freedoms where rights are denied, not to listen to offensive material" (Morrison, c1). While this commentator comes close to identifying a contextual feature of the reading – the position of the audience as "captive," which I consider below – his conclusion that "our freedom to choose what to read or listen to was violated" is empty without reference to what features gave the passages their offensive character and what distinguished the offensiveness of Crosbie's work from that of other material (all of which was being read *because* it had offended someone). It is to these kinds of contextual factors that I now turn to try to make some sense of this censorship controversy.

   One important contextual element is the particular relationship between the audience and the discourse in question, namely *Paul's Case*. By way of introduction to the reading, the audience probably would have been given some idea of the kind of book Crosbie had written. The work has been called a novel, but its fifty-two fragmentary chapters – which range from letters to cartoons to word puzzles – along with explanatory endnotes and a bibliography place it squarely in the genre of avant-garde literature. In her preface Crosbie announces: "This is a critical enterprise, an exploration of the crimes of Paul Bernardo and Karla Homolka as a work of historical fiction" (viii). Crosbie's choice of subject for her book may have made some audience members nervous from the start. After all, it was less than four years earlier that Paul Bernardo had been sentenced to life in prison after a notorious trial that made public details of his crimes that horrified the nation. How much more sensitive would a Toronto audience be to the treatment of these events, given that the shocking sex slayings of teenagers Leslie Mahaffy and Kristen French had occurred not more than a few hundred kilometres from where the reading was taking place. Thus the proximity (both in time and space) of the audience to the painful circumstances of the Bernardo crimes may have contributed to the offence felt by members of the audience.

In his column Saunders confirms this point, distinguishing between *Paul's Case* and other potentially offensive works: "Plenty of books, of course, contain scenes as harrowing as *Paul's Case* does ... But what troubled us was the fact that Crosbie's scenes were local. They described events with which the audience was deeply familiar, ones we tend to regard as sacrosanct and untouchable" (c1). Rather than sympathizing with those members of the audience who felt as if "burial plots [were] being desecrated," however, Saunders argues: "That was precisely the point behind the reading. It offended us" (c1). Like his questionable support for public readings of the works of Holocaust deniers and child pornographers, Saunders' defence of discourse that is more offensive because it is local rests on his desire to prove his commitment to free speech. But this is like telling a man to go out and murder to prove that he is free. I think it makes more sense to see the proximity of *Paul's Case* as a factor in determining the appropriateness of the PEN readings, in the same way that writers about the Holocaust felt a respectable amount of time needed to elapse before they tackled their subject, and in the same way that proximity to Catholics makes Orange parades in Drumcree very different from their marches in other parts of Northern Ireland.

If one key contextual factor in the PEN controversy is that some members of the audience were understandably sensitive to the passages being read, the second important element is the nature of the passages themselves. The two most controversial passages are "Mahaffy" and "Pornography." The first is a fictional diary entry by the fourteen-year-old victim Leslie Mahaffy on the night (14 June 1991) she is abducted. She finds herself locked out of her house after she returns late from a wake for a friend killed in a car accident, and repairs to the local corner store to record her thoughts. What strikes the reader about this passage, which one would expect to elicit the sympathy of the reader/audience, is the way Crosbie focuses so intently on Mahaffy's juvenile delinquency. Leslie begins her diary entry by noting that she has "just ripped off" (*Paul's Case*, 62) some candy from the store for her brother Ryan. The party she has just left was broken up by the police "after the fire we made got into the trees." Further vandalism is suggested by her carving "I Will Love You Always on a tree with Kelly's knife." At that party, she writes, "We were all drinking beer, and Mike was passing around that purple grass he calls Barney." She notes that she has been "wasted" in the past and in trouble with her parents, and adds: "I know they're both really mad at me now and I'm screwed because I reek of dope and it's really late" (62).

Characterizations of the real Leslie Mahaffy in reports about the Bernardo crimes generally agree that the teen was troubled, but the details vary: in his analysis of media coverage of the case Frank Davey traces the evolution of her image from "suspected runaway and shoplifter" to her later characterization, by Mr Justice Francis Kovacs (judge in the Homolka trial), as a girl "who lived beyond reproach" (32). Crosbie seems to have accepted the most negative depictions. Moreover, a closer analysis of "Mahaffy" suggests that the author has manipulated the various kinds of misdemeanours associated with the teenager so that examples of each of them occur on the night of her abduction. In reality on that night Leslie did not steal from the corner store; she had been arrested for shoplifting a cassette tape about two months earlier (Burnside, 21). While, according to some accounts, the real Leslie had been involved with alcohol and drugs in the past (Williams, 167), all agree she exhibited considerable self-discipline in the weeks leading up to her abduction (Williams, 169; Burnside, 22). Paul Bernier, one of Leslie's friends who was at the party described in the diary entry, reports that her drinking that night was minimal: "If she ever drank, it would be one, maybe two beers, maybe every other party" (Appleby, D3). No records of that party mention drugs. Furthermore, Crosbie takes a couple of incidents that did occur at the party and alters them in ways that make the teenager seem more disreputable. According to the book by Stephen Williams, a tree was set ablaze by a spark from "the fire the *guys* had built" (my italics), but there is no evidence that Leslie was directly involved, as Crosbie's description (in which it is "the fire we made") suggests. Also, Leslie did not carve her message to her dead friend into a tree, but wrote it harmlessly on a large rock (Appleby, D3).

There are two ways of viewing Crosbie's "fictionalizing" of Leslie Mahaffy's last night of freedom to focus on the teenager's misdeeds. In the most damning view, as Davey writes of early newspaper reports of a similar emphasis, "the weight of these stories was to suggest that Mahaffy had been to some extent responsible for her own death, courting danger, living on the margins of criminality, and making it difficult for parents or police to protect her" (31). I think it is more likely that Crosbie, like any artist, was trying to convey an essence of Mahaffy's character – which in her eyes was a troubled one – and, constrained by the form of the diary entry, which generally limits the narrative to the day's events, felt it necessary to concentrate the negative much more than might otherwise be necessary. Motivations aside, the point here is that the focus on Mahaffy's transgressions distracts from what is crucial in the girl's involvement in the Bernardo affair: her role as victim. While this misconstruction may be compensated for by other passages when the book is read as a whole, it is easy to see why, as the only portrait of Leslie Mahaffy at a public reading, the audience would feel a disservice was being done to her memory and object.

The second controversial passage, "Pornography," takes the form of an imagined letter by a female guard at the prison in which Bernardo is incarcerated. This letter is written for a fictional pornographic publication at its behest: "If it's nasty, send it in and turn our readers on!" (*Paul's Case*, 54). The letter is, to put it mildly, nasty, rivalling the explicit language and graphic sex scenes of the most extreme real pornographic magazine. By way of setting the scene for her letter, the guard begins by describing the normal tenor of her practices in the prison: "I spend a lot of time during my breaks frigging off after escorting some of these buffed and sex-starved specimens to the showers. I watch them, naturally, oozing into my panties as they soap their cock-shafts and piss-slits, their big hairy balls. I practically drool imagining all the cum they could shoot, but I'm all business when I'm with them (although I sometimes let them get a load of my full, milky tits when I bend down with the leg-irons)" (54). Imagine the 1,200 PEN members sitting in Roy Thompson Hall in Toronto – some of whom are already a bit jittery just from the fact that the book being read dredges up memories of Bernardo's disturbing crimes – being assaulted with this material. Yet this is only the beginning. The guard then embarks on a description, in equally explicit detail occupying several paragraphs, of the sadistic sexual acts to which she claims to have subjected Bernardo. Here is an excerpt: "He lay against the cot and spread his ass cheeks while I put on some of my favourite spiked rings. I ran my hand over my dripping gash and rammed my fist up his ass while ripping at his foreskin with my long fingernails. Meanwhile, I was straddling his legs and cumming like crazy as he bucked against me, his face buried in the pillows" (55). The guard will go on to talk of a noose around Bernardo's neck and "golden showers," but it is not difficult to see why, even by this point, at least one member of the audience would be prepared to call out "Enough!"

I am not advocating the censorship of Crosbie's book because it contains a passage like "Pornography." I acknowledge the possibility that the prison guard's letter is meant to embody the feelings of violent revenge many people secretly harbour towards Paul Bernardo. But it is one thing to indulge in this fantasy while reading in private, quite another to be exposed without warning or choice – to be "captive," according to the audience member quoted above – to pornographic material read aloud as part of a group exercise. It is the difference between enjoying one's sexual fantasies, however explicit, in private and the embarrassing and potentially painful sharing of those fantasies with friends and colleagues sitting nearby. The other difference between the private and public reading of "Pornography" is that, as with "Mahaffy," the former allows for the contextualizing of the passage, whereas the latter does not. Crosbie obviously means her fifty-two fragments – letters sent to Bernardo every week for a year, according to the book's cover blurb – to work as a whole, and this structure will imbue "Pornography" with a particular meaning, even if it is merely that this is one perspective and voice among many. But in the bald and deracinated public reading, in which the passage is one of very few read, this meaning will be lost, leaving the passage little more than an embodiment of its title.

This last distinction leads us to the question of why "Pornography" was chosen by PEN organizers to be read at all. It is not a representative passage in either perspective or language. Divorced from its context, it adds nothing to our understanding of the Bernardo crimes, neither enlarging on the events that took place nor exploring the motivations of the criminals or the feelings of the victims. As a reflection of the public's mood it misses the mark, as it sooner evokes disgust and embarrassment than emotional identity. Perhaps this last point is a clue to the choice of "Pornography" as a reading, for its effect, more than anything, is to shock. If the passage was read *because* it gives offence, then its selection, like Saunders' support of Zundel, was misguided. A public reading should not be a contest to see whose commitment to free speech is closest to an absolute principle (such a ploy is especially insulting to an audience of PEN supporters) but to show the value of a particular piece of writing: almost fifty other passages from Crosbie's book would have served this purpose better.

Had the recommendations I am making about contextual considerations been at the forefront of the decision-making process in the two cases I have studied here, I suspect they would have had beneficial results. In the Little Sister's affair, they likely would have rendered the long and costly legal proceedings unnecessary. In the case of the PEN reading, consideration of the context – of both the audience and the work – should have led to other passages' being chosen, thereby precluding the offence that was given to the audience and avoiding the protracted quarrel among the players in the controversy that resulted. I believe that censorship disputes in general would be resolved more easily and more fairly were these suggestions widely adopted. By foregrounding the context of each work in censorship disputes and bringing to bear as many sophisticated interpretive skills as possible, censorship will not be eliminated, but the judgments rendered in cases of censorship will be more reasonable. I do not pretend that I have provided a comprehensive explanation of *how* to make censorship judgments more just. That has not been the goal of this book. I do hope, however, I have shown it is the search for ways of making censorship judgments more just, and not the abstract debate over the evils of censorship, that is where the real work is to be done.

Notes

1 Discussion of censorship in areas of Canadian culture other than literature is limited as well. The most extensive of such discussions, produced
almost exclusively after 1985, appear in writing on pornography. See,
for example, Burstyn, Clark, Cole, Cossman, Kirsten Johnson, Dany
Lacombe, and McCormack. One of the first book-length academic studies of censorship in Canadian culture more generally, *Interpreting Censorship in Canada*, edited by Klaus Peterson and Allan C. Hutchinson,
appeared in 1999.
2 The most extensive of these is *Mind War: Book Censorship in English
Canada*, by Peter Birdsall and Delores Broten. Also see the special issue
of *Canadian Children's Literature* (vol. 68, 1992) as well as Schrader and
Jenkinson.

CHAPTER ONE

1 For a more nuanced (if more ambiguous) argument in favour of the
Enlightenment definition, see Kathleen Sullivan, 39–40.
2 Stanley Fish makes a similar point about First Amendment rhetoric
when he claims that the words "free speech" have been appropriated
by the forces of neo-conservativism: "'Free speech' is just the name we
give to verbal behaviour that serves the substantive agendas we wish
to advance; and we give our preferred verbal behaviors that name
when we can, when we have the power to do so, because in the

rhetoric of American life, the label 'free speech' is the one you want your favorites to wear" (102).

3 For similar constructivist reasoning (though without the emphasis on power) in the realm of sociology see, for example, Bourdieu; in anthropology see Douglas; in the philosophy of science see Kuhn.

4 For arguments similar to Jansen's, see Marilyn French (169) and Schiller.

5 Nicholas Harrison, for example, views censorship as the government exercise of state secrecy or of extraordinary powers during war, but also sees it manifest in issues of "literacy, … education, racism, and structures of media ownership and finance" (4); Annabel Patterson recognizes "the subtle intersections of state censorship with self-censorship" (17); and in answer to his own questions, "What is censorship? What sort of material does it seek to suppress?" David Tribe replies, "almost anything" (17).

6 This definition takes discourse not just to mean verbal expression in speech or writing but to include all modes of signification – a common poststructural usage (M.H. Abrams, 241). My use of the term "ideological predisposition" is consistent with the meaning of "ideology" found in standard dictionaries: "a system of ideas or way of thinking, usually relating to politics or society, or to the conduct of a class or group, and regarded as justifying actions, especially one that is held implicitly or adopted as a whole" (*Canadian Oxford Dictionary*, 702). I explain its relationship to censorship more fully later in this introduction.

7 A similar example would be a case in which the federal government, in trying to censor the producer of pornography under obscenity law, was told by a court that it must permit the pornography under a freedom-of-expression provision. In this case the government would be trying both to express a view (pornography is bad) and to censor that view at the same time (through its judiciary agent's invoking the free-speech provision). This example shows that, contrary to Schauer's distinction, public censorship can be as self-contradictory as private censorship.

8 Controversy over this kind of censorship erupted in the United States in 1989 when some politicians demanded that the National Endowment for the Arts, a federal arts-funding body, deny funding based on the content of some artists' work. For a discussion of the controversy, see Atkins, 33–4; Hoekema, 48; Parachini, 10; Pindell, 20–3; and Kathleen Sullivan, 39.

9 For discussions of the subject in which self-censorship is equated with censorship, see Marilyn French, 169–70; Holquist, 15, 20; Lamarche, 56–8; and Patterson, 17. Danilo Kis's article "Censorship / Self-Censorship" makes a particularly strong argument for viewing self-censorship as an even more pervasive and powerful form of censorship

than the more direct, overt forms. Where I differ from most of these commentators, however, is in my rejection of the idea that "self-censorship inevitably leads to artistic and human catastrophes" (Kis, 45), in favour of the view that self-censorship is an inherent feature of human expressive practices performed sometimes for good reasons, sometimes for bad ones.

10 See Foucault, "What is an Author," and Barthes.

11 I explore some concrete suggestions for making censorship judgments more just in my conclusion.

CHAPTER TWO

1 Findley does not restrict his concern regarding censorship to the realm of literature but engages in debates involving incidents in other media as well. A good example is his defence of the controversial CBC documentary *The Valour and the Horror*, a film that depicts a reckless and sometimes barbaric Second World War Allied command: "If it were not controversial, it would be worthless; it would be mere propaganda," writes Findley. "What has become of freedom of expression?" ("Valour," 197–8).

2 No doubt there are other factors that have made this issue central to Findley, including the interesting biographical detail (which he recounts in an interview with William Whitehead) of a relative who, when Findley was a child, was relegated to a mental institution for voicing ideas that "tampered with the protective walls thrown up by other people to keep the hurt of reality out" ("Alice," 18). This episode, which Findley calls "the first truly profound experience of my consciousness" ("Alice," 17), has implications for our understanding of his novel *Headhunter*, which I will be exploring in the second part of this chapter.

3 Abbreviated references in the text are to archival material listed in the Bibliography, Archives, Findley Papers.

4 Also in the file 17-4 of Ms/TsN is another page 149, on which appears, "Then tear the tails off your shirts," with the word "fucking" added before "tails" by Findley by hand. The same phrasing as that cited above occurs in TsC, file 17-7:151 and TsO, file 17-10:151.

5 See also TsC, file 17-6:96.

6 See also TsO, file 17-10:169.

7 "Fuck" is not the only potentially controversial word removed or altered in the text. When Robert visits the Lousetown whorehouse, his companion for the evening, Ella, remonstrates against his sexual disinterest. In a draft manuscript she says: "Dontcha un'erstand – if you don't screw me I don't get paid!" (TsC, file 17-6:48). In the published

version "do" (43) appears in place of "screw." Once again, Findley may have made the change because he believed the prostitute would be less crass than the word "screw" connotes, but as the evidence accumulates, it supports a band of chaste-tongued characters less and a concern for non-offensive language more.

8 Findley certainly recognizes a difference between "classics" and the "mass market paperback" (quoted in Benson, 111). I suspect he would not see *The Wars* as a work of the latter category, in which profanity is more common.

9 The incidents I describe here are the most widely publicized attempts to censor Findley's work. In the course of my research I have come across other incidents, especially numerous, it seems, at high schools where *The Wars* is taught, to suppress his writing.

10 Some, like liberal legal expert Ronald Dworkin, call for changes to American law that would make it more difficult for private citizens to sue the media for libel. Dworkin's view rests on the argument that rigorous libel laws endanger free speech and that "any censorship on grounds of content is inconsistent with [our] commitment ... to individual moral responsibility" (58). Dworkin rightly sees libel law as a kind of censorship, but wrongly, I think, sees censorship as always a greater evil than the violation of privacy.

11 Perry Nodelman makes the same point in the service of the provocative and, to my mind, ultimately untenable libertarian argument that all children should have access to any material in which they are interested, "no matter how offensive, how narrowminded, how boneheaded, or how dangerous I might personally find it" (122).

12 The neutralist conception of liberalism I describe here has its origins in Enlightenment thinking about such qualities as liberty, equality, and justice, and maintains that these qualities will be maximized only when the individual is free from state interference. This liberal approach rejects censorship, arguing that "We retain our dignity, as individuals, only by insisting that no one – no official and no majority – has the right to withhold opinion from us on the ground that we are not fit to hear and consider it" (Ronald Dworkin, 57). For a comprehensive discussion situating the neutralist among other kinds of liberals, see Blattberg.

13 In fact, the comparison to birds is the most prominent metaphor Bradbury uses for his burning books. In the pivotal scene in which a woman is incinerated along with her books, "A book lit ... [is] like a white pigeon ... wings fluttering"; the books fall around the woman "like slaughtered birds" (34). When firefighters burn down the house of Montag (the hero), his forbidden books are burnt as well: "there on the floor, their covers torn off and spilled out like swan-feathers, the

incredible books ... The books leapt and danced like roasted birds, their wings ablaze with red and yellow feathers" (102–3).

14 That Findley frowns on the censorship of someone like Slade is further suggested by his portrayal of the public reaction to the painter's work:

> The exhibit – and the Pollard Gallery – had been closed the next day by the police. Someone of influence had complained and Pollard was charged with showing indignities to the human body. Ultimately, the gallery owner had his day in court and was cleared. Julian Slade left the country and did what he had always wanted to do. He went to Spain and studied the works of Goya, and he went there a good deal wealthier than he had been before the Shreds exhibit. By the end of the third day following that event, every single one of the canvases had been sold.   (86)

All that attempts at censorship accomplish, this passage suggests, is to increase the demand for the offending art and to secure notoriety and monetary gain for the artist. Findley may be writing here from his own experience with the publication of *Famous Last Words*, which was delayed in England because of the threat of a libel suit. This censorship and the strong condemnation that met the book upon its eventual publication had the same effect as the closing of the gallery does on Slade's work: as Findley recalls in his memoir, "all the furor over the book has catapulted it onto the best-seller lists" (*Inside Memory*, 206).

15 Or as Edmund Burke more poetically put it, "Our inability to locate the precise point at which day ends and night begins does not detract from the utility of the distinction between day and night" (quoted in Schauer, 215n3).

16 In fact, there is a more general undercurrent in the novel that links both high and low art forms with victimization or harm. Ben Webster, a particularly offensive member of the Club of Men, fantasizes about his young nieces by invoking a song: "Long, long ago, there had once been a song that talked about sweet sixteen. The kid in the song was a kid that you met when you went to the village green. Ben was thinking the song could be updated, now. It would be about fucking green–teens. He began, in his mind, to hum the tune" (549). Music is again invoked in one of the scenes of child molestation in which "The finale was being performed on top of the piano" (595). Here artistic and sexual performance are conflated, and the source of music actually provides the site of degradation. This scene is also interesting for the effect the performance has on the spectators: "The watching men were electrified" (596). That an "electrifying" effect is precisely what Slade intends to impart through his paintings (85) suggests a link between his art and the novel's sexual predation.

CHAPTER THREE

1 Pride and humour are also Atwood's primary reactions in the account
  of the defence of her writing by her grandmother Killam in the
  Annapolis Valley, where Atwood says she was "increasingly beyond
  the pale." A neighbour had come to the older woman's house to
  demand how she could have "permitted her granddaughter to publish
  such immoral trash?" ("Great Aunts," 14). Atwood's grandmother
  gazed out the window and proceeded to speak about the weather, to
  the great amusement of Atwood's Aunt J., hiding behind the door, and,
  evidently, to Atwood herself.

2 In the 1990s Atwood turned from the critique of censorship based on
  economic pressures to the ridicule of a similar form of censorship
  based on political correctness. As Lynne Van Luven, reviewing *Good
  Bones*, writes: "Atwood audaciously swipes at the forces of censorship
  in 'There Was Once,' showing how an overly circumspect 'editor's
  voice,' which challenges every nuance of the Cinderella story, reduces
  the tale to bland unviability" (B6).

3 I discuss below the importance of images of hands in the novel.

4 For more in-depth essays on this motif in the novel, see Lucking and
  Carrington.

5 Atwood actually prefaces this comment by making a distinction
  between censorship and suppression: "I'll be careful when I use the
  word 'censorship,' because real censorship stops a book before it's even
  been published. Let us say 'suppression.'" Her distinction is artificial
  and inaccurate. As Barbara Hill Rigney recognizes, Atwood is saying in
  this passage that "it is the act of the censors which is, in fact, obscene"
  (Rigney, 134).

6 Commonly it is the boy who is told that his penis will fall off if he
  doesn't leave it alone. In the absence of this organ, Rennie may be
  transferring this sentiment to her hands.

7 Perhaps Rennie reacts so acutely to this depiction because there is a rat
  in the picture. It may remind her of her transgression as a child, for
  which she was thrust in the cellar: "Sometimes there were things down
  there, I could hear them moving around, small things that might get on
  you and run up your legs" (53). If it was a rat she was afraid of in the
  cellar and she associated it with her sexual misconduct, it may be the
  guilt that the image of the Black woman recalls that evokes such a
  strong reaction in her. The rat recurs as an emblem of sexual and
  political frustration in the novel: see 112, 199, 234, and 272.

8 Lucy Freibert notes that an interview Atwood gave to Jo Brans "suggests that Atwood was working on *The Handmaid's Tale* as early as
  1983" (290n5). Indeed, in an interview with Cathy Davidson published

in 1986, Atwood gives evidence of the early presence of at least some of the novel's ideas when she admits that she had "avoided writing this one for four years" (24).

9 Of this passage in which Offred repeatedly revises her story of her first sexual encounter with Nick, W.J. Keith remarks, "Seldom has the relativity of evidence … been exposed so blatantly" (127).

10 For similar readings, see Cathy Davidson, 24, and Freibert, 283.

11 It must have given Atwood a sense of vindication, only a couple of years after the publication of the novel in which she depicts the Commander, Fred, as a hypocrite and traitor in consorting with Offred, that Jim Bakker, his possible precursor, was revealed to be a fraud, having stolen money from his followers.

12 One of the insightful observations Larson makes to support this claim is that the repetition of the title "Night" for many of Atwood's chapters reminds us of *Night*, Elie Wiesel's moving Holocaust narrative (496).

13 We are probably also meant to see in the Nazi's mistress the character of Serena Joy. Offred makes careful note that the former wore "heavy mascara on her eyelashes, rouge on the bones of her cheeks" (137). Her last thought in this passage, "What I remember now, most of all, is the makeup" (138), symbolically conveys the self-delusion of the mistress and Offred when faced with the evil reality of their lovers, but primarily it reminds us of the heavy make-up used by Tammy Faye Bakker. This identification sets up a neat parallel between the rulers of Gilead and the Nazis.

14 See, among others, Bouson, 157; Keith, 125; and Michele Lacombe, 5.

15 It is true that, as Nathalie Cooke points out in her biography of Atwood, the novelist received a letter from a reader reporting that a religious sect in the United States "referred to its 'womenfolk' as 'handmaids'" (277), but this anecdote shows Atwood's prescient knowledge of the religious right more than it predicts that the practice of handmaids will become widespread in America.

16 There are comparisons of Gilead with other real-life regimes as well, such as the Ayatollah Khomeini's Iran: one of Professor Pieixoto's publications is "Iran and Gilead: Two Late-Twentieth-Century Monotheocracies, as Seen Through Diaries" (282).

17 "The Greater Evil" is the article that Margaret Laurence published in *Toronto Life* in September 1984, which, on the surface, manifests the same ambivalence that Atwood expresses in this passage.

18 It is unclear if Atwood is purposefully displaying her ambivalent feelings about censoring pornography or whether her penchant for the accurate portrayal of character is here eclipsing her political objectives.

19 Foucault makes a similar argument in volume 1 of his *History of Sexuality*.

20 Offred echoes this connection between illicit sex and outlawed discourse repeatedly in the novel. For example, she reflects on the ignorance of Nick, the chauffeur, regarding "what really goes on in there, among the books. Acts of perversion, for all he knows. The Commander and me, covering each other with ink, licking it off, or making love on stacks of forbidden newsprint. Well, he wouldn't be far off at that" (170; see also 136, 209).

21 Atwood makes a pun on "page boy" that adds to the analogy. Nick is a page-boy in his capacity as helper to the Commander, but he is also the agent through which Offred gains access to the forbidden pages of books and magazines in the Commander's study.

22 For other passages where Offred expresses her feelings of discontinuity, see 37, 97, and 183.

23 There is an underground in Gilead, of course, and Offred's tale is testimony to the survival of banned impulses, but suppressed ideas – individuality, freedom, etc. – have nowhere near the power in Gilead that they would were they not suppressed.

24 For a more sustained rebuttal to the claim that censorship is counter-productive, see Schauer, 75–8.

CHAPTER FOUR

1 While, for Atwood, the relationship between censorship and feminism mainly involved the anti-pornography feminists of the late 1970s and early 1980s, in this chapter I trace the connection between censorship and a feminism that, for Laurence, takes a less historically specific form, one that is characterized mainly by "the quest for physical and spiritual freedom, the quest for relationships of equality and communication" (Laurence, "Ivory Tower," 24).

2 She encountered censorious opposition from the start of her writing career. King reports that one of her earliest short stories, "The Merchant of Heaven," portrays the unsuccessful attempts of a preacher to proselytize his evangelical Christianity in Accra, Ghana. Publication of the story in the Vancouver-based *Prism International* was met by opposition on religious grounds, to which Laurence responded: "quite a number of people wrote to the newspapers here, regarding 'Prism,' and some of them were very concerned about the publication of irreligious material (i.e. my story). Very peculiar. I thought of it as quite religious" (quoted in King, 142). Her reaction here could easily be a response to the attacks on *The Diviners* fifteen years later.

3 Laurence had originally intended to call this novel *Dance on the Earth*, a title that, after abandoning the novel, she eventually came to attach to her memoir.

4 While I understand that the term "fundamentalist" can have pejorative connotations, I use it in its more neutral sense of "one laying stress on belief in literal and verbal inspiration of [the] Bible and other traditional creeds" (*Collins English Dictionary*, 172). Other Laurence scholars, such as King and Wainwright, also use this term (as does Laurence herself).

5 One passage in *The Diviners* that Laurence says, in her memoir (*Dance on the Earth*, 266), was singled out by her opponents finds Morag hot and bored in Prin's kitchen. The "offensive" line is "She is watching two flies fucking, buzzing while they do it" (35). In the later, 1985 controversy, one of the contentious passages, according to the *Toronto Star* (Contenta, A8), was a love scene between Jules and Morag:

> In an hour or so, Morag wakens, and puts her head between his legs, sweeping her hair across his thighs. She takes his limp cock very gently in her mouth and caresses it with her tongue, and it lengthens and grows hard before he is even awake. Then he wakens and says deeper. After a while, she disentangles and he raises her until she is looking into his face in the greylight of the room.
> "Ride my stallion, Morag."
> So she mounts him. He holds her shoulders and her long hair, penetrating up into her until she knows he has reached whatever core of being she has.   (*The Diviners*, 280)

6 Laurence writes: "when I had been writing about Africa I could never be sure [of accurately capturing speech]. It was not my culture, and of course we know things about our own culture, and about our own people that we don't even know we know" (quoted in Rosemary Sullivan, "An Interview," 68).

7 There are some striking similarities between Cary and Laurence regarding religion and their writing careers. As David Cecil describes in the introduction to *The Captive and the Free*,

> Cary was a profoundly religious spirit of that intensely individual and protestant kind which cannot find fulfillment in any corporate body; he had to carve out his creed by himself and for himself ... It was not orthodox; it was not Christian in any substantial sense. Cary did not identify God with Christ or with any kind of personal spirit. But experience had convinced him that man's apprehension of beauty and of human love was inexplicable on any purely rational or materialist terms. It was proof of some transcendental spiritual reality with which a man must relate himself harmoniously if he is to find satisfaction.   (7)

Laurence came to see herself as a markedly non-traditional Christian, valuing Jesus' gift of (artistic) grace and human love over his divinity:

> I have to look at myself as a kind of very unorthodox Christian, but a Christian all the same. The social gospel is what seems to matter to

me more and more. Why should any person say, as the fundamentalist born-again (?) Christians do, that saving one's own soul, by pro-
claiming Jesus as yr spiritual saviour, is ALL that is necessary in this
life? ... it seems to me that what still comes across, throughout those
thousands of years of history, is a message by a young Jew ... whose
new doctrine was simply another commandment ... "Thou shalt
love thy neighbour as thyself." (*A Very Large Soul* 73)

Both Cary and Laurence came to explore this humanist spirituality in
novels they struggled to complete before dying. While Cary was able
"at the end against appalling odds to win his tragic race with death"
(Cecil, 7), Laurence was not so favoured.

8 King makes a similar point when he writes, "a book about the fundamentalists would have required her to delve into the world of – and, in
the process, perhaps write sympathetically about – her enemies. Her
insecure side pulled her in the direction of a book in which to some
extent she would have explained and justified the conduct of her opponents. The strong, resilient side of Margaret ultimately resisted any
such impulse because it would have been a form of capitulation" (351).

9 Previous study of this material has been limited to King's brief discussion
of it in the end-matter of his biography and Nora Foster Stovel's recent
essay, "Mourning Becomes Margaret: Laurence's Farewell to Fiction."
    Abbreviated references in the text are to archival material listed in
the Bibliography, Archives, Laurence Fonds and Papers.

10 The draft fragments of the novel are not as painfully didactic as Laurence's initial choice of names – Hogg, the pig-headed master; Price,
the valuable saviour; and later, the Reverend Jake Flood, the preacher
who swamps Allie – would imply. In them, as in her Manawaka
novels, Laurence tackles difficult moral issues in a story told with
warmth and wit in which her characters' thoughts and feelings take
precedence over any political message.

11 That Taine sees Milton as sympathizing with Satan is implied by his
later argument that Satan is meant to embody many of the virtues and
sufferings of the Puritans, with whom Milton commiserated (1:451).

12 The allusions to Taine, Legouis, and Daiches appear in "Draft Ms."

13 Laurence was probably also heavily influenced, in her depiction of
Allie, by Gwen Pharis Ringwood's *A Remembrance of Miracles*. In this
play a high school English teacher is challenged (initially, like Allie, by
one of her students) over a list of books the young woman provides to
her class. Members of the small town demand that the books be
banned from the school and the teacher be fired. After a protracted
conflict that includes a combative school board meeting, the teacher,
broken by the controversy, finally resigns. Laurence wrote the foreword
for the collected plays of Ringwood, published in 1982, while she was

still working on Dance Draft. Therein she wrote of *A Remembrance of Miracles*: "I find this play almost unbearably poignant, as I happen to know only too well what the teacher is forced to go through" (Foreword, xiv). While it is clear that Dance Draft was to share much common ground with Ringwood's play, it is interesting to note that Ringwood in turn drew on Laurence's 1976 censorship controversy: proof of this is that one of the ten books on the teacher's list, all of which in reality have been banned at some point, is *The Diviners*.

14 Clara Thomas confirms the importance of Milton for Laurence when she reports that Laurence kept and cherished her mother's copy of *Paradise Lost*, which she turned to "repeatedly, before and during the composition of every novel" (87).

15 Though he stops short of equating Hagar and Satan, Robert D. Chambers has also found that "like Milton's Satan, Hagar begins with a deliberate act of rebellion against her father" and that, as Milton does with Satan and God, "Laurence renders the battle between [Hagar and her father] in magnificent terms" (23).

16 Allie's comments about the maturity of her students are also reminiscent of some of the comments Robert Buchanan made to defend his teaching of *The Diviners*: "These Grade 13 students are adults. They'll be reading *The Diviners* just weeks before they graduate" (quoted in Sallot, 3).

17 The behaviour of the fundamentalists in the *Diviners* controversy may also have reminded Laurence of the anti-Communist witch-hunts and conspiracy theories that were beginning to grow, especially in the United States in the late 1940s, when Laurence resigned from the *Winnipeg Citizen*. She may have conflated these attacks on free speech and on communism in the offensive against Allie.

18 Of the range of reactions Laurence exhibited, feeling hurt was probably the most profound. It is the response King notes in his first reference to the controversy, and the common theme of a variety of comments by writer friends of Laurence that Wainwright catalogues in his preface to *A Very Large Soul* (xvii–xviii). Of these comments, Timothy Findley's is the most direct: "The psychological effect of that whole [censorship] episode, both those episodes [1976 and 1985] on Margaret Laurence was devastating" (quoted in Wainwright, 87; parenthetical editing is Wainwright's).

19 Laurence's definition approximates that of *The Canadian Oxford Dictionary*, which indicates that the word has entered common parlance meaning "The mental capacity to accept as equally valid two entirely contradictory opinions or beliefs" (418).

20 As George Woodcock writes in a tribute shortly after Laurence's death, "the orator, the spokesman who articulates the group's sense of itself,

assumes a special and symbolic role, and I think this was the role that as the tribe of Canadian writers we all – consciously or half-consciously – accorded to Margaret" (31).

21 The connection between these two statements is more clear in the speech that preceded the article. That she allowed the non sequitur to materialize in abridging the speech suggests her attention was focused more on the harms pornography could engender than the dangers of censorship.

22 Nabokov makes a compelling defence of his novel by arguing that it lacks the "mediocrity, commercialism, and certain strict rules of narration" that he finds in pornography (315). His purpose in writing the novel, rather, is "aesthetic bliss, that is a sense of being somehow, somewhere, connected with other states of being where art (curiosity, tenderness, kindness, ecstasy) is the norm" (316–17).

23 In the speech she backs up this point with the example of the *Hustler* magazine cover that showed a woman being put, head first, through a meat grinder. "To me," writes Laurence, "this is obscene" ("On Censorship," 17).

24 For a highly compelling account, drawing on the thinking of J.L. Austin, of pornography as a speech act with real and potentially dangerous consequences in the world, see Langton. There has been copious debate on a more general level over the line between speech and action. Fish challenges the distinction between protected "political" speech and unprotected "fighting words," arguing that "every idea is an incitement to somebody … and therefore a candidate for regulation" (106). For a comprehensive rebuttal, see Haiman.

25 As a suggested way of making censorship disputes more reasonable, I present a similar argument in my Conclusion, calling it "setting the bar high."

26 While the 1976 *Diviners* controversy influenced Laurence's work, her writing on censorship may in turn have influenced governmental policy in Ontario. When Laurence was engulfed in the 1985 controversy, the leader of the provincial New Democratic Party, Bob Rae, sent her a copy of a speech he had delivered in the legislature shortly after the publication of "The Greater Evil." The speech (in Hansard #116) addresses proposed government amendments to portions of the Theatres Act dealing with obscenity and shares many of the sentiments expressed in Laurence's article. In an accompanying note to Laurence, Rae acknowledges the author's influence: "I am enclosing a copy of a speech I gave recently in the legislature on censorship. Our views are a little different, but I don't think dramatically so. As you can see, I am opposed to the current Tory government's attitude to censorship and yet am also dumbfounded by the spread of violent

pornography against which we need some protection, particularly from the criminal law. Thank you for helping me think through a perplexing subject." Like Laurence, Rae felt obscenity provisions were too blunt a tool as they were formulated at the time, but that a more context-sensitive censorship law was necessary.

27 By contrast, Atwood's novels about censorship issues are both set outside Canada (the first of this kind for the author). Did this geographical distance provide her with greater scope to explore issues that, on home turf, might have seemed more threatening?

CHAPTER FIVE

1 Sociologist Pierre Bourdieu discusses a similar concept of censorship in his essay "Censorship and the Imposition of Form." He writes of "structural censorship," which "is exercised through the medium of the sanctions of the field, functioning as a market on which the prices of different kinds of expression are formed; it is imposed on all producers of symbolic goods, including the authorized spokesperson, whose authoritative discourse is more subject to the norms of official propriety than any other, and it condemns the occupants of dominated positions either to silence or to shocking outspokenness" (138). Bourdieu's observations apply to social institutions in general, and, while my notion of socio-cultural censorship resembles Bourdieu's structural censorship, it is significantly more narrowly defined and applied specifically to writers in Canada.

2 Race is a slippery term used to describe groups that sometimes would be better classified by nationality (East Indian or Japanese, for example) or religion (Jews have been referred to as a race). I am also aware that race and ethnicity are fiercely debated as terms for these groups. Even within the "races" I have chosen to explore, the idea of a monolithic Native race (which includes status/non-status Indians, Métis, etc.) or a unified Black race (within which writers from Trinidad, whom I study, are only one group) is problematic. So my use of the term race applies loosely to a group of people whose members see themselves clustered around similar geographic, linguistic, and cultural traits.

3 While my approach with these writers is more anecdotal than scientific, I am aware of the error in some postcolonial studies in which, as Arun Mukherjee writes, "an unproblematic relationship is assumed between the representativeness of the writer and his or her ability to present an 'authentic' portrayal of 'the oppressed'" (xiv–xiv). I do not pretend that the writers I examine here speak for all of the members of the Native or Black communities in Canada, but contend that their work offers a window on to a set of experiences that many of these members encounter.

4 I use the present perfect tense here to indicate that this historical marginalization continues today, if to a less pronounced degree. Certainly strides have been made in recent years to allow marginal writers a less restricted voice in Canadian discourse.

5 Mary Ellen Macdonald reminds me that Native Canadians receive free tuition for post-secondary studies, so my argument applies mainly to other minority groups.

6 "Gatekeepers" has a tradition of usage that can be traced back to Dorothy Smith's use of the term in 1978. I employ it in a sense similar to scholars such as Gerson, Nelson, and Spender, for whom a gatekeeper mediates women's writing, but apply it to marginalized cultures.

7 "White," like "Black" and "Native," is a blunt and imprecise label. Nevertheless, I use it to designate those who can be considered members of the mainstream, dominant group in Canadian society.

8 Unless otherwise indicated, all references to Culleton's work are to this version of the novel.

9 Beatrice Culleton and the protagonists of her novel (April and Cheryl Raintree) are Métis. While some Métis consider themselves to be as different and sometimes as ostracized from Native communities as they are from White ones, the socio-cultural censorship of Métis people and culture is similar enough to that of Native Canadians to allow me to discuss them as one.

10 Greg Young-Ing gives some dramatic examples of ways in which "Aboriginal peoples have historically been blocked from equitable participation in the publishing industry" (181, 185).

11 For other Native authors who give first-hand accounts of being restricted by publishers' ideological agendas, see Jeannette Armstrong (in Williamson, 25) and Lenore Keeshig-Tobias ("Keepers of the Culture," 225).

12 Barton documents the teaching of the novel in grade schools (14), and Hoy analyses discussion arising from her use of it in one of her graduate university seminars (157–8).

13 Cheryl's prodigious memory, the rhythms of the speech, and her emotional style of telling it all point to her affinity for oral narration. I will discuss the dichotomy between oral and written Native story-telling and its relation to censorship below.

14 While Krupat makes his point about American writing, Robert Lecker makes similar observations about the Canadian literary canon, the mimetic nature of which he sees as "the appropriate instrument of power in an institution that seeks to verify its solidity and authority over time" (37).

15 An exception to this observation, of course, is Pauline Johnson, who has been regularly anthologized. As with publishers and critics,

however, anthologists have generally seen fit to approve only those of Johnson's poems that, according to Harry, "appealed to the romantic view of the Indian ... in which the Indian heroic emotions and virtues are compatible with those of the dominant white society" (151). Indeed, Johnson herself chose not to reprint one of the few poems in which she is self-critical of her participation in this romantic view ("His Majesty the West Wind") because she sensed the discomfort her stance would elicit in her audience (Brown, 145). This is a particularly ironic example of self-censorship.

16 For example, an early edition (1978) of *Canadian Short Stories* featured no Native writing; the latest edition (1991) contains one story by Daniel David Moses. *The Oxford Book of Canadian Short Stories in English* (1986) featured no Native writing; *The New Oxford Book of Canadian Writing* (1997) contains one story by Thomas King.

17 Of course, not all White writers feel this way. Anne Cameron argues: "I have not been censored or stifled, or denied any freedom of speech or expression; I have been asked to take a step or two to one side. Not down. To one side" ("The Operative Principle is Trust," 69). But as Daiva Stasiulis points out, this acquiescence in the face of Native demands is part of a "self-censoring climate" (48), and self-censorship, as I have shown in the Introduction and will discuss below, is not different in kind from traditional censorship.

18 See Brill de Ramírez for further discussion of differences between oral and written cultures, especially her comprehensive appendix of "Conversive Literary Structures" (221–3), in which she gives a referenced itemization of characteristics of the oral tradition in Native story-telling.

19 Culleton has gone so far as to agree to the suggestion that this internalization is a form of brainwashing (Lutz, 101).

20 For a more detailed account of the altered portions of the novel, see Hoy, 181n.

21 "African Canadian" is a label that does not adequately capture the nuanced identity of a writer who, like Harris or Brand, grew up in Trinidad-Tobago, a country of cultural transition between Africa and Britain. Godard refers to Philip as "African–Caribbean–Canadian" ("Marlene Nourbese," 153). I will refer to her as a Black Canadian.

22 In addition to the articles I cite, see David Marriott and McAlpine.

23 Note that Philip ironically uses Standard English and classical mythology, both cultural legacies of an imperialist education, to convey her opposition to the silencing of non-imperialist cultural expression.

24 We have seen that scenes of rape are pivotal in the censored works of Findley and Culleton; in her poetry Philip overtly uses rape as a metaphor for censorship.

25 It is in this conversation, in which Margaret asks Zulma to teach her "Tobago-talk," that Philip conveys the importance of Nation Language, suggesting the necessity of maintaining the freedom to use Black speech patterns in a foreign, colonial environment.

26 Professor Nathalie Cooke has pointed out to me that, in compiling the 1990 edition of *An Anthology of Canadian Literature in English,* she and the other editors were asked by the publisher (Oxford University Press) and agreed to exclude some mainstream writers in order to include members of visible minorities. This is a perfect example of anti-racist ideology driving socio-cultural censorship (in this case of writers from the dominant social group).

CHAPTER SIX

1 These two quotations are taken respectively from Section 2b ("Fundamental Freedoms") and Section 1 ("Guarantee of Rights and Freedoms") of the "Canadian Charter of Rights and Freedoms" contained in Part I of the *Constitution Act, 1982.*

2 A legal case featuring similar considerations arose from the decision by a group of neo-Nazis to march with swastikas through a section of Skokie, Illinois, largely populated by Holocaust survivors. The court decided that, under the First Amendment, the neo-Nazis had the right to march (Skokie v. National Socialist Party). In my opinion this is an example of a censorship dispute in which the nature of the audience was not adequately considered.

3 This point is raised by both Laurence and Culleton, as I have shown in chapters 4 and 5 respectively.

4 For an interesting but, I think, ultimately self-contradictory critique of this legislation, see Musgrave, D3.

5 A few often-cited studies are Donnerstein, Malamuth, and Zillman.

Bibliography

ARCHIVES

Findley, Timothy. Papers. National Archives, Ottawa, MG 31, D 196.
- "Additional Material, Notes and Revisions for Draft Two" (AM). File 19-4.
- "Filmscript, Typescript Draft, 'First Draft'" (Fts1). Files 18-4 to 18-6.
- "Filmscript, Typescript Draft, Notes" (FtsN). Files 19-5 to 19-7.
- "Manuscript/Typescript Draft, Notes" (Ms/TsN). Files 17-3 to 17-4.
- "Typescript Draft, Correspondence" (TsC). Files 17-5 to 17-7.
- "Typescript 'Original Typescript'" (TsO). Files 17-8 to 17-11.
Laurence, Margaret. Fonds. William Ready Archives, McMaster University, Hamilton, Ont.
- "Blue Notebook." 5th accrual, ser. 1, box 6, file 6.
- "Diviners Draft." 1st accrual, ser. 1, box 3, file 2.
- "Draft Manuscript." 5th accrual, ser. 1, box 6, file 3.
- "First Typescript." 5th accrual, ser. 1, box 6, file 7.
- "Manuscript Notes." 5th accrual, ser. 1, box 6, file 2.
- "Notes." 5th accrual, ser. 1, box 6, file 4.
- "Post-it Note." 5th accrual, ser. 1, box 6, file 2.
- "Research Material." 5th accrual, ser. 3, box 8, file 9.
- "Third Typescript." 5th accrual, ser. 1, box 6, file 8.
Laurence, Margaret. Papers. York University Archives, Toronto.
- Interview. *Morningside*. CBC Radio, Toronto, 1985. ML5, ser. 1, file 18.
- Letter to James Stark, 23 Aug. 1982. Accessions 3 & 4, ser. 1, box 5, file 136.
- "Notes and Research 'The Diviners' 1970–1974." Accession 3, box 22, file 153.

- "On Censorship ... A Speech Given to the Ontario Provincial Judges and Their Wives." Peterborough, Ont., 2 June 1983. ML5, ser. I, file 11.
- Letter from Lynn McDonald to Eric Cotton, 21 Jan. 1985. Accession 4, ser. 1, box 12, file 307.
- Letter from Bob Rae to Margaret Laurence, 18 Jan. 1985. Accession 4, ser. 1, box 12, file 307.

ANTHOLOGIES OF CANADIAN NATIVE LITERATURE

Brooks, Cheryl, and Dorreen Jensen, eds. *In Celebration of Our Survival: The First Nations of British Columbia.* Vancouver: UBC Press 1991.

Fife, Connie, ed. *The Colour of Resistance: A Contemporary Collection of Writing by Aboriginal Women.* Toronto: Sister Vision Press 1993.

Grant, Agnes, ed. *Our Bit of Truth: An Anthology of Canadian Native Literature.* Winnipeg: Pemmican Publications 1990.

King, Thomas, ed. *All My Relations: An Anthology of Contemporary Canadian Native Fiction.* Toronto: McClelland and Stewart 1990.

Maki, Joel T., ed. *Steal My Rage: New Native Voices.* Vancouver: Douglas & McIntyre 1995.

Moses, Daniel David, and Terry Goldie, eds. *An Anthology of Canadian Native Literature in English.* 1st ed. Don Mills: Oxford University Press 1992. 2nd ed. Toronto: Oxford University Press 1998.

Perrault, Jeanne, and Sylvia Vance, eds. *Writing the Circle: Native Women of Western Canada.* Edmonton: NeWest 1990.

Roman, Trish Fox, ed. *Voices under One Sky: Contemporary Native Literature.* Scarborough: Nelson 1993.

WORKS CITED

Abrams, M.H. *A Glossary of Literary Terms.* 7th ed. Fort Worth, Texas: Harcourt Brace 1999.

Abrams v. United States, 250 U.S. 616 (1919).

Acker, Kathy. *Empire of the Senseless.* New York: Grove 1989.

Adachi, Ken. "Atwood Takes a Chance and Wins." *Toronto Star,* 13 Oct. 1985, E1.

Aitken, Johan. "'Long Live the Dead': An Interview with Timothy Findley." *Journal of Canadian Fiction* 33 (1981–82): 79–93.

Allen, Lillian. "Poems Are Not Meant To Lay Still." In Silvera, ed., *The Other Woman.* 253–62.

"Angry Author Fights against Plan To Ban Her Books." *Toronto Star,* 20 Dec. 1984, A3.

Appleby, Timothy. "Aftermath." *Globe and Mail,* 20 July 1991, D3.

Armstrong, Jeannette. *Slash.* Penticton, BC: Theytus Books 1985.

– "The Disempowerment of First North American Native People and Empowerment through Their Writing." In Moss and Goldie, eds., *An Anthology of Canadian Native Literature in English*. 207–11.

Ashcroft, Bill, Gareth Griffiths, and Helen Tiffin. *The Empire Writes Back: Theory and Practice in Post-Colonial Literatures*. London: Routledge 1989.

Atkins, Robert. "A Censorship Time Line." *Art Journal* 50.3 (1991): 33–7.

Atwood, Margaret. *Bodily Harm*. Toronto: McClelland and Stewart 1981.

– "Amnesty International: An Address." *Second Words: Selected Critical Prose*. Toronto: Anansi 1982. 393–7.

– "An End to Audience?" *Second Words: Selected Critical Prose*. Toronto: Anansi 1982. 334–57.

– "Atwood on Pornography." *Chatelaine*, Sept. 1983, 61, 118, 126, 128.

– *The Handmaid's Tale*. Toronto: Seal Books 1986.

– "And They Said It Couldn't Happen." *Globe and Mail*, 18 Feb. 1988, A7.

– "Great Aunts." In *Family Portraits: Remembrances by Twenty Distinguished Writers*, ed. Carolyn Anthony. New York: Doubleday 1989. 1–16.

– Speech to Toronto Council of Teachers of English, Women's Club, University of Toronto, 25 May 1995.

Atwood, Margaret, and Robert Weaver, eds. *The Oxford Book of Canadian Short Stories in English*. Toronto: Oxford University Press 1986.

– *The New Oxford Book of Canadian Short Stories in English*. Toronto: Oxford University Press 1997.

Ayre, John. "Bell, Book and Scandal." *Weekend Magazine*, 28 Aug. 1976, 9–12.

Banerjee, Chinmoy. "Alice in Disneyland: Criticism as Commodity in *The Handmaid's Tale*." *Essays on Canadian Writing* 41 (1990): 74–92.

Bannerji, Himani. *Thinking Through: Essays on Feminism, Marxism and Anti-Racism*. Toronto: Women's Press 1995.

Barthes, Roland. "The Death of the Author." *Image, Music, Text*. New York: Hill and Wang 1977. 142–8.

Barton, Marie. "Write the Wrong." *Canadian Author & Bookman* 61.1 (1985): 14.

Bataille, Georges. *Erotism: Death and Sensuality*. 1957. Trans. Mary Dalwood. San Francisco: City Lights Books 1986.

Benson, Eugene. "Interview with Timothy Findley." *World Literature Written in English* 26.1 (1986): 107–15.

Birdsall, Peter, and Delores Broten. *Mind War: Book Censorship in English Canada*. Victoria: CanLit 1978.

Blake, William. *The Marriage of Heaven and Hell*. In *The Norton Anthology of English Literature*, ed. M.H. Abrams. 5th ed. New York: W.W Norton 1986. 2:60–72.

Blattberg, Charles. *From Pluralist to Patriotic Politics: Putting Practice First*. Oxford: Oxford University Press 2000.

Bourdieu, Pierre. *Language and Symbolic Power*. Ed. John B. Thompson, trans. Gino Raymond and Matthew Adamson. Cambridge: Polity Press 1991.

Bouson, J. Brooks. *Brutal Choreographies: Oppositional Strategies and Narrative Design in the Novels of Margaret Atwood*. Amherst: University of Massachusetts Press 1993.

Bradbury, Ray. *Fahrenheit 451*. 1953. New York: Ballantine 1966.

Brand, Dionne. "In the Company of My Work." Interview in Silvera, ed., *The Other Woman*. 356–80.

Brill de Ramírez, Susan Berry. *Contemporary American Indian Literatures and the Oral Tradition*. Tucson: University of Arizona Press 1999.

Brown, Russell, Donna Bennett, and Nathalie Cooke, eds. *An Anthology of Canadian Literature in English*. Rev. and abr. ed. Toronto: Oxford University Press 1990.

Brownmiller, Susan. "Let's Put Pornography Back in the Closet." In Lederer, ed., *Take Back the Night*. 252–5.

Brydon, Diana. "Caribbean Revolution and Literary Convention." *Canadian Literature* 95 (1982): 181–5.

– "'It could not be told': Making Meaning in Timothy Findley's *The Wars*." *Journal of Commonwealth Literature* 21.1 (1986): 62–79.

– *Writing on Trial: Timothy Findley's Famous Last Words*. Toronto: ECW 1995.

Burnside, Scott, and Alan Cairns. *Deadly Innocence: The True Story of Paul Bernardo, Karla Homolka, and the Schoolgirl Murders*. New York: Warner Books 1995.

Burstyn, Varda, ed. *Women against Censorship*. Vancouver: Douglas & McIntyre 1985.

Burt, Richard, ed. *The Administration of Aesthetics: Censorship, Political Criticism, and the Public Sphere*. Minneapolis: University of Minnesota Press 1994.

– "'Degenerate "Art"'": Public Aesthetics and the Simulation of Censorship in Postliberal Los Angeles and Berlin." In Burt, ed., *The Administration of Aesthetics*, 216–59.

– "Introduction: The 'New' Censorship." In Burt, ed., *The Administration of Aesthetics*, ix–xxix.

Butler, Judith. *Excitable Speech: A Politics of the Performative*. New York: Routledge, 1997.

Cameron, Anne. "Métis Heart." *Canadian Literature* 108 (1986): 164–6.

– "The Operative Principle Is Trust." In Scheier et al., eds., 63–71.

Caminero-Santangelo, Marta. "Moving beyond 'The Blank White Spaces': Atwood's Gilead, Postmodernism, and Strategic Resistance." *Studies in Canadian Literature* 19 (1994): 20–42.

Campbell, Maria. *Halfbreed*. Toronto: McClelland and Stewart 1973.

The Canadian Oxford Dictionary. Ed. Katherine Barber. Toronto: Oxford University Press 1998.

Carr, Brenda. "To 'Heal the Word Wounded': Agency and the Materiality of Language and Form in M. Nourbese Philip's *She Tries Her Tongue, Her Silence Softly Breaks*." *Studies in Canadian Literature* 19.1 (1994): 72–93.

Carrington, Ildiko de Papp. "Another Symbolic Descent." *Essays in Canadian Writing* 26 (1983): 45–63.

Cary, Joyce. *The Captive and the Free*. London: Michael Joseph 1959.

Casselton, Val. "Reality is Atwood's tool – and it includes a Utopia." *Vancouver Courier*, 22 July 1979, 16.

Cecil, David. Introduction to Cary, *The Captive and the Free*, 5–7.

Chambers, Robert D. "The Women of Margaret Laurence." *Journal of Canadian Studies* 18.2 (1983): 18–26.

Clark, Lorenne. "Pornography's Challenge to Liberal Ideology." *Canadian Forum* 59 (1980): 9–12.

Coetzee, J.M. *Giving Offense: Essays on Censorship*. Chicago: University of Chicago Press 1996.

Cole, Susan G. *Pornography and the Sex Crisis*. Toronto: Second Story 1992.

Collins English Dictionary. Canadian ed. Toronto: Totem 1981.

Comeau, Paul. "Hagar in Hell: Margaret Laurence's Fallen Angel." *Canadian Literature* 128 (1991): 11–22.

Contenta, Sandro. "'Ban Margaret Laurence' Group Says She's Too Disgusting for Schoolkids." *Toronto Star*, 3 Mar. 1985, A1, A8.

Cooke, Nathalie. *Margaret Atwood: A Biography*. Toronto: ECW 1998.

Copp, David, and Susan Wendell, eds. *Pornography and Censorship*. New York: Prometheus 1983.

Cossman, Brenda. *Bad Attitude/s on Trial: Pornography, Feminism and the Butler Decision*. Toronto: University of Toronto Press 1997.

Cowart, David. *History and the Contemporary Novel*. Carbondale: Southern Illinois University Press 1989.

Crosbie Lynn. "The Argument." *Globe and Mail*, 1 Dec. 1997, D1.

– *Paul's Case: The Kingston Letters*. Toronto: Insomniac Press 1997.

Culleton, Beatrice. *In Search of April Raintree*. 1983. Winnipeg: Peguis Publishers 1992.

– *April Raintree*. Winnipeg: Pemmican 1984.

Curry Jansen, Sue: *See* Jansen.

Daiches, David. *Milton*. London: Hutchison and Co. 1957.

Davidson, Arnold E. "Future Tense: Making History in *The Handmaid's Tale*." In *Margaret Atwood: Vision and Forms*, ed. Kathryn VanSpanckeren and Jan Garden Castro. Carbondale: Southern Illinois University Press 1988. 113–21.

Davidson, Cathy N. "A Feminist '1984.'" *Ms*, Feb. 1986, 24–6.

Davies, Frank. *Karla's Web: A Cultural Investigation of the Mahaffy-French Murders*. Toronto: Penguin 1995.

Deep Throat. Dir. Girard Damiano. Arrow Productions, c. 1971.

Deer, Glenn. *Postmodern Canadian Fiction and the Rhetoric of Authority*. Montreal: McGill-Queen's University Press 1994.

Diamond, Sara. "Pornography: Image and Reality." In *Women against Censorship*, ed. Varda Burstyn. Vancouver: Douglas and McIntyre 1985. 40–57.

Donnerstein, Edward, and Leonard Berkowitz. "Victim Reactions in Aggressive Erotic Films as a Factor in Violence against Women." *Journal of Personality and Social Psychology* 41 (1981): 710–24.

Donovan, Kathleen M. *Feminist Readings of Native American Literature: Coming to Voice.* Tucson: University of Arizona Press 1998.

Douglas, Mary. *Purity and Danger: An Analysis of Concepts of Pollution and Taboo.* London: Routledge and Kegan Paul 1966.

Dumont, Marilyn. "Popular Images of Nativeness." In *Looking at the Words of Our People: First Nations Analysis of Literature*, ed. Jeannette Armstrong. Penticton, BC: Theytus Books 1993. 45–50.

Dworkin, Andrea. *Pornography: Men Possessing Women.* New York: Penguin 1979.

Dworkin Ronald. "The Coming Battles over Free Speech." *New York Review of Books*, 11 June 1992, 55–64.

Emberley, Julia V. *Thresholds of Difference: Feminist Critique, Native Women's Writings, Postcolonial Theory.* Toronto: University of Toronto Press 1993.

Engel, S. Morris. *With Good Reason: An Introduction to Informal Fallacies.* 4th ed. New York: St Martin's Press 1990.

Fee, Margery. "Upsetting Fake Ideas: Jeannette Armstrong's 'Slash' and Beatrice Culleton's 'April Raintree.'" In New, ed., *Native Writers and Canadian Writing.* 168–80.

Findley, Timothy. *The Last of the Crazy People.* 1967. Harmondsworth: Penguin 1983.

– *The Wars.* Toronto: Clarke, Irwin 1977.

– "Better Dead than Read? An Opposing View." *Books in Canada*, Dec. 1978, 3–5.

– "Alice Drops Her Cigarette on the Floor ..." *Canadian Literature* 91 (1981): 10–21.

– *Famous Last Words.* New York: Delacorte 1981.

– *The Wars.* Dir. Robin Phillips. Torstar 1982.

– "Censorship by Every Other Name." *Indirections* 8.4 (1983): 14–20.

– *Not Wanted on the Voyage.* Toronto: Penguin 1984.

– *Inside Memory: Pages from a Writer's Workbook.* Toronto: HarperCollins 1990.

– "The Valour and the Horror." *Journal of Canadian Studies* 27.4 (1992–93): 197–8.

– *Chasseur des têtes.* Trans. Nésida Loyer. Montreal: Boreal 1993.

– *Headhunter.* Toronto: HarperCollins 1993.

– Letter to author. 5 Dec. 1998.

Fish, Stanley. *There's No Such Thing as Free Speech, and It's a Good Thing, Too.* Oxford: Oxford University Press 1994.

Fiss, Owen M. *Liberalism Divided: Freedom of Speech and the Many Uses of State Power.* Boulder, Colo.: Westview Press 1996.

Foucault, Michel. *Discipline and Punish: The Birth of the Prison.* Trans. Alan Sheridan. New York: Pantheon 1977.

– "What Is an Author?" *Language, Counter-Memory, Practice: Selected Essays and Interviews.* Ithaca: Cornell University Press 1977.

– *History of Sexuality.* New York: Pantheon 1978.

Fraser, Matthew. "Atwood Part of International Campaign to Bolster Support for Rushdie." *Globe and Mail,* 14 Feb. 1992, C1.

French, Marilyn. *The War against Women.* New York: Ballantine, 1992.

French, William. "The Good Book Versus Good Books." *Globe and Mail,* 15 June 1978, 16.

Frey, Rodney. Preface to *Stories that Make the World: Oral Literature of the Indian Peoples of the Inland Northwest as Told by Lawrence Aripa, Tom Yellowtail, and Other Elders,* ed. Rodney Frey. Norman, Okla.: University of Oklahoma Press 1995. xiii–xvi.

Friebert, Lucy M. "Control and Creativity: The Politics of Risk in Margaret Atwood's *The Handmaid's Tale.*" In McCombs, ed., *Critical Essays on Margaret Atwood.* 280–91.

Fuller, Janine, and Stuart Blackley. *Restricted Entry: Censorship on Trial.* Vancouver: Press Gang 1995.

Fung, Richard. "Uncompromising Positions: Anti-censorship, Anti-racism, and the Visual Arts." In *Suggestive Poses: Artists and Critics Respond to Censorship,* ed. Lorraine Johnson. Toronto: Toronto Photographers Workshop 1997. 137–49.

Gass, William. "Shears of the Censor." *Harpers,* Apr. 1997, 59–65.

Gerson, Carole. "Anthologies and the Canon of Early Canadian Women Writers." In *Re(dis)covering Our Foremothers: Nineteenth-Century Canadian Women Writers,* ed. Lorraine McMullen. Ottawa: University of Ottawa Press 1990. 55–76.

Godard, Barbara. "The Politics of Representation: Some Native Canadian Women Writers." In New, ed., *Native Writers and Canadian Writing.* 183–225.

– "Talking About Ourselves: The Literary Productions of Native Women of Canada." In *The CRIAW Reader: Papers on Literary Productions by Canadian Women,* ed. Diana M.A. Relke. Ottawa: CRIAW/ICREF 1992. 49–108.

– "Marlene Nourbese Philip's Hyphenated Tongue or Writing the Caribbean Demotic between Africa and Arctic." In *Major Minorities: English Literatures in Transit,* ed. Raoul Granqvist. Amsterdam: Rodopi 1993. 151–75.

– "Writing Resistance: Black Women's Writing in Canada." In Vevaina and Godard, eds., *Intersexions.* 106–15.

Goddard, John. "Personal Recollections of Controversy That Made Margaret Laurence Weep." *Montreal Gazette,* 10 Jan. 1987, B8.

Goldie, Terry. "Fresh Canons: The Native Canadian Example." *English Studies in Canada* 17.4 (1991): 373–84.

Govier, Katherine. "Margaret Atwood: 'There's Nothing in the Book That Hasn't Already Happened.'" *Quill and Quire* 51 (1985): 66–7.

Grant, Agnes. "Contemporary Native Women's Voices in Literature." In New, ed., *Native Writers and Canadian Writing.* 124–32.

Green, Hanna. *I Never Promised You a Rose Garden.* New York: Holt, Rinehart and Winston 1964.

Griffin, Susan. *Pornography and Silence: Culture's Revenge against Nature.* New York: Harper and Row 1981.

Haiman, Frank. *"Speech Acts" and the First Amendment.* Carbondale: Southern Illinois University Press 1993.

Harpur, Tom. "Atwood's Priority: How Do We Stop War?" *Toronto Star,* 5 Oct. 1981, D1, D3.

Harrison, Nicholas. *Circles of Censorship: Censorship and Its Metaphors in French History, Literature and Theory.* Oxford: Clarendon Press 1995.

Harry, Margaret. "Literature in English by Native Canadians (Indians and Inuit)." *Studies in Canadian Literature* 10 (1985): 146–53.

Hill Rigney, Barbara: *See* Rigney.

Hoekema, David A. "Artists, Humanists, and Society: Conservatives Have the Wrong Answers, and Liberals Ask the Wrong Questions." *Art Journal* 50.3 (1991): 45–8.

Hollingsworth, Margaret. "Musings on the Feminist Muse: *New Year's Day, 1990.*" In Scheier et al., eds., *Language in Her Eye.* 142–5.

Holmes, Michael. Letter. "Pen-to-PEN Combat." *Globe and Mail,* 10 May 1999, C1.

Holmes, Oliver Wendell: *See* Abrams v. United States.

Holquist, Michael. "Corrupt Originals: The Paradox of Censorship." PMLA 109 (1994): 14–25.

Howells, Coral Ann. "'Tis Sixty Years Since': Timothy Findley's The Wars and Roger McDonald's 1915." *World Literature Written in English* 23.1 (1984): 129–36.

– *Margaret Atwood.* New York: St. Martin's Press 1996.

Hoy, Helen. "'Nothing but the Truth': Discursive Transparency in Beatrice Culleton." *Ariel: A Review of International English Literature* 25.1 (1994): 155–84.

Hutcheon, Linda. *The Canadian Postmodern: A Study of Contemporary English-Canadian Fiction.* Toronto: Oxford University Press 1988.

Jacobsen, Sally. "Alabama Teacher Loses Job for Teaching Atwood Poem." *Margaret Atwood Society Newsletter* 18 (1997): 1–3.

Jansen, Sue Curry. *Censorship: The Knot that Binds Power and Knowledge.* New York: Oxford University Press 1991.

Jenkinson, David. "Censorship Iceberg: Results of a Survey of Challenges in Public and School Libraries." *Canadian Library Journal* 43.1 (1986): 7–21.

Johnson, Ken. "Attila Richard Lukacs at 49TH Parallel." *Art in America* 77 (1989): 204.

Johnson, Kirsten. *Undressing the Canadian State: The Politics of Pornography from Hicklin to Butler*. Halifax: Fernwood 1995.

Johnston, Basil H. "One Generation from Extinction." In New, ed., *Native Writers and Canadian Writing*. 10–15.

Keeshig-Tobias, Lenore. "The Magic of Others." In Scheier et al., eds., *Language in Her Eye*. 173–7.

– "Keepers of the Culture." Interview. In Silvera, ed., *The Other Woman*. 220–51.

Keith, W.J. "Apocalyptic Imaginations: Notes on Atwood's *The Handmaid's Tale* and Findley's *Not Wanted on the Voyage*." *Essays on Canadian Writing* 35 (1987): 123–34.

Kelly, Deirdre. "Sadism Doesn't Sit Well with PEN Supporters." *Globe and Mail*, 23 Apr. 1999, A7.

King, James. *The Life of Margaret Laurence*. Toronto: Knopf 1997.

Kis, Danilo. "Censorship/Self-Censorship." *Index on Censorship* 15.1 (1986): 43–5.

Klovan, Peter. "'Bright and Good': Findley's *The Wars*." *Canadian Literature* 91 (1981): 58–69.

Krupat, Arnold. "Native American Literature and the Canon." *Critical Inquiry* 10 (1983): 145–71.

– *For Those Who Come After: A Study of Native American Autobiography*. Berkeley: University of California Press 1985.

Kuhn, Thomas S. *The Structure of Scientific Revolutions*. Chicago: University of Chicago Press 1970.

LaBelle, Beverly. "Snuff – The Ultimate in Woman Hating." In Lederer, ed., *Take Back the Night*. 272–8.

Lacombe, Dany. *Blue Politics: Pornography and the Law in the Age of Feminism*. Toronto: University of Toronto Press 1994.

Lacombe, Michele. "The Writing on the Wall: Amputated Speech in Margaret Atwood's *The Handmaid's Tale*." *Wascana Review* 21 (1986): 3–20.

Lamarche, Gara. "Some Thoughts on the 'Chilling Effect.'" *Art Journal* 50.4 (1991): 56–8.

Landsberg, Michelle. *Women and Children First*. Toronto: Macmillan 1982.

Langton, Rae. "Speech Acts and Unspeakable Acts." *Philosophy and Public Affairs* 22.4 (1993): 293–330.

LaRocque, Emma. "Preface or Here Are Our Voices – Who Will Hear?" In *Writing the Circle: Native Women of Western Canada*, ed. Jeanne Perreault and Sylvia Vance. Edmonton: NeWest 1990. xv–xxx.

Larson, Janet Karsten. "Margaret Atwood's Testaments: Resisting the Gilead Within." *Christian Century*, 20 May 1987, 496–8.

Laurence, Margaret. "In the Air." *Winnipeg Citizen*, 22 Sept. 1948.

– *The Stone Angel*. Toronto: McClelland and Stewart 1964.

– "Ten Years' Sentences." *Canadian Literature* 39 (Winter 1969): 10–16.

– *The Diviners*. Toronto: McClelland and Stewart 1974.

- "Ivory Tower or Grassroots? The Novelist as Socio-Political Being." In *A Political Art: Essays and Images in Honour of George Woodcock*, Ed. W.H. New. Vancouver: University of British Columbia Press 1978. 15–25.
- "A Letter from Margaret Laurence." In *Stopping the Book Banners*. Book and Periodical Development Council, c. 1978. Courtesy of Atwater Library, Montreal.
- *The Christmas Birthday Story.* Illust. by Helen Lucas. Toronto: McClelland and Stewart 1980.
- "Gadgetry or Growing: Form and Voice in the Novel." *Journal of Canadian Fiction* 27 (Summer 1980): 54–62.
- Foreword. Ringwood, *Collected Plays*. xi–xiv.
- *Dance on the Earth: A Memoir.* Toronto: McClelland and Stewart 1989.
- "The Greater Evil." *Dance on the Earth: A Memoir*. 265–74.
- *A Very Large Soul: Selected Letters from Margaret Laurence to Canadian Writers*. Ed. J.A. Wainwright. Dunvegan, Ont.: Cormorant 1995.

Lecker, Robert. *Making It Real: The Canonization of English-Canadian Literature*. Concord, Ont.: House of Anansi Press 1995.

Leckie, Barbara, and Peter O'Brien. "Margaret Atwood." In *So to Speak: Interviews with Contemporary Canadian Writers*, ed. Peter O'Brien. Montreal: Véhicule Press 1987. 174–93.

Lederer, Laura, ed. *Take Back the Night: Women on Pornography*. New York: William Morrow and Co. 1980.

Legouis, Emile. *A History of English Literature*. 1926. Trans. Helen Douglas Irvine. London: Dent 1960.

Lennox, John, and Ruth Panofsky, eds. *Selected Letters of Margaret Laurence and Adele Wiseman*. Toronto: University of Toronto Press 1997.

Leo, John. "The Words of the Culture War." *U.S. News and World Report*, 28 Oct. 1991, 31.

Longino, Helen E. "Pornography, Oppression, and Freedom: A Closer Look." In Lederer, ed., *Take Back the Night*. 40–54.

Loury, Glenn C. *One by One from the Inside Out: Essays and Reviews on Race and Responsibility in America*. New York: Free Press 1995.

Lucking, David. "In Pursuit of the Faceless Stranger: Depths and Surfaces in Margaret Atwood's *Bodily Harm*." *Studies in Canadian Literature* 15 (1990): 76–93.

Lutz, Hartmut. *Contemporary Challenges: Conversations with Canadian Native Authors*. Saskatoon: Fifth House Publishers 1991.

Lyons, Bonnie. "Using Other People's Dreadful Childhoods." In *Margaret Atwood: Conversations*, ed. Earl G. Ingersoll. Willowdale, Ont.: Firefly Books 1990. 221–33.

McAlpine, Kirstie. "Narratives of Silence: Marlene Nourbese Philip and Joy Kogawa." In *The Guises of Canadian Diversity: New European Perspectives*, ed. Serge Jaumin and Marc Maufort. Amsterdam: Rodopi 1995.

McCarthy, Mary. "Breeders, Wives and Unwomen." *New York Times Book Review*, 9 Feb. 1986, 1, 35.

McCombs, Judith. "From 'Places, Migrations' to *The Circle Game*: Atwood's Canadian and Female Metamorphoses." In *Margaret Atwood: Writing and Subjectivity*, ed. Colin Nicholson. New York: St Martin's Press 1994. 51–67.

McCombs, Judith, ed. *Critical Essays on Margaret Atwood*. Boston: G.K. Hall and Co. 1988.

McCormack, Thelma. "Must We Censor Pornography? Civil Liberties and Feminist Jurisprudence." In *Freedom of Expression and the Charter*, ed. David Schneiderman. Toronto: Thomson Professional Publishing 1991.

McDonald, Lynn. Letter to Eric Cotton, 21 Jan. 1985. In Laurence, Papers, accession 4, ser. 1, box 12, file 307.

MacEwen, Gwendolyn. "Icarus." *Magic Animals: Selected Poems Old and New*. Toronto: Macmillan 1974. 11–13.

McKenzie, M.L. "Memories of the Great War: Graves, Sassoon, and Findley." *University of Toronto Quarterly* 55.4 (1986): 395–411.

McKenzie, Stephanie. Interview with Beatrice Culleton. Montreal, 26 Jan. 1994 (courtesy of the author).

MacKinnon, Catharine A. *Only Words*. Cambridge, Mass.: Harvard University Press 1993.

Malak, Amin. "Margaret Atwood's 'The Handmaid's Tale' and the Dystopian Tradition." *Canadian Literature* 112 (1987): 9–16.

Malamuth, Neil M., and Edward Donnerstein. "The Effects of Aggressive-Pornographic Mass Media Stimuli." *Advances in Experimental Social Psychology* 15 (1982): 103–36.

Maracle, Lee. "Native Myths: Trickster Alive and Crowing." In Scheier et al., eds., *Language in Her Eye*. 182–7.

Marriott, David. "Figures of Silence and Orality in the Poetry of M. Nourbese Philip." In *Framing the Word: Gender and Genre in Caribbean Women's Writing*, ed. Joan Anim-Addo. London: Whiting and Birch 1996. 72–85.

Marriott, John. "Culture as a Censorship Shell-game." In *Suggestive Poses: Artists and Critics Respond to Censorship*, ed. Lorraine Johnson. Toronto: Toronto Photographers Workshop 1997. 163–70.

Martin, Sandra. "Pen-to-PEN Combat." Letter. *Globe and Mail*, 10 May 1999, C1.

Matheson, Sue. "An Interview with Margaret Atwood." *Herizons* 4 (1986): 20–2.

Meiklejohn, Alexander. *Free Speech and Its Relation to Self-Government*. New York: Harper 1948.

Mellor, W.M. "Timothy Findley's True Fictions: A Conversation at Stone Orchard." *Studies in Canadian Literature* 19.2 (1994): 77–101.

Meyer, Bruce, and Brian O'Riordan. "The Marvel of Reality: An Interview with Timothy Findley." *Waves: A Decade of Fine Canadian Writing* 10.4 (1982): 5–11.

Mill, John Stuart. "On the Liberty of Thought and Discussion." *Utilitarianism, On Liberty, and Considerations on Representative Government.* Ed. H.B. Acton. London: Dent 1972. 78–113.

Milton, John. *Complete English Poems; Of Education; Areopagitica.* Ed. Gordon Campbell. 4th ed. London: Dent 1990.

Morley, Patricia. *Margaret Laurence.* Boston: Twayne 1981.

Morrison, Rod. Letter. "Pen-to-PEN Combat." *Globe and Mail*, 10 May 1999, C1.

Morton, Donald E. *Vladimir Nabokov.* New York: Frederick Ungar 1974.

Moss, John. *Sex and Violence in the Canadian Novel.* Toronto: McClelland and Stewart 1977.

Mukherjee, Arun. *Postcolonialism: My Living.* Toronto: Tsar 1998.

Musgrave, Susan. "A Crime against Criminal Writers." *Globe and Mail*, 3 May 1997, D3.

Mycak, Sonia. *In Search of the Split Subject: Psychoanalysis, Phenomenology, and the Novels of Margaret Atwood.* Toronto: ECW 1996.

Nabokov, Vladimir. "On a Book Entitled Lolita." *The Annotated Lolita.* Ed. Alfred Appel, Jr. New York: McGraw-Hill 1970. 313–19.

Nelson, Sharon H. "Bemused, Branded, and Belittled: Women and Writing in Canada." *Fireweed* 15 (1982): 65–102.

Nelson Canadian Dictionary of the English Language. Scarborough: ITP Nelson 1997.

New, W.H. *Native Writers and Canadian Writing: Canadian Literature Special Edition.* Vancouver: University of British Columbia Press 1990.

Nichols, John. "Feminist Author Looks at the Future." *The Blade*, 4 May 1986, E3.

Nodelman, Perry. "We Are All Censors." *Canadian Children's Literature* 68 (1992): 121–33.

Not a Love Story: A Film about Pornography. Dir. Bonnie Sherr Klein. National Film Board of Canada 1981.

Orwell, George. *1984.* Ed. Bernard Crick. Oxford: Clarendon 1984.

Oxford English Dictionary. Compact ed. Complete text reproduced micrographically. 2 vols. Glasgow: Oxford University Press 1971.

Pal, Sunanda. "Celebration of the Black Being in Claire Harris's *The Conception of Winter* and *Drawing Down a Daughter.*" In *Intersexions: Issues of Race and Gender in Canadian Women's Writing*, ed. Coomi S. Vevaina and Barbara Godard. New Delhi: Creative Books 1996. 131–41.

Parachini, Allan. "Speakeasy." *New Art Examiner* 20.4 (1992): 10–11.

Patterson, Annabel. *Censorship and Interpretation: The Conditions of Writing and Reading in Early Modern England.* Madison: University of Wisconsin Press 1984.

Peterson, Klaus, and Allan C. Hutchinson, eds. *Interpreting Censorship in Canada*. Toronto: University of Toronto Press 1999.

Petrone, Penny. *Native Literature in Canada: From the Oral Tradition to the Present*. Toronto: Oxford University Press 1990.

Philip, Marlene Nourbese. "Journal Entries: Against Reaction." In *Work in Progress: Building Feminist Culture*, ed. Rhea Tregebov. Toronto: Women's Press 1987.

– *Harriet's Daughter*. Toronto: Women's Press 1988.

– "Racism in the Book Business." Letter to the Editor. *Globe and Mail*, 17 June 1989, D7.

– *She Tries Her Tongue, Her Silence Softly Breaks*. Charlottetown: Ragweed Press 1989.

– "Managing the Unmanageable." In *Caribbean Women Writers: Essays from the First International Conference*, ed. Selwyn R. Cudjoe. Wellesley, Mass.: Calaloux Publications 1990. 295–300.

– *Frontiers: Essays and Writings on Racism and Culture*. Stratford, Ont.: Mercury Press 1992.

– "Publish + Be Damned." *Frontiers*, 160–7.

– "The Disappearing Debate; or, How the Discussion of Racism Has Been Taken Over by the Censorship Issue." In *Borrowed Power: Essays on Cultural Appropriation*, ed. Bruce Ziff and Pratima V. Rao. New Brunswick, NJ: Rutgers University Press 1997. 97–108.

Pindell, Howardena. "Breaking the Silence." *New Art Examiner* 18.2 (1990): 18–23.

"Pulp Fiction, Pulp Legislation." Editorial. *Globe and Mail*, 13 June 1998, D6.

Rae, Bob. Letter to Margaret Laurence, 18 Jan. 1985. In Laurence, Papers, accession 4, ser. 1, box 12, file 307.

Rahv, Philip. "The Unfuture of Utopia." In *Orwell's Nineteen Eighty-four: Text, Sources, Criticism*, ed. Irving Howe. New York: Harcourt Brace Jovanovich 1963. 181–5.

Réage, Pauline. *Story of O*. Trans. Sabine d'Estrée. New York: Ballantine 1965.

Rigney, Barbara Hill. *Margaret Atwood*. Totowa, NJ: Barnes and Noble 1987.

Ringwood, Gwen Pharis. *The Collected Plays of Gwen Pharis Ringwood*. Ed. Enid Delgatty Rutland. Ottawa: Borealis Press 1982.

Robertson, James R. "Obscenity: The Decision of the Supreme Court of Canada in *R. v. Butler*." Background paper. Ottawa: Law and Government Division, Library of Parliament 1992.

Rothstein, Mervyn. "No Balm in Gilead for Margaret Atwood." *New York Times*, 17 Feb. 1986, C11.

Rubenstein, Roberta. "Nature and Nurture in Dystopia: *The Handmaid's Tale*." In *Margaret Atwood: Vision and Forms*, ed. Kathryn VanSpanckeren and Jan Garden Castro. Carbondale: Southern Illinois University Press 1988. 101–12.

– "Pandora's Box and Female Survival: Margaret Atwood's *Bodily Harm*." In McCombs, ed., *Critical Essays on Margaret Atwood.* 259–75.

Ruppert, James. "The Uses of Oral Tradition in Six Contemporary Native American Poets." *American Indian Culture and Research Journal* 4.4 (1980): 87–110.

Salat, M.F. "Other Words, Other Worlds: Of Ruby Slipperjack." In Vevaina and Godard, eds., *Intersexions.* 75–89.

Sallot, Jeff. "Students 'Overwhelmingly against' High School Principal Who Opposes Munro Novel." *Globe and Mail*, 14 Feb. 1976, 3.

Sanders, Leslie. "'The Mere Determination to Remember': M. Nourbese Philip's 'Stop Frame.'" *West Coast Line* 22 (1997): 134–42.

Saunders, Doug. "Shock Treatment." *Globe and Mail*, 3 May 1999, c1.

Schauer, Frederick. *Free Speech: A Philosophical Enquiry.* Cambridge: Cambridge University Press 1982.

Scheier, Libby, Sarah Sheard, and Eleanor Wachtel, eds. *Language in Her Eye: Views on Writing and Gender by Canadian Women Writing in English.* Toronto: Coach House Press 1990.

Schiller, Herbert I. *Culture, Inc.: The Corporate Takeover of Public Expression.* New York: Oxford University Press 1989.

Schrader, Alvin M. *Fear of Words: Censorship and the Public Libraries of Canada.* Ottawa: Canadian Library Association 1995.

Scott, Jay. "Dialogue on *The Wars*: A Symphony of Firsts." *Globe and Mail*, 10 Nov. 1983, e5.

Scott, Susan, and Rudy Platiel. "Laurence Again Target of Book Ban." *Globe and Mail*, 26 Jan. 1985, 23.

Sechehaye, Marguerite. *Autobiography of a Schizophrenic Girl.* Trans. Grace Rubin-Rabson. New York: Grune and Stratton 1951.

Silvera, Makeda, ed. *The Other Woman: Women of Colour in Contemporary Canadian Literature.* Toronto: Sister Vision Press 1995.

Skokie v. National Socialist Party, 373 NE 2d 21 (1978).

Smith, Dorothy. "A Peculiar Eclipsing: Women's Exclusion from Man's Culture." *Women's Studies International Quarterly* 1.4 (1978): 281–96.

Smolik, Noemi. "Attila Richard Lukacs." *Artforum* 27 (1989): 145.

Spender, Dale. "The Gatekeepers: A Feminist Critique of Academic Publishing." In *Doing Feminist Research*, ed. Helen Roberts. London: Routledge and Kegan Paul 1981. 186–202.

Staels, Hilde. "Margaret Atwood's *The Handmaid's Tale*: Resistance through Narrating." *English Studies: A Journal of English Language and Literature* 76 (1995): 455–67.

Stasiulis, Daiva. "'Authentic Voice': Anti-Racist Politics in Canadian Feminist Publishing and Literary Production." In *Feminism and the Politics of Difference*, ed. Sneja Gunew and Anna Yeatman. Halifax: Fernwood 1993.

"Steamy Classroom Reading: A Catholic Student Quits Over a 'Disgusting' Assignment." *Western Report* 9.25 (1994): 27–8.

Steinem, Gloria. "Erotica and Pornography: A Clear and Present Difference." In Lederer, ed., *Take Back the Night*. 35–9.

Stoffman, Judy. "PEN Event Welcomes Iranian." *Toronto Star*, 23 Apr. 1999, D14.

Stovel, Nora Foster. "Mourning Becomes Margaret: Laurence's Farewell to Fiction." *Journal of Canadian Studies* 34.4 (1999–2000): 105–20.

Strossen, Nadine. *Defending Pornography: Free Speech, Sex, and the Fight for Women's Rights*. New York: Scribner 1995.

"Student Calls for Removal of Findley Book." *Globe and Mail*, 6 June 1991, C5.

Sullivan, Kathleen M. "The First Amendment Wars." *New Republic*, 28 Sept. 1992, 35–40.

Sullivan, Rosemary. "An Interview with Margaret Laurence." In *A Place to Stand On: Essays by and about Margaret Laurence*, ed. George Woodcock. Edmonton: NeWest 1983. 61–79.

– *Shadow Maker: The Life of Gwendolyn MacEwen*. Toronto: HarperCollins 1995.

Summers, Alison. "An Interview with Timothy Findley." *Malahat Review* 58 (1981): 105–10.

Sunstein, Cass R. *Democracy and the Problem of Free Speech*. New York: Free Press 1993.

Taine, Hyppolyte A. *History of English Literature*. Trans. H. Van Laun. 2 vols. Edinburgh: Edmonston and Douglas 1871.

Thomas, Clara. "Towards Freedom: The Work of Margaret Laurence and Northrop Frye." *Essays on Canadian Writing* 30 (1984–85): 81–95.

Thompson, Dawn. "Typewriter as Trickster: Revisions of Beatrice Culleton's *In Search of April Raintree*." In Vevaina and Godard, eds., *Intersexions*. 90–105.

Tribe, David. *Questions of Censorship*. London: Allen and Unwin 1973.

Twigg, Alan, ed. *Strong Voices: Conversations with Fifty Canadian Authors*. Madeira Park, BC: Harbour Publishing 1988.

Van Gelder, Lindsy. "Margaret Atwood, Novelist." *Ms*, Jan. 1987, 48, 50, 90.

Van Luven, Lynne. "Good Bones to Chew." *Ottawa Citizen*, 26 Sept. 1992, B6.

Vevaina, Coomi S. "Articulating a Different Way of Being: The Resurgence of the Native Voice in Canada." In Vevaina and Godard, eds., *Intersexions*. 55–73.

Vevaina, Coomi S., and Barbara Godard, eds. *Intersexions*. New Delhi: Creative Books 1996.

Wagner, Vit. "Timothy Findley: The Art of Controversy." *Toronto Star*, 8 Feb. 1992, J1, J10.

Wainwright, J.A., ed. *A Very Large Soul: Selected Letters from Margaret Laurence to Canadian Writers*. Dunvegan, Ont.: Cormorant 1995.

Weaver, Robert, ed. *Canadian Short Stories*. Toronto: Oxford University Press, 3rd ser., 1978; 5th serv., 1991.

Williams, Stephen. *Invisible Darkness: The Strange Case of Paul Bernardo and Karla Homolka*. Toronto: Little, Brown and Company 1996.

Williamson, Janice, ed. *Sounding Differences: Conversations with Seventeen Canadian Women Writers*. Toronto: University of Toronto Press 1993.

Wilson, Sharon Rose. "Turning Life into Popular Art: *Bodily Harm's* Life-Tourist." *Studies in Canadian Literature* 10 (1985): 136–45.

– *Margaret Atwood's Fairy-Tale Sexual Politics*. Jackson: University Press of Mississippi and ECW 1993.

Wood, Diane S. "Bradbury and Atwood: Exile as Rational Decision." In *The Literature of Emigration and Exile*, ed. James Whitlark and Wendell Aycock. Lubbock, Tex.: Texas Tech University Press 1992. 131–42.

Woodcock, George. "Speaker for the Tribes." *Canadian Woman Studies / Les cahiers de la femme* 8.3 (1987): 30–2.

Woollard, Ronald T. Letter. *Globe and Mail*, **14** Feb. 1976, 6.

Xiques, Donez. "Early Influences: Laurence's Newspaper Career." In *Challenging Territory: The Writing of Margaret Laurence*, ed. Christian Riegel. Edmonton, Alta.: University of Alberta Press 1997. 187–210.

Young-Ing, Greg. "Aboriginal Peoples' Estrangement: Marginalization in the Publishing Industry." In *Looking at the Words of Our People: First Nations Analysis of Literature*, ed. Jeannette Armstrong. Penticton, BC: Theytus Books 1993. 177–88.

Zillman, Dolph, and Jennings Bryant. "Pornography, Sexual Callousness, and the Trivialization of Rape." *Journal of Communication* 32 (1982): 10–21.

Zwicker, Heather. "Canadian Women of Color in the New World Order: Marlene Nourbese Philip, Joy Kogawa, and Beatrice Culleton Fight Their Way Home." In *Canadian Women Writing Fiction*, ed. Mickey Pearlman. Jackson, Miss.: University Press of Mississippi 1993. 142–69.

Index